The Mandela Brief

Also by Thomas Grant

Jeremy Hutchinson's Case Histories
Court Number One, The Old Bailey

The Mandela Brief

Sydney Kentridge and the Trials of Apartheid

THOMAS GRANT

JOHN MURRAY

First published in Great Britain in 2022 by John Murray (Publishers)
An Hachette UK company

I

A CIP catalogue record for this title is available from the British Library

Hardback ISBN 978-1-529-37286-1
Trade Paperback ISBN 978-1-529-37297-7
eBook ISBN 978-1-529-37300-4

Typeset in Bembo MT by Hewer Text UK Ltd, Edinburgh
Printed and bound in Great Britain by Clays Ltd, Elcograf S.p.A.

John Murray policy is to use papers that are natural, renewable and recyclable products and
made from wood grown in sustainable forests. The logging and manufacturing processes
are expected to conform to the environmental regulations of the country of origin.

John Murray (Publishers)
Carmelite House
50 Victoria Embankment
London EC4Y 0DZ

www.johnmurraypress.co.uk

To Orlando, Ottilie and Artemis

Contents

Preface

I FIRST MET SYDNEY Kentridge in 2015. He had written to tell me that he had enjoyed a book I had recently published about a centenarian barrister called Jeremy Hutchinson. To receive such a letter was enough to set the heart aglow. At the time I knew him, from afar, as the greatest constitutional and commercial barrister at the English Bar of the last thirty or so years, a figure spoken of in reverential terms in legal circles. I also knew, though more dimly, that Sydney had had a previous career of equal note in his native South Africa. I suggested a meeting. During the hours we spent together I discovered I was in the company of a man who had lived an extraordinary life.

A few years later a mutual friend, Edwin Glasgow QC, collared me and told me in tones of deadly seriousness that I had a public duty to write about Sydney, whom Edwin described as the greatest advocate of the twentieth century. Edwin Glasgow is not a man you say no to, so I said yes, subject of course to Sydney's views. I had no particular expertise in the political and legal history of South Africa, though I at least knew that it was not a subject to be engaged with casually. The project, if undertaken, would involve a substantial investment of time and energy. Edwin, Sydney and I met up for a number of lunches. Sydney initially protested that 'no one will be interested in a book about me' and that, anyway, his memory was failing. Only time will tell whether the first objection is sound: if this book does not attract interest it will be my failure, not that of my subject. As to the second it became clear that it was groundless. Sydney could remember moments that occurred in a courtroom in the 1950s as if they were yesterday. He eventually agreed to the project on the understanding that any book would not be a biography. This was a relief given that Sydney was by this stage ninety-six years old.

Preliminary investigations demonstrated that, both in South Africa and England (and indeed in other jurisdictions), Sydney had been involved in a vast plethora of litigation of the greatest significance. The years of research that followed have confirmed Edwin's description. It is rare that, on closer acquaintance, a person touted as a 'great' man or woman conforms to his or her initial description. In Sydney's case the two and half years of my friendship with him and my labours in the archives have proved the exception. The longer I have spent in his company, both on the page and in person, the more I have come to realise that Edwin was right. I have also realised that Sydney's work as an advocate in South Africa, putting aside everything he did afterwards, was of seminal and historical importance. Readers who are expecting a critique of my subject, turn away now.

As I explain in the introductory first chapter, I quickly made a decision to concentrate on Sydney's South African work. Hence this book is devoted to the decades of the 1950s through to the mid-1980s, the central years of apartheid, and in particular a series of extraordinary cases Sydney appeared in. In having made that decision I am conscious that it involves ignoring Sydney's great contribution to English law. But a book has to have its limits and, as the title indicates, this book is devoted to the practice of law in the South African courts and in particular the role of the law in the enforcement of, and resistance to, apartheid and its legal apparatus. I have briefly delved into the biographical in Chapter 2, with an account of Sydney's early life which I thought was so interesting as to defy omission. The chapter will also, I hope, contextualise the chapters that follow. I leave it to somebody else to take up the baton of Sydney's later years.

The title *The Mandela Brief* is a reference to Sydney's work in the late 1950s and early 1960s in achieving the acquittal of Nelson Mandela and his co-accused at the so-called Treason Trial, and his later cases acting on behalf of Winnie Mandela in the 1970s and 1980s. It was given a further meaning when, towards the end of writing this book, I spoke with Sir Alan Ward. Now a distinguished retired Court of Appeal judge, Ward was born in Pretoria in 1938. Fresh out of school, he had started working for a firm of attorneys in the mid-1950s and recalled receiving telephone calls from Nelson Mandela, then the partner in a firm of Johannesburg attorneys, asking him to assist in appeals being heard in the Palace of Justice at Pretoria. The advocate who Mandela had briefed on a number of these cases was a certain Mr Kentridge, then in his mid-thirties. Ward, who eventually left South Africa for England after the Sharpeville massacre in 1960, still remembers Sydney's crystalline advocacy from those distant days. In an interesting role reversal, Sydney would eventually appear as counsel before Ward himself when he was sitting in the English Court of Appeal. He told me simply, 'Sydney has always been my legal hero.'

This is not a book directed solely to a professional legal readership. In fact it is for any reader interested in the history of state oppression and resistance to it. It is a book about the interaction between the courtroom and the political world; about human courage and resilience; about the outrage of state-sanctioned racism. It is above all about how lawyers can make a difference to the life of a nation and its inhabitants. It is also a portrait of a great advocate and a great man.

Sydney turned ninety-nine in November 2021. I am conscious that this is my second attempt at a study of a lawyer of great age. I look around and, fortunately for me, see nobody who can stand shoulder to shoulder with Sydney Kentridge or Jeremy Hutchinson. So I am pleased to say this will be my last foray into the, admittedly rarefied, field of centenarian advocates.

I publish this book with a certain amount of diffidence. The testimony of my bookshelves is eloquent: there is a huge library dedicated to the practice of law in apartheid South Africa. While interviewing numerous South African lawyers I have come to realise what serious students they are of their history. As I mention in the acknowledgements section of this book, I have obtained immeasurable benefit from those interviews and have made some lasting friendships. I hope they will think this book, albeit written by an outsider, a worthwhile addition to that library.

I have referred to Sydney Kentridge by his first name in this preface. In the chapters that follow he will be Kentridge.

Thomas Grant
Westminster, May 2022

The Mandela Brief

I

Sydney Kentridge at Ninety-Nine

O N 5 NOVEMBER 2012 fifteen barristers gathered in Court One
of the recently opened Supreme Court building in London's
Parliament Square. They had come to argue an abstruse but important point of law in the context of a substantial tax case: whether
clients who obtain legal advice from accountants can assert legal
professional privilege over that advice. For one of those barristers it
was a significant occasion not only because of the momentousness of
the issue which was about to be argued. That day Sir Sydney Kentridge
QC, who was representing the Law Society, was celebrating his ninetieth birthday. He was the oldest person ever to argue a case before
the United Kingdom's highest court. The hearing lasted three days, a
wearying experience for someone in their fifties, let alone for a man
entering his tenth decade. Kentridge's argument prevailed.[1] It would
be his last significant case: on 17 April 2013 he formally retired from
the Bar. Kentridge had been practising as an advocate for precisely
sixty-four years. I cannot say for sure whether his is the longest ever
legal career, but if it is not, it must surely come close. What is certain
is that it is the longest span of time any man or woman has maintained
a consistent and active legal practice at the highest level.

Life as a barrister is arduous. It requires constant application and
concentration. There are moments of stress, anxiety, even dread. It
involves the sacrifice of evenings and weekends. Most barristers –
unless they have found a relatively safe haven as a judge – have retired
(or have been retired by the market) by the age of seventy. Being an
effective advocate requires not just stamina but nimbleness; every
relevant fact in the case must be there at the forefront of your mind;
every document must be at your fingertips. By their late sixties most
barristers are simply worn out. Kentridge was not unaware of the

fact that age can blunt the lawyer's faculties. He asked his head of chambers and friend, Jonathan Sumption, to be frank with him if he ever felt that Kentridge was past it. Sumption, not a man known for lack of candour, never had to advise Kentridge that the time had come to retire.

In fact it was Sumption who left the Bar first. In January 2012 he had become a justice of the Supreme Court and was part of the panel of judges now hearing Kentridge on his ninetieth birthday. Also in court that day was (Lord) David Pannick QC, representing the appellant in opposition to Kentridge's case. When Pannick stood up to address the court that morning, instead of launching straight into his appeal, he offered a handsome tribute to his opponent and wished him a happy birthday – sentiments unheard of in, at any rate, an English court of law – concluding that all this was 'without prejudice to my right to submit that his case is entirely without merit'.

What is most remarkable about Kentridge's professional longevity is the fact that, right up to his retirement, he retained his towering pre-eminence at the English Bar. From the late 1980s until well into the twenty-first century he was generally considered the leading barrister in England. Yet Kentridge had been born in Johannesburg and had spent the first thirty (and more) years of his career practising in the South African courts. London was for him the place to forge a second career: he was called to the English Bar in 1977 at the age of fifty-four, joining chambers at 1 Brick Court, and for the next ten years or so shuttled between London and Johannesburg, building a new practice in one country while maintaining a distinguished practice in another. Perhaps this explains that professional longevity. When I asked Kentridge how he had been able to carry on working at the highest level to such a great age he gave a simple answer: having started practising at the English Bar only in the late 1970s, he felt he was beginning his professional life anew; it was as if, in his mid-fifties, he had reacquired the energy of a man in his early twenties. On that chronology, Kentridge retired at the tender age of sixty.

This book is about that first phase of Sydney Kentridge's career. Although many of Kentridge's English cases stand as landmarks in the

law, they are in the main of interest to the lawyer or political historian. The work he did in South Africa stands on a different level.
Kentridge was called to the South African Bar in 1949, a year after the
institution of the apartheid state following the surprise victory of the
National Party in the 1948 general election. In the years that followed,
from his chambers in central Johannesburg, Kentridge practised
almost exclusively in South Africa, during the darkest days of the
apartheid regime. Throughout those decades Kentridge appeared in
many of the most important political trials heard in South Africa,
becoming the country's pre-eminent advocate (the South African
term for barrister) and achieving worldwide recognition not only for
his remarkable forensic skills but also for his willingness to take on the
state in cases of acute political and moral significance.

It has been remarked that South Africa during this time presented
a paradox. The apparatus of apartheid, and the ever more oppressive
and draconian laws enacted to maintain the subjugation of the black
population, meant that South Africa acquired the hallmarks of a
police state. Yet, at least for some part of the malign rule of the
National Party, the country's legal system remained largely intact,
most of its judges stayed broadly independent and its procedures
preserved at least the semblance of fairness. South Africa in the first
half of the twentieth century had acquired an enviable international
reputation for the quality of its judges and jurisprudence.[2] That reputation was founded on deep-rooted legal ideals which did not simply
wither after 1948. Despite that standing, lacking the legal power to
strike down unconstitutional laws, the courts were obliged to apply
the apartheid legislation which then flooded the statute books. Some
judges did their best to blunt its full sting, but whenever some loop-
hole was identified and exploited by the judiciary to preserve the
rights of the individual against the might of the state, it would be
swiftly closed by a new act of parliament or regulation.

A turning point came with the Terrorism Act 1967, enacted after
the assassination of Prime Minister Hendrik Verwoerd in 1966, by
which the state plumbed the depths of oppressiveness. The Act gave
the police a power of arrest and indefinite incommunicado detention
which the courts were prohibited from examining; effectively a
person could be detained at the will of the police without any right

3

of challenge. The Act also created a catch-all offence of terrorism which encompassed, in essence, any act committed 'with intent to endanger the maintenance of law and order in the Republic', and which carried a potential death sentence. The Terrorism Act features heavily in the chapters of this book. In the years that followed its enactment Kentridge, alongside many other lawyers, often anxiously asked himself whether, by continuing to participate in the South African legal system, he was lending it, and the state itself, a degree of credibility. He discussed this moral problem in a lecture delivered in the late 1970s:

> What are we, as counsel, doing in these courts – are we really defending the rule of law or what remains of it or, as some persons both abroad and in South Africa have said of us, are we helping to give a spurious air of respectability and fairness to a procedure which is fundamentally unfair?[3]

A number of lawyers did opt out of the system and left their country to pursue careers in England or the United States. Some did not go voluntarily but were hounded out by state harassment and menace. But Kentridge stayed for another decade and more, and when he did establish a foothold in London in the late 1970s he remained in practice in South Africa for another ten years after that.

The answer Kentridge gave to his own question was the alternative option open to the political lawyer:

> And this does turn, to an extent, on the attitude of those who find themselves accused of terrorism or similar offences. In general, they do not want to use the court to make simply a political demonstration; what they want is to be defended and acquitted, if it is at all possible. And if they must go to prison, they would rather go for the minimum of five years than for ten or fifteen years. And so they want to be defended. They want advocates to be there to defend them, and are they not entitled to an advocate's assistance, however little he can do for them? And if the advocate is told that he is lending respectability to an obnoxious system, must he not simply accept this as an additional burden on his calling?[4]

It is vital to understand when reading this book that, for all the iniquities of government policy and legislation after 1948, the South African courts were far removed from the sham tribunals of Nazi Germany, the Soviet Union or Maoist China. Although the law was distorted so that it became a caricature of basic concepts of fairness, it was still possible (with capable and determined representation) to obtain at least the semblance of a fair trial. The judges, whatever their political viewpoint, still nurtured – albeit to varying degrees – respect for the rule of law. Although judges were increasingly hand-picked by the government on the basis of political affiliation, a former minister of justice could still ruefully comment that these state placemen, once safely installed on the bench, quickly came to convince themselves that they had been appointed on merit alone, and acted accordingly. What this meant was that an accused's case could be properly deployed in a public court by skilled lawyers in trials which, apart from the absence of a jury (finally abolished in South Africa in 1969),[5] were conducted according to procedures similar to those of English or American criminal trials. As some of the chapters of this book demonstrate, a defendant accused of a political crime had at least a hope, and (if well represented) a fighting chance, of being acquitted. That would certainly not have been the case in a Nazi or Soviet 'people's court'.

Another paradox – one shared with many oppressive regimes – is that the apartheid state was built upon law and a slavish respect for its processes.[6] The law is not inherently progressive. In apartheid South Africa it was an engine of repression. A state organised, as South Africa was, on the basis of strict segregation of people, in every aspect of their lives, according to their 'race' (a concept which, since it lacks any scientific basis, must be a creature of the law) requires an elaborate edifice of rules: first, to categorise each person within that taxonomy;[7] then in accordance with it to regulate where that person may live, whom they may marry or co-habit with, what work they may do, where they may go, and what services they may use. Those rules had to carry with them penalties sufficiently heavy to ensure compliance. The criminal law thus extended its tentacles into every corner of human experience and activity. It was a crime for a black person to swim at a beach reserved for white people; it was a crime for a black person to have sex with a white person; it was a crime for a black or a 'coloured' person (that is, a person categorised under the race laws as neither 'white' nor 'native', to use the statutory language of the time) to live or work in particular areas. It was also a crime for newspapers to publish articles about certain subjects. As Kentridge himself said in 1986:

> Apartheid brings into conflict with the law people who in the ordinary way would not be classified as revolutionaries, let alone criminals. I can illustrate this from my own personal experience. In my time at the South African Bar I have defended in almost every type of criminal case, from drunken driving through fraud to murder. But I have also had among my clients – and here I am not speaking of libel actions or suchlike, but of criminal cases properly so called where the accused stands in the dock – at least seven of the editors of leading and respectable South African newspapers, two law professors, a leading QC, and an Anglican dean.[8]

Between 1948 and the late 1980s the South African courts were the front line of an unceasing battle between a state determined to preserve and enforce the racist system by which it defined itself and the dissenters who sought to challenge it. Those years generated litigation of extraordinary significance, drama and pathos. The Treason Trial of 1958–61, the Sharpeville inquiry of 1960, the Rivonia Trial of 1964 and the Steve Biko inquest of 1977, to name just four legal proceedings, resonated around the world and have each generated a substantial literature. In the chapters of this book I recount some of those seminal cases, and Kentridge's role in them. They are the great set pieces of the legal struggle against apartheid: cases which made the headlines not just in South Africa but internationally.

Beyond these legal landmarks there were thousands more cases daily decided by the courts where the law was deployed against those who challenged the status quo. The South African apartheid state was not all-powerful. Increasingly it was riven by paranoia, conscious of the fragility of an ordering of society which privileged a minority over an unwilling majority. A stable state can tolerate dissent. A state in permanent fear of its destruction lashes out at dissenters. To give a flavour of the way the law was used against people who in some way, however small, fell victim to that paranoia, here are some examples of cases, in each of which Kentridge appeared as counsel. They give a vivid indication of the sinister and sometimes bizarre legal dispensation which persisted in South Africa during those years and how it could affect those who lived and worked there.

Kentridge recalls a case where a young black attorney (equivalent to an English solicitor) had been called as a witness by the prosecution to give evidence against a (black) friend on trial in Natal for offences under the Terrorism Act.[9] By the time he was produced at court, the attorney, who was accused of no offence, had already spent eight months in solitary confinement under section 6 of the Terrorism Act. His evidence related to some minor fact in the prosecution case – that the accused had been in possession of a particular car at a particular time. He refused to give evidence. As Kentridge explains:

> he told the court that he believed, however serious the crime the accused had committed, it was a crime of conscience. In his own community, as he explained to the judge, the accused was not regarded as a criminal. And in any event he could not bring himself to give evidence against his close friend.

The attorney knew that this brave refusal exposed him to a prison sentence; and on the application of the prosecution, he was sentenced to three years' imprisonment for contempt of court. The Law Society of Natal, possibly under pressure from the state, moved to strike the young man off the roll of attorneys; in short, to deprive him of his profession and his livelihood. Kentridge was retained by the attorney and argued that although his client's refusal to give evidence may have been unlawful, his behaviour had been frank and honest, and dictated by his conscience, not by disrespect for the court. By a majority of two to one Kentridge's argument was accepted by the court.

Another case involved John Dugard, then a professor of law at the University of the Witwatersrand. In 1978 Dugard was invited to participate in a symposium on education in South Africa. Two hours before it was due to start, one of his co-participants, Dr Nthato Motlana, who would later become one of the most well-known businessmen in South Africa, was made subject to a banning order. (Banning orders, issued at the discretion of the government to prevent individuals from going to or living in particular areas or participating in particular activities, could turn lives upside down at the stroke of a pen.) The order prevented Motlana from giving his paper, and Dugard, furious at the government's actions, read it out himself. Dugard was prosecuted for conniving in breaching the banning order. Simply speaking someone else's words could be a criminal offence in South Africa.[10]

A third case involved an equally distinguished academic, Professor Barend van Niekerk. In 1969 Van Niekerk published an article in the *South African Law Journal*, a journal as reputable as it sounds, entitled 'Hanged by the Neck until You Are Dead', pointing out that black defendants were far more likely to be sentenced to death than white defendants convicted of similar crimes (mainly murder and rape) and arguing that this differential treatment by the judiciary was the product of deliberate bias. For this statement of the obvious he was charged with contempt of court. The fact that Van Niekerk was acquitted shows that the judiciary still retained a vestige of independence in 1970.[11] But he was not so lucky the next time: two years later he was found guilty of contempt after, at a public meeting, calling on the judiciary to denounce the iniquities of the Terrorism Act and to refuse to admit evidence procured from interrogations under it.[12]

A final example dates to the Soweto uprising of 1976, when schoolchildren boycotted classes and engaged in mass protest. Under emergency powers legislation the state had almost unlimited ability to declare a state of emergency and to introduce regulations to control it. One such regulation brought into force in 1976 in response to the uprising made it a crime for a schoolchild to be outside their classroom during school hours. It also permitted the detention by a police officer of 'any person if in his opinion it was necessary to do so to maintain or restore law and order'. A police major drove past a school in Soweto and saw a group of children in the playground. He summoned a squad of police and some lorries. When they arrived, not only the children in the playground but also the children who remained in their classrooms and their teachers were arrested, bundled into the lorries and taken to police cells. An application for habeas corpus was issued and Kentridge was briefed. He argued that, at least as regards the children who had been in their classrooms and their teachers, the major could not rationally have believed (since no reasonable person in his position would believe) that it was necessary to arrest them. The major filed an affidavit simply stating that he did, indeed, believe their arrest necessary 'to maintain or restore law and order', without any further explanation. The judge decided that he could not question or go behind the police officer's opinion on the matter and dismissed Kentridge's application.[13] Kentridge still remembers the case with barely concealed rage.

Lawyers are often derided today as overpaid leaches. Perhaps it has always been so. Jack Cade's murderous statement of intent – 'First thing we'll do, let's kill all the lawyers' – dates back hundreds of years and is still quoted, sometimes only half in jest.[14] I am not going to mount a general defence of the legal profession. Yet sometimes lawyers deliver services which not only profoundly affect for the better their clients' lives but also change the political weather. In South Africa during the apartheid years the practice of law could actually matter. Lawyers could not only save lives from personal ruin and, not infrequently, the gallows (Kentridge's advocacy saved many from the hangman's noose); they could also expose the brutality and malice of the state. In a pre-internet age it was often through what was said in public South African courtrooms that the world came to hear the truth of what was happening in a country which tried hard to project a positive image of placid coexistence and whose government cynically proclaimed apartheid as merely a 'policy of good neighbourliness'.[15] That was never truer than during the Sharpeville inquiry and the Steve Biko inquest, where Kentridge's devastating cross-examination of state witnesses – parties to, respectively, a massacre of sixty-nine peaceful black protestors and the beating to death in custody of a young black political leader – were reported around the globe. It was also often only in the courtroom that the voices of political dissenters could be heard, whether through their counsel or directly. Most such dissenters were subject to orders which banned their words being quoted in print. But what was said in a courtroom was sacrosanct. It was Nelson Mandela's evidence in the Treason Trial (see Chapter 3), reported at length in the newspapers, which projected his politics to a national and international audience.

From the vantage point of the twenty-first century it is easy to forget that what has become known as human rights law was, in an earlier age, not the glamorous discipline it is now. In the 1950s and 1960s in South Africa – just as much as in England – an advocate could make a very good living practising commercial law. Kentridge worked in a wide range of legal areas – and became one of the great commercial lawyers both in South Africa and England – but devoted much of his professional energy to poorly paid and anxious cases acting for those considered by many to be enemies of the state. In the late 1950s there was nothing fashionable about defending Nelson Mandela or Chief Albert Luthuli, men whom most whites at the time viewed not as visionaries but as terrorists. One of the people I interviewed for this book, Wim Trengove SC, identified one of Kentridge's greatest achievements as having taken on, as one of South Africa's most eminent advocates, deeply unpopular causes. Kentridge could have sequestered himself in the comfortable world of insurance, mining and business litigation, offending nobody and earning a lot of money. Instead he chose to make the representation of dissenters and supposed enemies of the state an integral part of his practice. By doing so, Kentridge, alongside other great names such as Isie Maisels, Vernon Berrangé, Bram Fischer, Rex Welsh, George Bizos, Denis Kuny, Ismail Mohamed and Arthur Chaskalson, legitimised this as a field of legal activity all lawyers should participate in with honour and pride. Kentridge and almost all of the names I have mentioned share one characteristic. They were white. It was a fact of the South African legal world throughout the time of Kentridge's practice there that it was an almost exclusively white – as well as male and middle-class – preserve. This was a function of the values of the period as well as the almost insuperable legal and practical obstacles placed before black men and women aspiring to practise law. It was one of the extraordinary early achievements of Nelson Mandela to have operated a firm of attorneys in Johannesburg in the 1950s. As we have seen in the preface to this book, before he represented him at the Treason Trial, Kentridge received briefs from Mandela's firm. The first black advocate to be admitted to the Transvaal Bar was Duma Nokwe, who qualified in 1956. Nokwe's attempts to build a practice were stymied by the prohibition imposed by apartheid legislation on his occupying chambers in Johannesburg and also by the fact that for three years he was an accused, alongside Mandela, in the Treason Trial, and so another of Kentridge's clients. After his acquittal Nokwe was subjected to state harassment which eventually forced him into exile. His experience was hardly an inspiring precedent for aspiring black lawyers. Although this is a book about a white advocate operating in a white professional world, it is also a book about some of the extraordinarily brave black men and women whom Kentridge represented.

The so-called cab rank rule, under which an advocate cannot choose the clients they act for by reference to their political views or other characteristics, is a principle about which many platitudes have been uttered and which, in England, has been as much honoured in the breach as in the observance. In South Africa in the apartheid years, it actually meant something. Political defendants obtained the benefit of first-rate representation by the very best lawyers practising in that country. Kentridge once observed:

> During the long years of apartheid in South Africa, I believe that one of the things which kept the flame of liberty flickering was that opponents of the apartheid regime charged with offences including high treason were able to find members of the Bar to defend them with such skill as they had and with vigour.[16]

Kentridge is emphatic that, while he abominated the apartheid regime, he was never a political activist in South Africa, although for a while he was a member of Alan Paton's Liberal Party (which would eventually be effectively outlawed by the state).[17] His status as an anti-apartheid icon derived predominantly from his role as a lawyer and his work within the legal system. Kentridge's liberal views were of course no secret and he did not confine his public utterances to the courtroom: as the vice chairman and, in 1972/3, chairman of the Johannesburg Bar Council, he was vocal in criticising the excesses of the government. But his professionalism in the courtroom, devoid of theatrics or speechifying, ensured that his standing before the judiciary – who actually decided virtually all cases, whether civil or criminal – and so his effectiveness on behalf of his clients was never diminished. Judges could not dismiss Kentridge as an agitator using the courtroom to pursue a wider agenda. As Kentridge has often said, defendants on trial for their lives want effective representation from their counsel, not airy displays of rhetoric.

Above all Kentridge was an advocate. Careful and deliberate, he was never melodramatic or declamatory. His calm, seemingly irresistible flow would be punctuated with flashes of modulated anger, irony or wit. (When Kentridge once objected to an opponent who was developing an argument with excessive prolixity, the judge responded, 'We must allow Mr X a little latitude'; to which Kentridge gave the immortal retort 'It's not the latitude I am objecting to, it's the longitude.') He was also blessed with a beautiful voice. In an article about the so-called Prisons Trial of 1968–9, the *Observer* created this pen portrait of Kentridge: 'Mr Kentridge was easily the most sophisticated person in court, with the face and bearing of an upper-class Regency buck speaking Afrikaans whenever he was obliged to with what sounded like a Knightsbridge accent.'[18] Although Kentridge would demur at its being located to Knightsbridge, that voice, authoritative and smoothed over by the softest of South African accents, is undoubtedly very pleasing on the ear.

Many of the people I have spoken to, themselves barristers of long standing and high reputation, unhesitatingly name Kentridge as the greatest courtroom advocate they have ever seen. Anthony Sampson, describing Kentridge in his biography of Nelson Mandela, caught this quality of inexorability when he referred to Kentridge's 'relentless rationality'.[19] Kentridge, aged only forty-five, appeared in the seminal case of *Madzimbamuto v Lardner-Burke*[20] in the Privy Council in London in 1968. His argument took a full six days to develop, involving the citation of hundreds of legal authorities and texts. It was the first time he had ever argued a case in England. Lord Reid, one of the most brilliant judges of the twentieth century and who delivered the majority judgment in the case, was said to have later described Kentridge as the finest advocate he had ever heard. Gilbert Marcus SC, whom Kentridge led on a number of occasions, spoke of his ability to reduce a seemingly complex case to its essentials: 'He had the capacity to distil both fact and law to their essence, and then present his conclusion to the court with absolute conviction. Judges were very hesitant to challenge him.' It was said to be a running joke among South African judges that they should always reserve judgment on cases that Kentridge argued; in the moment of their utterance his arguments sounded so compelling that it was essential to take the time to ponder them further. Dikgang Moseneke, later the deputy chief justice of South Africa and whom Kentridge represented in the early 1960s when Moseneke was still a teenager, recalled being thrilled by his counsel's 'swagger and fearlessness'.[21] David Pannick QC recalled a case he argued against Kentridge in England, William Rees-Mogg's ill-fated challenge to the constitutionality of the Maastricht Treaty, describing Kentridge's approach as akin to a polite invitation to the judges to make themselves comfortable in the back of a very well-appointed limousine: 'I was reduced to running alongside that limousine, struggling to keep up.' Jeremy Gauntlett SC QC, who was Kentridge's junior in various political cases in the 1980s, recalls thinking, as he sat in court, 'only Merlin himself could cast such a spell'. Speaking about the art of advocacy, Sir Alan Moses referred to the paradox that the more dramatic the lawyer the less effective he or she is likely to be. Reaching for his ideal advocate, Moses invoked Kentridge, describing his 'placid recitation of fact in a quiet voice with the sudden moment of steel . . . it makes the hairs stand up on the back of your head'.[22] In a speech to commemorate Kentridge's ninetieth birthday, his old friend Jonathan Sumption referred to the 'mesmerising quality of his advocacy, the low bass, the measured cadences, the caustic irony, the striking turns of phrase'. Kentridge was the master of Sumption's first rule of advocacy: 'when you start a sentence the tribunal should never be quite sure how it is going to end'.[23]

The other aspect of Kentridge's advocacy which requires mention was his acerbic bravery in the face of fiercely pro-apartheid judges, who generally detested the clients he was representing. In 1977 Kentridge was retained by Denis Goldberg and several other prisoners serving sentences for political crimes. Goldberg had been sentenced to life in prison at the Rivonia Trial and for the previous thirteen years had been deprived of any news relating to the outside world. The prisoners brought a claim against the minister of prisons challenging the decision to prevent them from reading newspapers or otherwise receiving information concerning political events. The issue turned in part on whether prisoners had a right to news or whether it was a privilege which could be withheld at the discretion of the authorities. A Brigadier du Plessis had prepared an affidavit responding to the application and in it had himself referred to the 'right' to such reading matter. When Kentridge relied on this seeming admission in his submissions, the judge, a notoriously government-friendly figure, responded by saying that the brigadier was not a lawyer and was using language in a loose sense. Kentridge retorted with heavy irony, 'Come, come, My Lord, this is after all a *grown-up* Brigadier'.[24] Geoff Budlender, then a young attorney sitting behind counsel, remembers his astonishment that anyone would have the temerity to talk to a judge like that.[25] Benjamin Pogrund, the campaigning journalist, recalled Kentridge's demeanour during the marathon Prisons Trial towards an equally establishment-minded judge:

> When Kentridge pursued cross-examination, the judge's face went red and his head tilted back as he visibly struggled to control his temper. Kentridge dealt with him without ever raising his voice. He would turn sideways and address [the judge] with cold contempt. In Kentridge's mouth, the ritual phrase 'As Your Lordship pleases,' sounded a total insult, and [the judge] knew it and would burst into shouting. Then, realising he had lost control he would abruptly adjourn the court, stalk out, and return a few minutes later.[26]

I could quote a host of others who saw Kentridge in action. But to attempt a description of an advocate's qualities is like trying to convey a theatre actor's stage presence. Words fall short. Ultimately you had to be there. Fortunately, for many of the cases I discuss in the chapters that follow, verbatim transcripts are available. Using Kentridge's own words I have sought to bring the force and magic of his advocacy to life.

Readers can also see Kentridge on screen. Although none of Kentridge's courtroom appearances were filmed he was finely portrayed by Albert Finney in a 1984 television version of John Blair's play about the Steve Biko inquest. The man himself can also be seen in wig and gown in a mock trial of George Washington which was conducted in the Old Hall of Lincoln's Inn in 1990 before a large audience of visiting American lawyers. It was a rare example of

Kentridge in the role of prosecutor and it will not surprise anyone to learn that he did not obtain a conviction.[27]

Yet there is something more about Kentridge the lawyer than courtroom brilliance or legal acumen. Jonathan Sumption identified it with exactitude: it is moral stature, something that, as Sumption put it, 'no amount of forensic technique can impersonate'. Kentridge acquired that stature not simply through longevity and accumulated experience. He was already demonstrating it in his thirties when judges listened to him with respect and care. It was gained through a combination of characteristics: absolute professional integrity, intellectual rigour and courtesy. Moral stature is something few advocates attain. It is a quality which not only redounds to the credit of the advocate but also to their client or case. I have no doubt that it is this quality that served to imbue in Kentridge's cross-examination and submissions in the Biko inquest the gravitas that turned that proceeding into the seminal event it became. His words echoed round the world.

Today professionals are encouraged, almost required, to actively market themselves to potential clients. Throughout his career Kentridge never lifted a finger in that direction. The very thought of self-promotion filled him with horror. Newspaper articles of the time lament his fastidious refusal ever to grant interviews. For Kentridge, an advocate's reputation should be founded solely on the work they undertake. In his lecture 'The Ethics of Advocacy' he expressed the hope that the 'distinction between a profession and a business still . . . remains'.[28] Although Kentridge wrote articles for legal journals and gave numerous lectures (in the early 1970s he even spent a term as a visiting scholar at Harvard Law School), there was otherwise a remoteness which separated him from his clientele. A newspaper profile of Kentridge published in 1977 (naturally, without his co-operation) reported that it was 'just as terrifying to be his client as it is to face him in the witness stand'.[29]

This adamantine rectitude may explain an interesting episode dating from the late 1970s in which Kentridge was involved. In 1977 Dr Percy Yutar, the former attorney general of the Transvaal, applied to join the Johannesburg Bar, so that he could engage in private practice as an advocate. Yutar, once memorably described by R. W.

Johnson as the apartheid regime's Vyshinsky,[30] had been the senior prosecutor in the Rivonia Trial, which resulted in life sentences being imposed on Nelson Mandela, Walter Sisulu and other senior African National Congress (ANC) members. He had also prosecuted Breyten Breytenbach, the radical Afrikaans poet, who had been sentenced to nine years in prison for treason in 1975. Yutar had achieved notoriety for the 'venom and viciousness' with which he prosecuted political cases,[31] and also for his addiction to publicity. He freely gave interviews to newspapers, lauding his own supposed achievements and inveighing against some of the defendants he had prosecuted. He had earned the enmity of the legal profession for his unprecedented personal attack on Alan Paton when the writer had given evidence in mitigation on behalf of the Rivonia defendants in 1964.

For Kentridge, Yutar represented the very antithesis of how a professional person should behave. He also had personal reason to despise Yutar. When Kentridge's wife Felicia was a young advocate in the late 1950s, she found herself defending a man on a murder charge which Yutar was prosecuting. Yutar offered to accept a guilty plea to culpable homicide (the equivalent of manslaughter) and tried to pressurise Felicia (who was twenty years his junior) to persuade her client to agree to plead guilty to the lesser charge which, unlike that of murder, did not carry the death penalty. But Felicia's client insisted he was innocent and refused to plead guilty to anything. When the case came before the court, Yutar announced that the state's witnesses could not be traced and so he was withdrawing the prosecution. Kentridge himself had direct experience of Yutar's professional ethics. When Yutar was prosecuting a prison guard for providing newspapers with information about the torture of prisoners at the notorious Cinderella Prison at Boksburg, east of Johannesburg, he made a false and entirely gratuitous attack on the integrity of the well-known *Rand Daily Mail* journalist Benjamin Pogrund. Kentridge represented Pogrund in his successful libel action against Yutar, which led to a damages award.[32]

So when Yutar made his application to join the Johannesburg Bar, Kentridge took the unheard-of step of opposing it. A hearing was convened, presided over by senior members of the Bar Council, at which Kentridge laid out his reasons why Yutar should be denied admission. In the transcript of the hearing one can detect a streak of understated rage permeating Kentridge's submissions and cross-examination. The time he devoted to this proceeding, from which he could gain nothing personally, takes us to the heart of Kentridge's personality: the passionate belief in comporting oneself in accordance with rigorous professional and personal principles; the self-discipline in seeing something through; the contempt for those who compromised their integrity to gain advantage. The sixty-eight-year-old Yutar was eventually permitted to join the Bar, but subject to the humiliating condition that he carry out a pupillage with an established advocate so that he could relearn the rudiments of professional ethics.[33]

No proper account of Kentridge's work can ignore his wife. Felicia was born in 1930 to Irene Geffen, the first female advocate in South Africa. She and Sydney married in 1952 and had four children. Felicia was herself only the eighth or ninth female advocate called to the South African Bar. She practised from another Johannesburg group (a 'group' is the equivalent to an English set of chambers), although in South Africa in the 1950s and 1960s motherhood made private practice very difficult. In 1973 she founded the Law Clinic at Witwatersrand university, where law students would provide pro bono legal advice to mainly black clients in relation to employment, housing, family and criminal issues. In a country with virtually no legal aid system, the Law Clinic offered vital services to those who would otherwise have no access to legal assistance. Out of that project in the late 1970s Felicia, alongside Arthur Chaskalson (later South Africa's chief justice) and Geoff Budlender, founded the Legal Resources Centre (LRC), which, with the assistance of advocates willing to give their services gratis, provided representation to the otherwise legally disenfranchised and brought a number of seminal test cases concerning restrictions on the working and living arrangements of black people, the outcomes of which changed for the better hundreds of thousands of lives. Sydney was one of the LRC's first trustees, and he says that, through her work for it, Felicia did far more to mitigate the iniquities of apartheid than he ever did.[34] In honouring her tireless contribution to the LRC (which continued throughout Felicia's life), Nelson Mandela, then president of South Africa, said that 'This remarkable institution perhaps did more than any other in the 1970s and 1980s to challenge executive abuses, and to be a legal voice for the voiceless.'[35] The LRC continues in existence to this day.[36]

Press photographs of Kentridge outside court in the sixties and seventies show a countenance of intense, almost saturnine, seriousness. A newspaper profile in 1977 described his 'cold glittering eyes under bushy eyebrows and a forehead knitted in a permanent frown'.[37] Former colleagues recall a man with a forbidding presence not given to small talk or levity when preparing his cases. His juniors told me of anxious weekends spent in the study of his house discussing tactics for forthcoming trials or appeals. His close friend and fellow advocate Ivor Schwartzman recalled giving Kentridge lifts to his chambers in the 1960s: 'We would often drive in total silence. Sydney would be cogitating on some legal point, entirely oblivious to the world.'

But there was – and is – another side to Sydney Kentridge. Ever since he went to see *La Traviata* in war-torn Naples in 1944, he has been a devoted opera-goer. I was surprised to hear that he was an enthusiastic participant in chorus rehearsals of amateur productions of Gilbert and Sullivan in the 1950s. His children remembered that he would assiduously read them the great novels of the English canon in the evening, impersonating with gusto the various voices of Dickens's or Stevenson's characters, before retreating to his study to continue his legal work. Kentridge's daughter Eliza recalled this in her poetry collection *Signs for an Exhibition*:

WHO WANTS A CHAPTER?
US, US
WE ALL DO

There was always a book on the go
I fell asleep to Dickens and Nesbit
Year after year in the feathered room of your voice

'Sign Poem 6'

In their private lives Felicia and Sydney Kentridge were a glamorous couple of 1960s and '70s Johannesburg, living in a large house surrounded by beautifully tended gardens on Houghton Drive (the house lodged in many people's memories and is now the studio and home of Kentridge's son, the internationally renowned artist William Kentridge). Writers, lawyers, journalists and intellectuals visiting South Africa would often be found at their dinner table. Their circle included the novelist Nadine Gordimer, the politician Helen Suzman, the writer Mary Benson and the artist Cecil Skotnes. Gordimer was said to have used many of the people she socialised with as models for her fictional characters, and some have discerned a portrait of Kentridge in her 1966 novel *The Late Bourgeois World*.

In 2013 Kentridge's daughter Catherine published a memoir of her childhood, *The Book of Cathy: A South African Childhood*. It contains a vivid child's-eye view of her parents. Catherine recalls her parents' sociability, their being frequently out at the theatre or dinner parties, and annual New Year's Eve parties for which a band would be hired; there was dancing on a specially rented wooden dance floor, and Dante, 'a very popular and famous Italian bartender', would serve elaborate cocktails. Friends remember a fine dancer and tennis player as well as an enthusiastic participant in games of charades. A lifelong lover of cricket, Kentridge can still recall going, at the age of eight, with his father to see England play South Africa in the second test at Newlands, Cape Town, in January 1931. With the lawyer's dedication to detail he can remember the precise number of runs each player made.

Although he sat as a temporary judge at various times,[38] Kentridge never crossed over to become a full-time member of the judiciary. Many have remarked that, in other circumstances, Kentridge would have ended his career sitting in the highest court of South Africa or England. But becoming a judge in apartheid South Africa was not something he could contemplate. The thought of having to apply apartheid legislation was repugnant to him. And Kentridge started out too late in England for it to be feasible that he might join the English judiciary.[39] Nonetheless in 1994, although by then in full-time practice in London, Kentridge was invited by Arthur Chaskalson to sit for two terms as an acting judge of the newly formed South

African Constitutional Court.[40] (Chaskalson, the court's first president, was apparently delighted that Kentridge agreed to participate and spoke of the 'shock to the South African legal establishment [of having] this great figure . . . come out from England to sit with us in our Court'.)[41] Created by the post-apartheid Interim Constitution, the court was a cornerstone of the new multiracial era. Kentridge attended the opening ceremony to hear Nelson Mandela say, 'the last time I entered a court of law was to find out whether or not I would be sentenced to death'.[42]

It was fitting that Kentridge delivered the Constitutional Court's first judgment, in which he ruled unconstitutional an apartheid-period law that placed on the accused the burden of proving that a confession had not been voluntarily obtained.[43] (This was no technical point: for decades the state had relied in prosecutions on confessions extracted by violence or threats.) He was also a member of the panel which heard the first case argued in the Constitutional Court, in which two convicted murderers sentenced to hang invited the court to declare that the death penalty was unconstitutional.[44] It was perhaps the most momentous case ever to be heard by the Constitutional Court, which held unanimously that capital punishment was indeed incompatible with the new constitution. The result was that over 300 other convicted prisoners then under sentence of death and awaiting execution had those sentences commuted. Kentridge, who in his early days in practice had heard the death penalty pronounced on many of his clients, concluded his judgment in the following way:

> [T]he choice . . . is not between the death penalty on the one hand and the condonation of the murderer's act on the other. The choice is between the death penalty and a long term of imprisonment which might in appropriate cases include life imprisonment in the fullest sense of the term. As a civilised society it is not open to us, in my opinion, to express our moral outrage by executing even the worst of murderers any more than we could do so by the public hangings or mutilations of a bygone time.
>
> In conclusion . . . the striking down of the death penalty entails no sympathy whatsoever for the murderer, nor any condonation of his

crime. What our decision does entail is a recognition that even the worst and most vicious criminals are not excluded from the protections of the Constitution. In 1910 Mr Winston Churchill speaking in the House of Commons said this: 'The mood and temper of the public in regard to the treatment of crime and criminals is one of the most unfailing tests of the civilisation of any country. A calm dispassionate recognition of the rights of the accused, and even of the convicted criminal, against the State . . . tireless efforts towards discovery of curative and regenerative processes: unfailing faith that there is a treasure, if you can only find it, in the heart of every man. These are the symbols which, in the treatment of crime and criminal, mark and measure the stored-up strength of a nation, and are sign and proof of the living virtue in it.'[45]

★

In his later life Kentridge has had many honours bestowed on him. He has been deluged with honorary degrees and awards. In 1999 he was knighted 'for services to international law and justice'. At a dinner at the Banqueting House in London to celebrate the occasion, he was described as 'simply the most highly regarded advocate in the Commonwealth'. On other occasions he has been described as 'the advocate of the century'.[46] The then lord chief justice, Lord Phillips, once described Kentridge as 'the most brilliant advocate of his generation or perhaps of his generations'. At a dinner in South Africa in 2000 honouring the joint contribution of Sydney and Felicia Kentridge to law and justice in South Africa, Nelson Mandela gave a speech where he said of Kentridge, recalling his appearance in the Treason Trial, that 'his brilliance shone out and with it, the promise of the career to come. His manner was always understated, controlled and relentlessly rational. His cross-examination was devastating.'[47]

In 2012 lectures that Kentridge had delivered over the course of thirty years were collected in a book, *Free Country*, edited by two chambers colleagues, David Lloyd Jones and George Leggatt (both of whom have gone on to become Supreme Court judges). In 2013 Kentridge appeared on BBC Radio 4's *Desert Island Discs*.[48] Despite these laurels he remains a very modest man. The one boast, if you can call it that, which I have ever heard him utter is that, perhaps uniquely for any lawyer, he has acted during his career for three winners of the

Nobel Peace Prize – Chief Albert Luthuli, Nelson Mandela and Archbishop Desmond Tutu. When I quote to him some plaudit aimed in his direction, he likes to quote Adlai Stevenson – 'Flattery is fine, as long as you don't inhale.'

This book is not a biography of Sydney Kentridge. To embark upon the life of a (at the time of writing) ninety-nine-year-old man would be a daunting task. Nor is it an attempt to give a comprehensive over-view of the legal work he has been involved in. That would also be a vast undertaking: in England alone Kentridge argued almost fifty cases in the House of Lords or Supreme Court,[49] to say nothing of his many appearances in other courts. Instead this book focuses on the key political cases in which Kentridge appeared from the 1950s to the 1980s. My purposes are various: to provide, through the lens of the courtroom, an insight into South Africa at an extraordinary time; to explain how the law operates at moments of crisis; to show how advocacy can challenge an oppressive state; and to celebrate the work of Sydney Kentridge. The lives and work of great men and women deserve to be memorialised, and the writing of this book has led me to the unequivocal conclusion that Kentridge is among them. He has inspired many throughout his life and I hope this book might continue that inspiration into the future.

I started this introduction with Kentridge's last case in the Supreme Court. In fact, a few years later, aged ninety-six, he returned to Parliament Square to speak at the valedictory ceremony of a Supreme Court judge, Lord Mance.[50] Addressing the court for ten minutes without notes, Kentridge noted that Mance was retiring at the 'ridicu-lously early age of seventy-five' and advised him that, to get the best out of retirement, one had to develop a 'talent for idleness'. Kentridge's retirement has been shorter than most but he has followed his own advice. His nineties have been filled with cricket (of the spectating kind), opera, family and friends, and a remarkable tolerance for my ceaseless rounds of questions about the details of cases he litigated many decades ago.

2

The Early Years

THE UNION OF South Africa into which Sydney Kentridge was
born on 5 November 1922 was then in its infancy. It had been
created twelve years earlier, in the wake of the Second Boer War of
1899–1902, through a union of the older British possessions of the
Cape Colony and Natal with the newly annexed Afrikaans-speaking
Boer republics of the Transvaal and Orange Free State. The South
Africa formed in 1910 was a self-governing dominion of the British
Empire but in practice still closely tied to what its white English-
speaking population – a minority among a minority – regarded as the
mother country.[1] Its four provinces each had their own parliaments
(elected by whites only) but were overseen by a Union administration
headed by a governor general appointed by the British crown. A trigger for the Boer War had been the discovery of gold in and around
Kentridge's birthplace, Johannesburg (then only a mining camp in
what was at that time the independent Transvaal), in the 1880s.
Thereafter South Africa had rapidly industrialised and urbanised. In
1899 the Witwatersrand region produced a quarter of the world's
gold; by 1921 it produced half. South Africa was badly hit by the
Spanish influenza pandemic of 1918–19: in some towns mortality
reached 25 per cent, and among the fatalities was Sydney's paternal
grandfather Woolf Kentridge, who had been born in Lithuania before
emigrating with his family to England in the 1880s and then to Natal
at the turn of the century.[2] But the growth of South Africa's economic
base, largely owned by English-speaking whites, was not halted. In its
largest conurbation the population was growing exponentially: in
1904 Johannesburg had had a population of only 60,000, rising to
102,000 in 1911 and well over 500,000 in 1921. Kentridge was born
into a dynamically changing country.

Kentridge has no recollection of the house, in the eastern Johannesburg suburb of Kensington, where he was born.[3] Shortly after his birth the family moved to his maternal grandparents' house in another obscure suburb, to the south of Johannesburg, Forest Hill: the first house that he can remember. His father Morris was by the early 1920s both an attorney (the South African equivalent of a solicitor) and a prominent Labour member of the national parliament. Having followed his parents to South Africa in 1902 after completing his studies at the universities of St Andrews and Glasgow, Morris had started work as a lawyer in Natal, and had long been active in politics. His early years provide an exemplary story of resilience in the face of reverses of fortune: seats won at one election only to be lost at the next, but without any loss of resolve. Morris finally secured a firm foothold in national politics when he was elected in 1924 for the Johannesburg constituency of Troyeville. He remained its MP until he retired in 1958, by which time he was Father of the House: the longest serving member of parliament. He published *I Recall*, his memoirs, a year later. 'Public service was one of the things we took for granted,' recalls Kentridge of his childhood. Although Morris would become one of the grand old men of South African politics, in his early life he was known as a firebrand. During the so-called Rand Revolt of early 1922 Morris provided legal advice to the rebels and a car in which he was travelling with his pregnant wife May was shot at by government soldiers (Kentridge was almost lost to the world before he entered it). Martial law having been proclaimed, Morris was detained without charge for several weeks.

Kentridge's mother May was born in London in 1899, after her family had emigrated to England from Russian-occupied Poland. She was brought to what would become South Africa as a young girl by her parents, who, like many other emigrants, were lured by the promise of a more prosperous life. The movements of Kentridge's parents and grandparents speak to a period of extraordinary cross-continental human migration, driven in many cases by racial intolerance and a willingness to risk all to forge new lives in new worlds. Eighteen years younger than Morris, May married him in 1921.[4] Although his maternal grandfather Leon died in the late 1920s, Kentridge still remembers him as a fine carpenter who made toys for the young Sydney and took him for his first visit to a cinema (or 'bioscope', as they were then called in South Africa) to see a Charlie Chaplin film.

Morris was prominent in Jewish affairs as vice president of the Board of Deputies of South African Jews, and May was equally active in Jewish charities as an organiser of fundraising events. While both his parents were Orthodox Jews, they were – Kentridge recalls – 'not particularly observant. My father went to the synagogue on what were called the High Festivals – the Jewish New Year, the Day of Atonement and so on. And we were brought up to learn about them and to do the same, but we didn't observe Sabbath or anything of that sort.'

Many families like the Kentridges in Johannesburg's large Jewish community traced their immediate ancestry to eastern Europe, from where parents or grandparents had been driven by rising and, at times, violent antisemitism under Russian rule. British South Africa was, for them, a haven of tolerance and opportunity. Some renounced their religion altogether; for many others, their faith remained in the background, part of their cultural identity but rarely at the forefront of family life. 'We always knew that we were of the Jewish religion and never thought of being anything else, but I don't think that religious belief played any real part in my father's or mother's life, nor in ours.' Until the age of fifteen or sixteen Kentridge would go to synagogue with his mother and father, but usually only for high festivals. 'There were traditions we observed because they were traditions, but we never spoke about God. My parents had a Jewish marriage, the family had Jewish burials, my own marriage was a Jewish marriage and my children were brought up in the Jewish faith . . . but like Tony Blair, our mantra was "We don't do God."'

Kentridge was the eldest of three brothers.[5] In 1931, when he was eight years old, the family moved to Yeoville, a more middle-class suburb to the north-east of Johannesburg. The house in Yeoville, small and neat, was to be Kentridge's home, apart from the years he spent abroad in the mid-1940s, for more than twenty years until he married in 1952.

Although the Kentridges were by no means wealthy, they had, as all but the poorest white families did in interwar South Africa, black servants who lived in a room in their backyard. 'We usually had two:

a man who did the heavy cleaning, and a woman who did the cook-
ing, and sometimes a white nanny,' he recalls. The domestic help the
Kentridges had said more about the entrenched racial divides of South
Africa as a whole than it did about his family's economic circumstances. 'We lived in comfort, but my mother and father were not well-
off.' Because of his all-consuming commitment to politics Morris
Kentridge did not have a substantial legal practice and, as in Britain in
the same period, the salary of a member of parliament in South Africa
was fairly meagre.

The early 1920s was a formative period for South African politics,
when the foundations were laid upon which full-blown apartheid
would later be built.[6] In 1922 Jan Smuts's government brought in the
Apprenticeship Act, which excluded black people from becoming
apprentices. In 1923 a Native Urban Areas Act decreed that blacks
could only live in urban areas temporarily, and that they should only
be allowed to rent, not own, property. At the same time, their collective bargaining rights at work were curtailed. Later that year the
African National Congress was formed, effectively by a renaming of
the Native National Congress. The new ANC was far less trustful
of Jan Smuts than its predecessor had been. After Smuts abruptly
dismissed a delegation demanding equal rights and an end to segregation, the ANC resolved that South Africa's long-term future lay
outside the British Empire, which it concluded could no longer be
trusted to extend civil rights.

In 1931 – the year that South Africa gained full independence from
Britain – the young Sydney started in the preparatory department of
King Edward VII School, where he was to stay for the next eight
years. It was then and (according to Kentridge) remains Johannesburg's
most prestigious boys' school. It resembled many other grammar
schools across the British Empire: a school for the academically able
sons – all of them, in South Africa, white – of aspirational parents. In
1933 Kentridge passed the exam to progress from King Edward VII's
preparatory department to its senior school. His favourite subjects
were now English and history, and later classics. He never enjoyed
the compulsory Afrikaans lessons that continued until the end of his
schooldays. Kentridge is modest about how well he performed

academically: 'I would say, well, but not brilliantly; I was never top of the class.' But at high school he found himself first or second in the class at Latin, and his precociousness soon meant that he was moved up a year.

With the Great Depression at its height, the South African Party (SAP), led by Jan Smuts, and the National Party, led by J. B. M. Hertzog, pledged to unite ahead of the 1934 election. The result was the United South African National Party, whose cumbersome name was soon shortened to the United Party. In 1932 Morris Kentridge left the Labour Party and joined General Smuts's new 'big tent'. Although Morris Kentridge was normally away in Cape Town, where the national parliament sat, for five months of the year, the family home remained in Johannesburg. The family sometimes went down to Cape Town (a long train journey from Johannesburg) while parliament was sitting, so Sydney and his brothers could see their father speak there. Kentridge would sometimes accompany his father to political meetings: he recalls his father being heckled during campaigning for the 1938 election, and giving as good as he got. Kentridge still remembers the excitement of hearing General Smuts speaking in support of his father in Johannesburg, the meeting kept in order by a cadre of burley bouncers procured from a local boxing gym.

In his latter school years Kentridge specialised in the classics. He loved the logic of the Latin language and learning about classical civilisation. His English master, Cecil Williams, who seemed more interested in discussing politics in the classroom, left a profound impression on the young man, who recalls vigorous discussions about the Italian invasion of Abyssinia in 1935. (Williams later became a professional actor and a leading member of the Communist Party and the Congress of Democrats. Nelson Mandela was arrested in August 1962 in the same car as Williams, masquerading as his chauffeur.)

Boys normally matriculated at the age of seventeen, but as he had been moved up a year Kentridge sat his matriculation examinations in December 1938, shortly after his sixteenth birthday. A few weeks later he began a bachelor's degree at the University of the Witwatersrand ('Wits' to its students), studying a combination of political philosophy and classics. He was gripped by the momentous events of 1939. The outbreak of war in September reopened the old fissures of South

African politics. 'The war, and what South Africa was going to do about it, divided the country. In parliament there was a division between those who followed General Smuts – all the English-speaking members – and those who followed General Hertzog, who were Afrikaner nationalists.' Parliament voted by a narrow majority in favour of following Britain and declaring war on Germany. Hertzog resigned as prime minister after the governor general, Sir Patrick Duncan, refused to allow him to call a general election. In Hertzog's place Smuts formed a government wholeheartedly committed to the war effort.

There were historical reasons why many Afrikaners opposed joining Britain's war against Germany. There were old ties of cultural kinship with Germany, including the fact that the Calvinist Afrikaners felt closer to German Lutheranism than to the Anglican Church. The bitter humiliation of the Boer War and its aftermath was within living memory; there had been harsh and, in some cases, inhumane treatment at the hands of British troops and administrators, while Wilhelmine Germany (with imperial ambitions of its own in southern Africa) had supported the cause of Boer independence. A number of prominent South African politicians, however, went further: they were openly sympathetic to German and Italian fascism. In the 1930s Oswald Pirow, who served as minister of both justice and defence, had twice visited Hitler. He returned home a great admirer of the Führer and an active advocate of a Nazi-style dictatorship for South Africa. (Twenty years later an unrepentant Pirow, as lead advocate for the prosecution, would face Kentridge in a former synagogue in Pretoria at the marathon Treason Trial (see Chapter 3).)

Kentridge is generous towards those South Africans who disagreed with Smuts and backed neutrality in the war: 'I wouldn't say they were Nazis, and while there were some who committed treason, they were a small minority. But certainly those on the Nationalist Party side were hoping for a German victory, and were very cock-a-hoop when the Germans were winning.' There was no question of the Kentridge family's stance: they supported the war effort and Smuts's government. Kentridge's father Morris remained a loyal MP throughout the war.

These parliamentary divisions were reflected in the country at large and at its universities. Wits was almost entirely English-speaking, although there was a minority Afrikaner element that opposed South African participation in the war. Kentridge recalls the febrile mood of student life at this time of world crisis and the debates that raged on campus. He soon became politically active at Wits and enjoyed the freedom of student life so much at first that the studiousness he had shown at King Edward VII eluded him. By the end of his second year Kentridge's academic application had returned: he got firsts in all his subjects, and his parents rewarded him with a radiogram – an enormous wireless set with a built-in gramophone. But he found time for the debating society and for two years he wrote for a weekly student newspaper, *WU's Views* (WU being the university's acronym). Thinking that he might become a journalist after graduation, in his second year Kentridge got a Saturday job working for the news editor of what was then Johannesburg's only Sunday paper, the *Sunday Times*. At the tender age of seventeen, he became its university correspondent. Kentridge downplays the achievement: 'it didn't mean much because there wasn't much news'.

Some of Kentridge's closest friends at Wits were medical students, and most were engaged, like him, in student politics or journalism. In mid-1940 Italy entered the war, threatening British Kenya and, potentially, countries even further south from its bases in Ethiopia. Many of his fellow students started enlisting in the South African forces, but Kentridge was still too young to join them. Instead he got stuck into the most contentious domestic question of the day for students: the 'colour question' at universities. While Kentridge was studying at Wits there was still no law against blacks or 'coloureds' enrolling. The university was considering segregating the tiny number of black and coloured students from their white fellows. Kentridge had been elected to the student representative council, which in 1941 voted against race segregation, so that black students could continue to participate in sport and university functions. The governing body agreed, but found that the predominantly Afrikaner University of Pretoria then refused to play Wits at rugby on the grounds that blacks might be watching, or – worse still – playing. 'Many English-speaking students felt that it was more important to have sporting relations

with Afrikaans universities than to have blacks, and favoured segregation. This caused a great deal of debate and division in our university,'
recalls Kentridge, who was for the first time confronted head-on by
the painful realities of racial politics in South Africa. These would
become even more acute with the onset of apartheid by the end of
the decade. The modest racial diversity of South Africa's English-
speaking universities did not survive for long: by the end of the 1950s
Wits (which Nelson Mandela attended in the late 1940s) had, along
with the others, been made whites-only.

By December 1940 some 137,000 South African men and women
were under arms. As in the First World War, blacks were officially
barred from combat roles, but many thousands joined the Native
Military Corps. In 1941 South African troops played a key role in
defeating the Italian forces in East Africa. Many of them then headed
north to the Libyan desert, only to be captured at the Second Battle
of Tobruk in 1942. In May of that year South African forces assisted
in the capture of the port of Diego Suarez in Madagascar from the
Vichy French, and in July 1943 they joined US, British and Canadian
forces in the invasion of Sicily.

The By the war's end some 335,000 South Africans had served in the
Allied war effort, more than a third of them black or coloured. Among
them were Kentridge's mother May, a volunteer army lorry driver in
South Africa in her early forties. From January 1942 Kentridge too was
in uniform, in the South African Air Force. Barely nineteen, he had
gained his Bachelor of Arts degree in December 1941 and immediately
volunteered. (South Africa never instituted any form of conscription
during the war.) He had no hesitation about doing so: 'I was for Britain
and against Germany. It was what I believed in, and it was automatic
that I should volunteer as soon I had finished my degree. The age for
going into the forces then was eighteen, so I could have gone earlier,
but my father felt that I should finish my degree.'

The recent graduate reported for a medical examination in the
middle of January 1942. A few weeks later Private Kentridge was of
the Air Intelligence Liaison, initially at a military camp outside
Pretoria. After basic training – 'marching and that sort of thing' – his
unit was sent in May 1942 to East Africa on a troop ship from Durban

up to Mombasa in Kenya. It was the young man's first time at sea and he was dreadfully seasick. It was also his first experience of real danger. Because Japanese submarines were known to be marauding in the Indian Ocean, the troop ship was escorted by a British destroyer. At dusk one evening the destroyer came alongside. A disembodied voice, carried by loudhailer, explained that a Greek tanker had been sunk by a submarine thirty miles away; the destroyer was going to look for survivors. Kentridge recalls the parting words of the destroyer's captain – 'Good luck!' – and the feeling of dread that descended on the troop ship, which hurried on up the coast, now unguarded and defenceless against Japanese torpedoes. There was actually a war on.

They arrived safely at Mombasa, which was by mid-1942 a busy naval base. After the Japanese had sunk the British battleships *Prince of Wales* and *Repulse* off Malaya in December 1941, the British Indian Ocean fleet had been withdrawn from Colombo to Mombasa, further away from the relentless advance of the Japanese. Kentridge recalls 'doing very little for a year' near Mombasa between mid-1942 and mid-1943. But he was soon promoted to corporal, and then to sergeant.

Kentridge, who had mostly only ever really encountered black people as domestic servants, now saw them perform a wide range of military roles in East Africa, and later in Italy: not just as batmen, mess servants, waiters and cleaners but also as engineers in the pioneer battalions. In South Africa in those days there was a common racist axiom – 'No black man should have liquor, or a gun, or the vote' – and while there were no black South Africans in a combatant capacity, Kentridge soon saw soldiers from India and West Africa bearing arms, 'an entirely new phenomenon' for him. While enforced segregation meant he had little interaction with black South African troops, for the first time he got to know Afrikaans speakers properly. Kentridge had spent all of his childhood in the big cities of Cape Town and Johannesburg, being educated alongside fellow English speakers, not Afrikaners. 'I remember sharing a tent with a couple of Afrikaans-speaking people, farm boys. They were very nice, very decent, and it was quite a revelation to me.'

Kentridge's unit was involved in coastal reconnaissance, scanning the ocean for signs of Japanese naval activity. While he soon realised that he would never be a pilot, he hoped to be a navigator; but he was chronically airsick, 'so that was the end of that thought'. Instead he found himself in 'a sort of jumped-up office job, conveying intelligence from headquarters to our unit, and vice versa, and making reports of operations'. In fact there was never anything to report. 'We were on the lookout for Japanese submarines, but none were ever sighted.'

In mid-1943, after an indolent year in Kenya, Kentridge was relieved to be sent on a troop ship up to Egypt. He was transferred to another unit that went through the Western Desert, from where by now the Axis forces had been finally routed. After a brief spell at a camp on the Libya–Tunisia border, Kentridge left the African continent for the first time in his life and sailed to Malta. A few weeks later he participated in the Allied invasion of Sicily, landing just south of Syracuse on D-Day plus four. It was here that Kentridge had his only moment of direct physical danger throughout the war. He recalls the terrifying experience of German Stukas attacking the recently captured airfield he was stationed at, and the bullets of snipers singing around his ears.

The invasion of Sicily had started on 9 July 1943. Just over a month later the whole island was in Allied hands. Kentridge's unit proceeded northwards at pace, through Catania and Taormina, which Kentridge found time to be charmed by.[7] In September he crossed the Straits of Messina from Sicily into the toe of Italy, enjoying a swim in the clear blue waters. His arrival was an epiphany of sorts. 'Italy was the first part of mainland Europe I'd ever seen, and from that time on, I loved it. That exposure to Italy was one of the important things in my life.' The first Italian city Kentridge explored properly was Bari, where his unit arrived in October, and he was enthralled to discover that the Allies, keen to restart civil life in the Italian cities they liberated, were about to reopen its opera house. Kentridge already had a love of opera, drawn mostly from gramophone records (there was not much live opera in Johannesburg, apart from amateur productions and the occasional visiting company). He went on to Naples, a 'really beautiful city but as dirty then as it is now', memorably captured in Roberto Rossellini's 1946 film *Paisan*, documenting the Allied liberation of Italy; there he attended his first professional opera performance: *La Traviata* at the San Carlo opera house. (More than sixty years later, in 2005, Kentridge saw his son William's production of *The Magic Flute* in the same auditorium.)

In February 1944 Kentridge was recalled to SAAF headquarters in Pretoria, where he was commissioned as a second lieutenant at the beginning of 1945 before being sent back to Italy. (He had never sought promotion: 'It was gazetted and you were simply told . . . one hoped for it, but never applied.') Rome had by now been liberated, and Kentridge visited the city which was to become his favourite world capital. On VE Day, 8 May 1945, Kentridge found himself 'in a very romantic place, halfway between Mantua and Verona'. A lorry was dispatched to a local brewery to ensure this momentous event was properly celebrated. Although the war in Europe was now over, the newly minted lieutenant found himself stuck in Italy for another eight months, until February 1946, when he was finally demobbed. He was just twenty-three. Kentridge spent a month or so in Cairo before flying to South Africa. Once back in Johannesburg, he was rather overwhelmed by his new-found freedom. For four years he had been told where to go and what to do: 'You didn't have to go and book a ticket, it was all done, and you never had to worry about where you were going to stay,' Kentridge recalls. 'And then you come out of the forces and find you've got to do things for yourself. You've got to go and buy your own clothes, and you've got to choose what you're going to wear.'

Kentridge decided that he wanted to return to university, but this time in England. White South African young men were eligible for an ex-serviceman's grant to study at just about any British university they liked, with a generous grant of £750 and an interest-free loan of £500: a total of £1,250, equivalent to about £50,000 today, and seen as 'untold riches' by Kentridge at the time; certainly enough to cover two years of undergraduate living.

Kentridge had nurtured an ambition to go to Oxford.

Everything we had in the way of language and culture came from Great Britain. One simply grew up with the knowledge that the premier universities in the world were Oxford and Cambridge, and particularly Oxford, because of Rhodes Scholarships which had originated in South Africa. I'd often heard of South Africans who had gone to Oxford on Rhodes Scholarships, which was the ultimate accolade for a student.

While still in uniform in Italy in the winter of 1945/6, Kentridge had unsuccessfully applied for a Rhodes Scholarship. But he did not lose hope. He later met a vice principal of Witwatersrand, who was visiting South African troops in Europe to encourage them to apply to university. The vice principal told Kentridge that Wits' principal, Humphrey Raikes, had previously been the sub-rector of Exeter College, Oxford. Kentridge had got to know the principal reasonably well through student politics, and he was now informed that Exeter would take anyone whom he recommended. 'I applied, and was accepted.' It was a route to university which is today unrecognisable.

Kentridge had decided to study jurisprudence, a degree that ex-servicemen were allowed to complete in two years instead of the usual three. His choice of subject was not motivated by his father's long career as an attorney. If anything, Morris discouraged his eldest son from following in his footsteps: 'He didn't particularly enjoy being an attorney, and he would have thought it terrible if I'd wanted to become one myself,' Kentridge recalls. 'Politics was much more his life than the law. Although he kept up his practice as an attorney alongside being a member of parliament, politics was really his life.'

Kentridge's interest in the law was inspired by an experience in Italy in late 1945. While stationed at South African Air Force head-quarters in Bari, he was approached by a major, a qualified South African lawyer in charge of running court martials. 'He came to me out of the blue one day, and said "You've got a university degree, haven't you?" I said "Yes." He said "Well, we've got two court martials coming up, and all my legal officers have gone back to South Africa. Would you like to do the prosecution?"' Kentridge pointed out that he did not have a degree in law and knew nothing about military tribunals. 'Don't worry about that,' the major replied. 'I'll tell you what the procedure is, and I'll give you a little book I've got on criminal law.' When the two hearings came up – one a case of danger-ous driving in which a serviceman had run over and killed an Italian civilian, the other for theft – the major was the presiding judge-advocate alongside three other officers. 'I remember thinking that this was a very exciting sort of thing to do, to lead your witnesses' evidence, cross-examine, and address a court. It occurred to me that this was what I could do for a living. So that's what tipped me into the law.'

Another reason why Kentridge chose to study law was the integrity of South Africa's judicial system in the mid-twentieth century. Despite the state's racial policies, its judiciary had remained remarkably independent. 'As early as 1832 in the Cape Colony, judges were appointed to hold office *quamdiu se bene gesserit* (during good behaviour) and not merely *durante bene placito* (at the King's Pleasure),' Kentridge noted in a lecture in 1986.[8] Although the young Sydney may not have been aware of this distinction forty years earlier, South Africa's legal system was not simply a tool of the state. It had a long record of scrutinising, and standing up to, the executive. Alan Paton described it as follows:

> In South Africa men are proud of their Judges, because they believe they are incorruptible. Even the black men have faith in them, though they do not always have faith in the Law. In a land of fear this incorruptibility is like a lamp set upon a stand, giving light to all that are in the house.[9]

Kentridge's first encounter with the judiciary was a happy one; after he returned from Italy in early 1946 he served as a clerk to a high court judge, Mr Justice Roper, who exemplified Paton's ideal.

The choice of whether to pursue the law or journalism as a career had nonetheless been a close-run thing. 'I think I could have become a good investigative journalist and quite a good leader writer. But in those days, although journalists were respected, journalism was somehow not regarded as a regular profession,' he recalls.

> When people ask me 'Why did you become a lawyer?' one of the reasons is that I knew I had to earn a living and I couldn't really think of anything else that I was competent to do. I wasn't a scientist and I would have shuddered at the thought of becoming a doctor. I had no artistic ability and I couldn't become an architect. In those days, if you were going for a profession it was law, medicine, architecture or accounting. As I had no interest in figures, that was really it.

It was on this slender and haphazard basis that one of the great legal careers of the century would be founded.

Kentridge still entertained the notion that he might become a journalist later: 'Some of the journalists I knew had been barristers for a short time and then dropped out and had gone into journalism.' But in the meantime, newly arrived at Exeter College, Kentridge was allocated a room of his own, overlooking Broad Street, and threw himself headlong into studying law.

Oxford had been untouched by wartime bombing; the same could certainly not be said of London, which Kentridge visited regularly between 1946 and 1948. Although he had witnessed some devastation in Italy, few of the cities he visited, such as Naples, had been bombed heavily beyond their rail yards; and the historic centres of Rome and Florence had been spared. London was the first city shattered by war that he had seen: 'I was appalled and shocked at the bomb damage in London: the empty sites, the ruins of buildings they had only just started clearing up.' But he soon fell in love with London, and he would end up living there in later life for over forty years. 'Because all the literature we read in South Africa was English literature, we knew all the names: Baker Street, where Sherlock Holmes lived, The Strand, Piccadilly and Pall Mall, from when I had played Monopoly in South Africa as a boy,' Kentridge recalls. 'I knew that Mayfair was a very expensive place, and the Old Kent Road was a very cheap place, and so they were. It was amazing to arrive in what had been magical places during my childhood, and to discover that they really existed.'

Kentridge's closest friends at Oxford were other ex-servicemen who had been given preference in the post-war admissions process. Many of them were four, five or six years older than students who had been too young to serve in the war and had arrived fresh from school. His cohort seemed even older, given their wartime experiences. Just as in the Air Force, Kentridge encountered very few women ('there was no particular girl I knew at Oxford,' he says chastely).

But overall he loved the course, which was mostly English law, although he chose to do an optional course in Roman–Dutch law, on which the common law of South Africa is based. Luckily a Professor

Leigh, who was one of the great exponents of Roman-Dutch law and had written the textbooks on the subject, was at Oxford at the time. As only a handful in Oxford studied the subject, Professor Leigh's lectures were 'really more like tutorials or seminars. You had to make sure you learned what you wanted to learn by your own efforts, but I found that very stimulating.'

Kentridge made the most of his time in England, travelling extensively around the country. In Oxford 'there was always so much going on by way of music, lectures and theatre'. The London theatre, meanwhile, was 'a revelation': he went to the New Theatre in St Martin's Lane, where he saw Laurence Olivier's *King Lear*: 'standing room at the back, but quite remarkable'. He also saw Alec Guinness in *Richard II* and Ralph Richardson in *Cyrano de Bergerac*, both classic productions. 'It was a quality of theatre I'd never dreamed could have existed': Johannesburg theatre in the 1930s had been only semi-professional. Although Covent Garden had yet to reopen with its own company, Kentridge saw the San Carlo Opera perform there, and got standing tickets to hear the celebrated Norwegian soprano Kirsten Flagstad in *The Valkyrie* and *Tristan and Isolde*: 'Somehow in those days I could stand through a Wagner opera: now I cannot always sit through one,' he observed sixty years later. His parents visited London and Sydney found himself invited with them to tea at 10 Downing Street, as Clement Attlee's guests.

Keen to escape England's harsh winter of 1946/7, Kentridge and a South African friend who had also been in Italy during the war and was now studying at Cambridge, took the train to Rome. It was 'a most dreadful winter, especially for a South African, with a fuel shortage. There were times when the gas was simply cut off, and electricity was rationed too.' As South Africans, they escaped the strict post-war exchange controls which prevented British nationals from taking more than fifty pounds abroad a year; they could afford to stop off in Paris, which Kentridge had never visited before. Their third-class return tickets to Rome cost the princely sum of three pounds apiece. Kentridge recalls his Roman New Year's Eve: 'Some Italians then would celebrate the new year by firing guns in the street. I was in my hotel bedroom when a bullet flew through the window past my head and lodged in my bedstead.'

Kentridge's finals in late May and early June of 1948 were, as is usual at Oxford, concentrated into an eight-day period, with three-hour papers each weekday morning and afternoon.

> The extraordinary thing for me was that you had to dress up for examinations in a gown, a mortarboard, a dark suit, white shirt and white bow tie, which struck me as partly ridiculous and partly very delightful. This is what they'd been doing for two hundred years or so at Oxford, and you just didn't query it or revolt against it, it was just one of those things.

A few weeks later he had to return to Oxford for an oral examination, normally offered to candidates on the borderline between a second and a first. His viva was before a panel of examiners presided over by a Professor Waldock, a professor of international law whom he had not met before. Kentridge had been 'expecting an ordeal' but the anticipated grilling turned out to be a formality. Waldock asked the student, 'Did you see in this morning's *Times* what Mr Churchill has to say about capital punishment?' When Kentridge sheepishly confessed that he had not, the professor said, 'Well, we haven't any other questions for you.' That was it. A few weeks later Kentridge learned, to his surprise, that he had obtained a first.

After another holiday in Italy and Switzerland that summer, Kentridge returned to South Africa in August 1948. Although he later had a long career at the English Bar, he never considered joining it in the late 1940s after he had graduated from Oxford, though with his first that would surely have been an option. But it would have required another year's study. Kentridge was nearly twenty-six and a sense of urgency was intruding into his mind, the desire to get on and earn a living.

Anyone with a degree in law from Oxford, Cambridge or London universities was automatically qualified to practise at the South African Bar: all they needed to do was sit simple supplementary examinations on certain aspects of South African law. While waiting to sit the exam Kentridge undertook a quasi-pupillage with Simon Kuper, a member of the Johannesburg Bar whom his father knew and who allowed Kentridge to sit with him in his chambers and accompany him to court.[10] After passing his final law examination in February 1949, Kentridge was called to the South African Bar in Pretoria on 17 April 1949.

The South Africa to which Kentridge returned in August 1948 was very different to the country he had left as an Air Force private in January 1942. Its economy had boomed in wartime, thanks largely to arms manufacturing: by 1945 a significant proportion of the machine gun and rifle ammunition used by the Allied armies was produced there.[11] South Africa's ports benefited from the Allies' preference for the Cape route over the Mediterranean and Suez Canal, where shipping was more vulnerable to submarine and air attack. The domestic economy was further boosted by a fall in imports from Europe, where manufacturing had largely been either turned over to the war effort or disrupted by its ravages.

In America, the Second World War had spurred a burgeoning Civil Rights movement. US armed forces, like those of South Africa, were still segregated; but the experience of combat and President Roosevelt's rhetoric contrasting American ideals of diversity and tolerance with the evils of Nazi racism gave momentum to demands for desegregation and an end to the Jim Crow laws. The road was a hard one, but within two decades of the war's end President Johnson introduced comprehensive civil rights legislation. There was no such post-war liberalisation in South Africa. While some pass laws were relaxed from 1942 to allow blacks to move to cities more easily for work in manufacturing, this proved to be a temporary measure. Once the war was over, these concessions were reversed and there was an ever-louder clamour among much of the white population, especially Afrikaner Nationalists, for segregation to be extended.

With Smuts's United Party re-elected in 1943, the newly formed Reunited National Party (soon to become the National Party) started laying plans to secure victory at the next election, due in 1948. The National Party's manifesto for the election of May 1948 introduced a new name for its vision of how South Africa should be organised: *apartheid* (Afrikaans for 'separateness'). The programme for which it stood did not constitute a fundamental break with the past; rather, it was a more overtly racist and radical version of policies that Smuts had already been pursuing, together with a revival and extension of

Hertzog's segregationist measures of the 1920s and 1930s. Although the Nationalists' victory is rightly seen as a watershed moment in the history of South Africa, their share of the popular vote (37.7 per cent) was considerably smaller than that for Smuts's United Party (49.2 per cent); Daniel Malan's party was able to form a government only through quirks of the first-past-the-post electoral system (which gave them seventy seats to the United Party's sixty-five) and by forming a coalition with the small Afrikaner party.

Once in government the Nationalists' first moves were not against the black population but to limit white immigration from Europe, particularly Britain, in a bid to prevent dilution of the Afrikaners' demographic advantage. The United Party, stunned by its unexpected election defeat, did little to oppose the new government's more draconian measures, such as the 1949 Mixed Marriages Act, criminalising marriages between whites and coloureds (marriages between white and black had already been illegal since 1923). A tide of legislation then ensued, and in short order the building blocks of the apartheid state were laid. In 1950 the Population Registration Act provided for the formal, individual classification of every South African into one of three racial categories ('white', 'native' and 'coloured'). That same year, in pursuit of a malign fantasy of racial purity, the Immorality Act outlawed any form of sexual relations – in or out of marriage – between those categories, while the Group Areas Act further restricted the places in which black or coloured people were permitted to live or work. In 1951 the Prevention of Illegal Squatters Act gave the police powers to remove 'surplus natives' from farmland to emergency camps. In 1952 the deceptively named Natives (Abolition of Passes and Co-ordination of Documents) Act in fact strengthened pass laws and the Native Laws Amendment Act revived Hertzog's old rule that blacks could live in urban areas only temporarily, and then only for reasons of employment.

No other state – arguably, not even Nazi Germany – had ever created so vast and comprehensive a legislative apparatus for the segregation of the population in every aspect of life according to a theory of race, together with the absolute privileging and supremacy of the minority deemed to belong to one of those supposed races. Under a veneer of rhetoric about 'separate but equal' coexistence, the purpose of the system was clear: to ensure the permanent subservience of the non-white majority.

White opposition to apartheid at first came from an unlikely source: a 'Torch Commando' of English-speaking Second World War veterans who strongly opposed the removal of the 'Cape Coloured' population's remaining democratic rights and which Kentridge joined shortly after his return from England. There was speculation in 1953 that the Torch Commando might be planning a military coup, but the organisation soon foundered because of an internal split over, ironically, whether coloured people should be admitted as members. Even anti-apartheid movements were riven by disagreements over which racial groups should be allowed to join them.

Kentridge's home city of Johannesburg was still growing fast. In the late 1940s alone, the number of blacks working in Witwatersrand's factories doubled. By 1951 Johannesburg had a population of 920,000, half of them black. Despite the efforts of the apartheid government and its predecessors, the black population of South Africa had been transformed between the 1930s and 1950s from primarily rural to primarily urban. South Africa's huge mining industry began to diversify beyond coal, gold and diamonds: the annual value of other metals extracted in the country grew from £22 million in 1945 to £100 million a decade later, including much of the uranium needed for the West's nuclear weapons and atomic power plants. But by 1954 many blacks were permitted to enter 'white' urban areas for twelve hours at a time, and then only for work, before being compelled to return to the austere so-called 'townships' of cramped, overcrowded basic housing designated for them beyond the city limits.

South Africa has always followed the English system of a split legal profession made up of attorneys and advocates (solicitors and barristers, in English parlance). At the time the Johannesburg Bar was made up of 'groups': sets of self-employed advocates who banded together to share the rent and secretarial expenses, similarly to the way English barristers' chambers operate. There were, however, significant differences from the English system. First, there were no clerks: advocates negotiated their own fees and managed their own diaries. To the English barrister who inherits an aversion to any discussion of money with the solicitor who instructs him or her, this is a startling – indeed disconcerting – thought, but Kentridge recalls that the system worked perfectly well. Second, newly qualified advocates did not then undergo a formal pupillage. An English barrister must spend a year as pupil to one or more barristers in chambers, learning the ropes and witnessing live court cases, before being let loose; in the 1940s, as soon as a South African advocate joined his group, he (and it was at this time almost uniformly a he) was on his own. In the 1940s, all the Johannesburg groups were housed in the magnificent art deco His Majesty's Building, which still stands on Eloff Street. It was a very small world: in the late 1940s there only were about a hundred advocates practising in South Africa's largest city.

Simon Kuper had evidently been impressed by Kentridge, and he invited the newly qualified advocate to join his group; Kentridge duly became a member of Group 621 (named somewhat prosaically after the number of the group's reception room, on the building's sixth floor) on the same day as his call to the Bar. The group, formed in 1913, was the oldest and most prestigious in Johannesburg, containing some of the great advocates of the period: Norman Rosenberg, Vernon Berrangé, Oscar Rathouse, Harold Hanson and Bram Fischer.

Kentridge received his first brief on the very day he was called to the Bar; remarkably, it was to defend a black man on a murder charge. There was at the time no proper system of legal aid in South Africa, and although anyone on a capital charge could be represented by an advocate paid for by the state, he or she was invariably represented by a novice like Kentridge, paid five guineas a time (a level of fee which ensured that only the recently qualified would defend in cases which were otherwise so momentous). The advocate did not have the benefit of assistance from an attorney. In such cases, where the defendant might not speak English, it would be up to the advocate to arrange for an interpreter at both the pre-trial interview and in court. 'I was thrown in at the deep end,' Kentridge recalls, before adding gloomily that his first client was duly convicted and sentenced to hang. As in Britain in the late 1940s, the death penalty was still on the statute book; in South Africa, it would remain there for many decades to come. Many people were executed – on average about 120 a year – and reprieves were rare. Until the end of apartheid, South Africa frequently held the ignominious annual world record for the number of judicial executions.

Kentridge defended in many murder trials in his early years at the Bar, most of them sordid or commonplace affairs involving drunken stabbings or robberies in which someone had been killed. Alan Paton's classic novel *Cry, the Beloved Country*, published in 1948 just a year before Kentridge started in practice, provides a vivid description of the type of trial the young advocate defended in during his early years. Three black men enter the house of a white man intent on burglary. They believe the owner will be absent. In fact he is in his study, and hearing a noise he goes into the corridor to investigate. One of the intruders, carrying a revolver, fires in panic. An everyday tragedy; yet at the heart of each case a man's life was at stake. 'I worked harder preparing those cases than I ever did again for any other sort of case. It was a terrible responsibility, but one did one's best.' Speaking decades later, Kentridge recalled the awful procedure, following immemorial English practice, of the judge donning the black cap before sentencing the accused 'to be taken from here to a place of execution and there be hanged by the neck until you are dead. And may the Lord have mercy upon your soul.' Paton evokes the scene that followed the sentence of death, the authenticity of which Kentridge sadly confirms:

> The Judge rises, and the people rise. But not all is silent. The guilty one falls to the ground, crying and sobbing. And there is a woman wailing, and an old man crying, *Tixo, Tixo* [God, God]. No one calls for silence, though the Judge is not quite gone. For who can stop the heart from breaking.[12]

★

In those early days briefs tended to arrive haphazardly by word of mouth. One drew on connections where one could, and Kentridge's first civil brief came from an older cousin, who practised as an attorney in Johannesburg. By this time Kentridge's father had virtually given up his practice, but a former partner of his also sent the young advocate a small case early on. Rules against any form of touting were very tight in South Africa at the time; an advocate had to be essentially a passive recipient of instructions whose practice could only

grow by the quality of their work and by whatever social or professional connections they were able and willing to exploit. The young
advocate could not afford to be choosy. Kentridge took any work that
came his way, whether in the criminal, civil or divorce courts. The
eclecticism of his practice would be unthinkable in the modern age
of specialisation, but it would generate advocacy skills that stood him
in good stead in the years to come.

The Johannesburg Bar was an almost entirely male environment.
When Kentridge started in practice there were only three women
advocates practising there (and the London Bar was not doing much
better). As at Oxford, Kentridge found a strong camaraderie of
ex-servicemen.

> Not only during the war but for many years after, there was always a
> gap between those who had served in the war, and those who hadn't.
> Even when I came to the Bar in Johannesburg my friends were for the
> most part people who had served in the war, not only because of our
> age but because somehow it created a bond.

Kentridge's father had long had a particular interest in labour
matters as a politician and knew a number of leading white trade
unionists in South Africa. He introduced Kentridge to Solly Sachs,
then general secretary of the Garment Workers Union in the
Witwatersrand. Sachs and his union were often in litigation with
the government or embroiled in libel actions against pro-Nationalist
newspapers who had defamed the general secretary. During
Kentridge's first year at the Bar, Sachs instructed his attorney to brief
him on a small matter and to appear before a tribunal that was investigating his union. Kentridge clearly impressed Sachs because, a few
months later, he found himself acting in a much more serious case.
Sachs's passport had been arbitrarily cancelled by the minister of the
interior, Eben Donges, one of the architects of apartheid, just before
he was due to go to France to attend an international conference of
trade unionists. Sachs challenged the lawfulness of the cancellation
and, having lost in the lower court, took the matter to the Appeal
Court of South Africa (otherwise known as the Appellate Division),
which sat in Bloemfontein. Kentridge was asked to provide an

opinion on whether the state had a prerogative power to take away a person's passport. Kentridge's advice was clear: there was no such power under South African law. When the case came before the Appeal Court at the end of 1949, Sachs engaged a KC from Cape Town, with Kentridge appearing as junior counsel. It was the first of countless occasions on which he would appear before South Africa's final court of appeal.

Although he sat quietly behind his leader in court, the argument presented to the five judges was, in essence, one that Kentridge had crafted, and it prevailed. In a judgment of great length and learning, the court held by a majority that there was no prerogative power to remove Sachs's passport.[13] The victory became a cause célèbre but proved to be Pyrrhic: in response, the Nationalist government simply brought in legislation arrogating to itself an unfettered power to issue and withdraw passports at will. Within a few months of being called to the Bar, Kentridge was already in the thick of the apartheid state's running battle through the courts against those who opposed it. His success in the passport case soon led to more trade union work, for both Sachs's union and others. Increasingly, he found himself challenging banning orders that effectively prevented people from participating in a trade union by requiring them not to address, or in some cases even attend, meetings and gatherings. While Kentridge still did general criminal work, by the early 1950s he was already specialising in human rights, constitutional, and administrative law, a specialisation that would lead to him being engaged as a junior counsel in the so-called Treason Trial, the most famous and important case of the time, before the decade was out.

3

The Treason Trial (1958–61)

IT IS AUGUST 1960. In a converted synagogue in Pretoria three judges sit on a raised platform looking down on a score of lawyers arrayed around desks which make up a straight-lined horseshoe. A young advocate, his hair sleeked back and enveloped in a black gown, is questioning a tall, powerfully built man, who stands confidently in the witness box. Behind the lawyers dozens of men and women, the ranks of the accused, sit in several rows of benches, surrounded by uniformed police officers. Press reporters look down from the gallery.

Q: There have been references in various speeches and documents
   that you've heard sitting in this Court to the possibility that the
   police will use violence against passive resistance, or against ANC
   members although they themselves are peaceful. Did you yourself
   believe that?
A: Yes, I did.
Q: Now, you have told us, you were arrested in 1952?
A: That is so.
Q: When you were arrested where were you taken?
A: I was taken together with about fifty others to Marshall Square.
Q: What occurred at Marshall Square?
A: We were put in the cells and as we were walking into the cells a
   police officer pushed one of the defiers down the steps. I think his
   name was Sam Mkai. He pushed him down the steps and he fell
   and broke an ankle. I was walking next to him at the time and I
   immediately turned to the officer and I protested, and demanded
   to see senior officers in order to report the matter. He was very
   angry with me and he immediately kicked me and ordered me to
   keep quiet. I would not keep quiet and I pushed him aside and

banged at the door, in order to draw attention to this matter. Eventually some senior police officers including Col. Prinsloo, who is now the head of the Special Branch in the Union, came and I made a report to him. I made a report both about the assault on Sam Mkai and on the assault on me. Col. Prinsloo then asked me to show him the marks where I was kicked and I did so. We were locked in and for the whole night groaning in pain Sam Mkai slept with us. He was only removed to hospital the after-noon of the following day. That was an experience of violence which I had personally, and which I witnessed on a colleague of mine.

Q: From your own personal knowledge is rough handling of Africans by the police unusual?

A: It's a very common occurrence.

Sydney Kentridge is thirty-seven years old. He has been practising at the Johannesburg Bar for eight years and is now participating in one of the seminal legal and political events of the decade. The man he is questioning is his client, Nelson Mandela, accused of treason and on trial for his life. The short exchange quoted above relates to the Defiance Campaign, a programme of mass civil disobedience which Mandela had spearheaded in 1952. Mandela's measured answers demonstrate those qualities of courage and selflessness for which he would later become celebrated. One of Mandela's co-accused, sitting on a bench at the back of the courthouse, admiringly described how he spoke 'with authority, unequivocally ... Nelson was adamant, unshakeable'. For several days Mandela remains in the witness box, expounding his political philosophy and ideals, unfolding an account of his life as an activist, explaining his hopes for a future multiracial South Africa. The trial has just entered its third year.

The Treason Trial, as it is universally known, was in every respect gargantuan. There were more defendants than in any other South African legal proceeding before or since, each on charges carrying a potential death sentence. The case, from initial charge to final verdict, lasted in total for a marathon four and a half years, from the end of 1956 to the spring of 1961. At one stage in its byzantine course the minister of justice warned: 'This trial will be proceeded with, no matter how many millions of pounds it costs . . . What does it matter how long it takes?' When, after almost three years of preliminary wrangling, the trial proper finally started, the prosecution called 211 witnesses, the defence a further 25. One witness testified for almost thirty court days. Nelson Mandela, who would become the most famous of the defendants, devotes almost eighty pages of his 1994 autobiography *Long Walk to Freedom* to the case. It took up three years of Sydney Kentridge's professional life and propelled the junior member of the Johannesburg Bar to the forefront of legal practice in South Africa.

The scale of the trial matched the ambition of the state in launching the prosecution. By 1955 seven years had elapsed since the National Party's surprise success in the 1948 election. Opposition to its policy of apartheid had coalesced into an organised platform which crossed political boundaries. The deluge of race legislation of the early 1950s inundated the lives of all South Africans classified as non-white: passbooks became mandatory, regulating where people could live and work; the education system was severely undermined; forced resettlements of whole populations were made to segregated townships.

Many were politicised by the experience. In June 1955, on a football field in the township of Kliptown, near Soweto, there was a mass gathering of some 3,000 activists known as the Congress of the People. Delegates of all ages, races and social backgrounds had converged from across the country, by foot, by bus, by bicycle, some on horseback: representatives from a host of organisations, with the purpose of discussing and adopting the so-called Freedom Charter, a manifesto for a different vision of South Africa. The text of the charter had been drawn from an exercise in grassroots consultation over a period of two years. Now, in a joyous outdoor gathering, it was being debated, the elation of the delegates undimmed by the menacing presence of onlooking police officers. Nelson Mandela was at the time an attorney in his late thirties. Until recently the head of the Transvaal ANC, he and his partner Oliver Tambo ran the only black-owned law firm in the country.[1] A banning order made it illegal for Mandela to belong to the ANC or to leave Johannesburg, but still he came to Kliptown. Fellow lawyer and anti-apartheid activist Joe Slovo, similarly barred from participating, recalled 'lying on a tin rooftop with some of my comrades some 150 metres from the main square, observing through binoculars this festival of democracy, and hearing the cheers and the singing which punctuated the adoption of each clause'.[2] The charter began with these heady words:

> We, the People of South Africa, declare for all our country and the world to know: that South Africa belongs to all who live in it, black and white, and that no government can justly claim authority unless it is based on the will of all the people; that our people have been robbed of their birthright to land, liberty and peace by a form of government founded on injustice and inequality; that our country will never be prosperous or free until all our people live in brotherhood, enjoying equal rights and opportunities; that only a democratic state, based on the will of all the people, can secure to all their birthright without distinction of colour, race, sex or belief. And therefore, we, the people of South Africa, black and white together – equals, countrymen and brothers – adopt this Freedom Charter. And we pledge ourselves to strive together, sparing neither strength nor courage, until the democratic changes here set out have been won.

The Freedom Charter was a high-minded document, echoing the phrasing of the United States Constitution and the Charter of the United Nations. It was sprinkled with idealistic generalisations about a future South Africa, in places studiedly vague so as to attract the support of as wide a constituency as possible. The one proposition that shone through with absolute clarity was the insistence on a multiracial state in which the franchise was extended to the entire adult population. In this respect Nelson Mandela described the document as a 'great beacon for the liberation struggle'.[3]

For two days – clear and sunny, as Mandela recalled them – the festivities continued. Speeches were delivered and songs sung. Stalls sold pamphlets and makeshift kitchens served soup. Banners were held aloft. Ebullience and optimism bound the delegates together. Then the police moved in, announcing that they were investigating supposed 'high treason'. The pamphlets were confiscated, arrests were made and names taken. Mandela managed to slip away disguised, so legend has it, as a milkman.

After the delegates had made their way back to their homes throughout South Africa the state started laying plans for the destruction of the leadership of the Congress of the People and with it, so it was hoped, any organised resistance to the ongoing project of apartheid. It moved slowly, deploying an army of plain-clothes police to gather evidence and note down the contents of speeches given at meetings across the country. Then, in pre-dawn raids on 5 December 1956, 140 people – most of them members of the ANC, the South African Communist Party or black trade unions, all united by their adherence to the Freedom Charter – were arrested. The event was described in one of the earliest chronicles of the Treason Trial:

> police knuckles and police batons hammered at the doors of 140 homes all over the Union of South Africa; the doors of luxury flats and the tin entrances of hessian shanty pondokkies [shelters], the oak of a parson's manse and the stable openings of farm labourers; doors in comfortable white suburbs, in grim African locations, in Indian ghettoes, in cities, in villages and on farms far out on the veld.[4]

Many of those arrested were dragged from their beds by police officers carrying sub-machine guns, bayoneted rifles and truncheons. The experience remained imprinted on Nelson Mandela's memory for the rest of his life. For forty-five minutes three police officers turned his house upside down before he was driven away, leaving behind his uncomprehending children. A week later sixteen further arrests were made in various parts of the country. The detainees were flown in military transports to Johannesburg, where they were held at the forbidding Old Fort Prison, one of the citadels of Afrikanerdom since the time of Paul Kruger. Almost the entire ANC high command had been detained in one swoop. Those arrested included a university professor – Z. K. Matthews, the originator of the Freedom Charter – a member of parliament, clergymen, lawyers, doctors, trade unionists and journalists. They also included the greatest names of the anti-apartheid struggle: not only Nelson Mandela but also Chief Albert Luthuli (the president of the ANC), Walter Sisulu, Duma Nokwe,

Joe Slovo, Ahmed Kathrada and dozens of others. For Luthuli the arrests were 'deliberately calculated to strike terror into hesitant minds and impress upon the entire nation the determination of the governing clique to stifle all opposition'.[5]

The government's timing had been carefully planned. Some of those detained were Communists or had Communist ties. The South African Communist Party had been officially banned in 1950, and as the Cold War dragged on a particularly intense brand of McCarthyite paranoia lived on in South Africa. Two events far from South Africa – Egyptian President Nasser's nationalisation of the Suez Canal in July 1956 and the brutal suppression of the Hungarian uprising by Soviet tanks in November – fuelled anti-Communist sentiment. The South African state could sell the prosecution to the world at large as a continuation of the West's counter-attack against Communist expansionism. The irony was that many South African Communists had historically opposed black liberation, and in return some anti-apartheid activists were deeply suspicious of communism. But irony was easily lost on South Africa's white leaders, and they found it all too convenient to portray the 156 detainees as Communists and fellow travellers intent not only on toppling the apartheid state but also installing a Marxist–Leninist government in its place through violent revolution. Although the world's media expressed concern about the 156 arrests – even the conservative *Daily Telegraph* in London and *Time* magazine in the United States reacted with distaste, while other papers noted uncomfortable parallels with the infamous 1933 Reichstag fire trial in Nazi Germany – the diplomatic fallout for South Africa was slight: most Western governments were not going to stand in the way of the South African government rounding up supposed Communist agitators.[6]

The principal charge against those detained was high treason. In England treason is the most serious of offences known to the law and can only be committed in time of war. The last person convicted of treason in an English courtroom was William Joyce – the Nazi broadcaster known as Lord Haw-Haw – and he had been hanged in 1946. But the South African concept of treason, derived from Dutch-Roman law, had a much wider reach; it was, according to the leading criminal law textbook of the time, committed by those who 'with a hostile intention disturb, impair or endanger the independence or safety of the state'. The accused were charged with participation in a conspiracy to overthrow the government by violent means. The innocuous Freedom Charter would turn out to be one of the central pieces of evidence deployed to prove this supposed conspiracy.

The 156 people arrested in December 1956 were all eventually released on bail. The level of bail was, like most things under apartheid, differentiated by race, although uniquely in this instance privilege ran in the other direction: £250 for whites, £100 for Indians and coloureds, and £50 for blacks. Yet when the accused arrived at the Drill Hall in Johannesburg, a vast barnlike structure dating from the Edwardian era which had been requisitioned for the purposes of the preparatory examination against them, they found that the authorities had fashioned a new form of temporary incarceration: a huge wire cage had been constructed to house them. In an act of droll defiance one of the accused fixed a sign reading DANGEROUS, PLEASE DO NOT FEED to it. The cage was only dismantled after the lead counsel initially retained by the 156 threatened a walkout by the defence legal team. 'The cage,' he remonstrated, 'in which the prisoners have now been placed makes them appear before this court like wild animals or beasts.'[7] The authorities partially relented.

The police were taking no chances outside the courtroom either. Five hundred armed officers surrounded the Drill Hall to guard it against demonstrations. Shots were fired that first day, and a baton charge left twenty-eight protestors – who had held placards declaring WE STAND BY OUR LEADERS – injured. There then unfolded a seemingly interminable legal process which ate up the whole of 1957 and glacially spilt over into 1958. The preparatory examination was a necessary prelude to a criminal trial: a magistrate would consider the prosecution evidence to assess whether it was sufficiently strong to permit it to proceed to a full trial. Week after week government prosecutors droned on, reading out speeches given by various of the accused or pamphlets they had written. An endless stream of plain-clothes police officers testified to what they had heard at countless political meetings across the country over the previous five years.

The 156 had to sit through all of it. Nelson Mandela did his best to keep his law practice going. After the end of the afternoon session he would rush from the Drill Hall to his offices across town on Fox Street to attend to his legal work. But the prospects for his professional life looked bleak. In his autobiography Mandela recorded that his firm had 'gone from a bustling practice that turned people away to one that was practically begging for clients'. Others of the accused were cast into unemployment and consequent poverty, supported by handouts from the Treason Trial Defence Fund, which had been founded by the Bishop of Johannesburg and was funded predominantly by British supporters including the philosopher and peace campaigner Bertrand Russell, the novelist Compton Mackenzie and the Liberal politician Jo Grimond. Yet the 156 found a kind of strength in adversity. One of them recalled that their predicament turned a 'company of strangers into something more like an extended family'. A group photograph of the 156 shows most of them smiling defiantly, like school-leavers posing for their graduation portrait.

As the first year of the ordeal ground on, relations between prosecutors and prosecuted grew increasingly fractious. Whenever a police detective went into the dock to identify a defendant, whom he claimed to have witnessed making some allegedly seditious speech, by tapping him on the shoulder, another defendant would pointedly wipe the same shoulder with a handkerchief, prompting fury from the prosecution counsel. Joe Slovo, a practising advocate alongside his other life as a political activist, had chosen to defend himself and would rile the magistrate, a Mr F. C. Wessel, with his punctilious insistence on his legal rights. Eventually Wessel cracked and fined him for contempt, with six weeks' imprisonment in default of payment. Sydney Kentridge's first involvement in the Treason Trial (he was not part of the team representing the accused in the Drill Hall) came with a brief to represent Slovo – who was a friend and colleague – on his appeal. He succeeded, persuading the judge that there had simply been a misunderstanding. Kentridge later recalled that the magistrate's patience had been sorely tested by counsel for most of the accused, the fiery Vernon Berrangé (and one of the iconic figures in the struggle against apartheid), and Slovo had taken the heat.[8]

The case bled into 1958. Without warning the prosecution announced that it was dropping charges against sixty-one of the accused. These included – to general bafflement – some of the biggest names in the dock, including Albert Luthuli, Joe Slovo and Oliver Tambo. But an impassioned plea by Berrangé could not stop the magistrate deciding at the end of January 1958 that the remaining ninety-five – '17 Europeans, 18 Indians, 2 Coloureds and 58 Africans', as the newspapers dutifully described and ranked them in the racially saturated parlance of the time – should be committed to be tried in the Supreme Court. Almost a year of evidence had culminated in one bland judicial sentence intoned by the magistrate: 'there was sufficient reason for putting all the accused on trial on the main charge of high treason'. And so the case lumbered onto its next phase: a full trial, to be held before a 'Special Court' of three judges, starting in August.

In the period of respite before the beginning of this next act of the drama Nelson Mandela, still on bail, married Winnie Madikizela. While the newly-weds enjoyed the semblance of a honeymoon in June 1958, for which Mandela had to obtain a relaxation of his banning order from the authorities, Sydney Kentridge was sitting in his chambers in Johannesburg poring over the indictment – the formal prosecution document setting out the alleged facts giving rise to the offences with which the accused were charged. Kentridge had been briefed to appear at the trial alongside a galaxy of legal talent: Israel ('Isie') Maisels QC,[9] Bram Fischer QC,[10] Vernon Berrangé, Rex Welsh, H. C. Nicholas, Chris Plewman, John Coaker and Tony O'Dowd. Each was already, or would become, a revered name in the annals of South African law. Kentridge later recalled Maisels as the most brilliant advocate he ever saw. The two men had an affinity with each other: one the son, the other the grandson of Jewish immigrants from Lithuania, both had inherited a detestation of racial prejudice.[11] Maisels would later describe the defence team around him as probably the strongest that had ever appeared in a South African court.[12]

That team had been brought together by Michael Parkington, a remarkable English lawyer, who had emigrated after meeting his South African wife-to-be at Cambridge.[13] A fierce anti-Communist, Parkington was not an obvious choice of attorney for the Treason Trialists. But his conservatism embraced an equally impassioned anti-racism and sense of fairness. Kentridge had been introduced to Parkington by his chambers colleague Bram Fischer; the attorney had instructed them in a case concerning an ANC-led boycott of cigarettes made by Afrikaner businessman Anton Rupert's Rembrandt Group, whose advertising boasted that only 'white hands' had made them.[14] 'Gigantic of stature, with a rapier tongue, and a delightfully bawdy wit, he was the arch "conspirator",' wrote one of the trialists of Parkington. Kentridge recalls a man who would habitually drink a glass of gin and water during the afternoon sessions in court, brought to him by a barman from a nearby hotel.

When the trial finally opened on 1 August 1958 its location was no longer Johannesburg but Pretoria, South African's executive capital and the spiritual home of Afrikanerdom. Pretoria is some thirty-six miles to the north-east of Johannesburg and at the time the two cities were linked by a poorly maintained and narrow road. The decision to shift venue was an inconvenience for the defence legal team, who were all based in Johannesburg; but, much worse, a crushing blow for the accused, none of whom had any connection with Pretoria. To get to court for a 10 a.m. start meant a pre-dawn rise to reach the centre of Johannesburg, where there was laid on an ancient and spartan wooden-seated bus. Each day all the trialists would spend four or five hours jolting along in this charabanc – inevitably it became known as the 'treason bus' – singing songs and playing games in an effort to keep up morale. Helen Joseph, one of the accused, recalled in her account of the trial *If This Be Treason* that 'the daily journeys became almost intolerable at times. Because we were human beings, not angels, disputes arose about seats, trifles took on the importance of earth-shattering events, [and] tempers flared.'[15] Whatever ability the defendants previously had to keep up jobs while simultaneously facing a treason prosecution was now snuffed out. Being on trial for your life in Pretoria was a full-time occupation, even if the prospects of promotion were not exactly rosy. Although the prosecution sought to justify the shift of venue on the ground that anti-government protests would be more likely to erupt in Johannesburg – 'the safety of the state is more important than the convenience of the Accused', sniffed the Crown counsel – it was difficult not to interpret it as a simple act of malice against those on trial. Whatever the outcome of the prosecution, they would have at least this punishment.

The location for the trial was a former synagogue recently converted into a courtroom. As will become evident, the Old Synagogue on Paul Kruger Street in Pretoria was a place which came to dominate Kentridge's professional life for the next twenty years. Completed and consecrated in 1898, the former synagogue was flamboyant in its architecture, drawing on Byzantine, Gothic and Moorish influences.[16] It had been purchased by the Department of Public Works in 1952 for use as a special 'security' court, a euphemism for political prosecutions. Everywhere the trappings of racial segregation were present: the public galleries, waiting rooms and lavatories strictly demarcated between 'European' and 'Non-European'. But the vestiges of a former place of worship had not been completely erased. Still present were ornate columns, elaborate mouldings and high galleries looking down on the proceedings below. Although the Ten Commandments had been boarded up, there remained discernible a Star of David. (In Kentridge's archive there is a letter anonymously sent to him during the trial which contains two blurry photographs of the proceedings illicitly taken from the public gallery. One of them is reproduced in this book. Kentridge is distinctly visible.)

It was in the mahogany formality of the Old Synagogue that the Treason Trial began. Above the judges' heads the Union Coat of Arms – bearing its absurd motto *Ex Unitate Vires*, 'Unity is Strength' – had been affixed to the wall. Technically the proceedings were entitled *Regina v Adams and others*, an uncomfortable reminder that prosecutions were still brought in the name of the Head of State, Queen Elizabeth II.[17] Kentridge recalls the packed public and press galleries, journalists attending from across the world; the ninety-one remaining accused (the previous ninety-five had been further whittled down by illness or political calculation by the prosecution) squeezed into the makeshift dock; the sense of anticipation as the teams of lawyers arranged themselves at their desks for what was to be, up to that point, the most momentous criminal trial in South African legal history. Into the courtroom processed the three judges making up the special treason court, Justices Rumpff, Ludorf and Kennedy, each personally nominated by the minister of justice.

The defence team took the initiative immediately. Isie Maisels stood up to make an application requiring courage: he submitted that both Rumpff and Ludorf should recuse themselves from the proceedings for apparent bias. (Few things are more likely to antagonise a tribunal ahead of a trial than unsuccessfully accusing it, in open court, of being unfit to hear the case.) The judges – 'immobile in their scarlet robes' – listened. Ludorf was a political appointee to the bench who had stood unsuccessfully as a National Party parliamentary candidate some years earlier. While at the Bar he had prosecuted some of the current accused on political charges and, during the war, had defended Robey Leibbrandt, an Olympic boxer and Nazi sympathiser who had plotted to assassinate General Smuts and was found guilty of treason in 1943. The case against Rumpff was more tenuous and he testily rejected any suggestion that he might be biased; but in an early victory for the defence Ludorf reluctantly agreed to step down. He was replaced by a much more liberal judge: Simon 'Tos' Bekker.

The prosecution was now led by the sixty-seven-year-old Oswald Pirow QC, a former minister of justice who had gained notoriety before the war for his overt admiration of Hitler. After meeting the Führer on an official visit to Germany Pirow had pronounced him 'the greatest man of his age' and the ensuing years had barely diluted the strength of his devotion. Pirow's retainer as lead prosecutor was a calculated and unabashed statement by the government of the purpose of this trial – the destruction of organised opposition to the apartheid system. He was a man who represented everything to which Kentridge was opposed; and yet, sixty years on, he remembers Pirow without rancour, indeed with something approaching respect for the man's qualities as a lawyer. Kentridge recalls that the advocates from both sides of the court would sometimes congregate in a local Pretoria café. On one occasion, while some of the defence team were discussing a recent politically motivated judicial appointment, Pirow joined them at their Formica table. He looked back on his own political appointments of judges, observing acidly that 'the trouble was that within two weeks of arriving on the bench they began to think that they had been appointed on merit'. On another occasion when the English barrister and Communist D. N. Pritt – a recent recipient of the International Stalin Peace Prize – came out to South Africa as an observer to the proceedings, Kentridge introduced him to Pirow. 'Ah, Mr Pritt,' purred Pirow. 'My good friend Oswald Mosley has told me much about you.'[18]

Despite his Nazi past, Pirow even won the grudging respect of some of the accused. Nelson Mandela wrote that he 'developed a certain affection' for Pirow, if only because he referred to the accused as 'Africans' rather the more derogatory 'Natives', which was then the common currency of official vocabulary. (In private, of course, even more demeaning racial terms were frequently used.) Even in desperate circumstances one could find a bleak enjoyment in the human comedy. Mandela recalled with wry amusement seeing the Communist Bram Fischer reading the anti-apartheid weekly *New Age* at his table during the trial as Pirow, sitting a few yards away, studied the newsletter which he continued to publish to propagate his particular brand of far-right politics, *New Order*.[19]

There followed weeks of legal wrangling over the indictment which had been drawn up against the remaining accused. Running to 406 pages, it was a document of byzantine complexity, attempting to implicate ninety or so disparate people from across the country, some of whom had never met each other before the trial, as participants in some vast malign conspiracy of subversion. It began thus:

> The Accused acting in concert and with common purpose in breach and violation of allegiance to the Queen and the South African Government, wrongfully, unlawfully and with hostile intent against the State, namely to subvert or overthrow the State or to disturb, impair or endanger the existence, independence, security, safety or authority of the State did in their individual capacities . . .

There followed a deluge of supposed 'hostile and overt acts against the State', including 'active preparation for a violent revolution against the State' and the 'establishment of a Communist State in place of the existing State'. Copious use of 'and/or' and 'inter alia', those catch-all formulations of belt-and-braces legal drafting, meant that the accused were, according to Kentridge's calculation, facing a staggering 498,015 separate allegations of treasonous conduct. Many of these related to meetings that they had not attended or documents that they had neither written nor published, or even necessarily read, but had merely at some point had in their possession – itself a slippery legal concept. Having got rid of Ludorf as one of the judges, the next step was, therefore, to attack the indictment in all its Kafkaesque over-complexity.

Although Maisels was the dominant figure in the trial's opening weeks during the late summer of 1958, the more junior members of the defence team also had spells in the limelight. 'Sydney Kentridge used to delight us with his lively exchanges with the judges and with the Crown,' recalled Helen Joseph. 'Within the first three weeks of the trial, he dealt effectively with the alternative charges under the Suppression of Communism Act.' In her account of the trial Joseph described Kentridge's advocacy: 'When Kentridge was on his feet we would listen expectantly, for he would fearlessly challenge any suspected infringement of the rights of the accused and Counsel. His argument was lucid, positive, deliberate, delivered in a clear cool voice, the very absence of emotion making it even more effective.'[20] But he was not averse to using humour to make his point and on one occasion (24 August 1958) the South African *Sunday Express* awarded him the 'quote of the week' prize:

> KENTRIDGE: My learned friend [Gustav Hoexter, one of the Crown counsel] suggested that it might be necessary to apply surgery to the alternative charges. I submit, My Lord, that they should be buried.
> MR JUSTICE BEKKER: There's still life in them yet.
> KENTRIDGE: Then I would suggest, My Lord, that Your Lordships should quietly put them out of their misery.

Then came an extraordinary moment. In October 1958, after the court had ordered the Crown to provide further particulars of what precisely it alleged against the accused,[21] Oswald Pirow stood up in court to announce that the prosecution was withdrawing the entire indictment: apparently a first in South African legal history. Jubilation followed. Joe Slovo threw an impromptu party at his house in Johannesburg, which the trialists and their lawyers attended.

Even in this moment of private celebration the police would not leave them alone. As the evening wore on they arrived, friendly press photographers in tow from Afrikaner newspapers, supposedly investigating breaches of the Liquor Laws (it was at the time a criminal offence to serve alcohol to a black person except in limited circumstances). The next day those newspapers led with photographs of party-goers looking on dejectedly as grim-faced police officers broke up the festivities. The Afrikaner *Die Burger* expressed its horror at this exercise in social miscegenation. Kentridge attended the party with his wife Felicia and a grainy newspaper photograph might show the couple moments after their dancing had been peremptorily interrupted. He recalls the officers bursting into bedrooms in search of illicit interracial sexual activity while the black guests poured their wine into a large vase, before refilling their glasses with ginger beer.[22]

The celebrations were, in any event, premature. After licking its wounds the Crown returned to the fray with a fresh indictment. Crucially, there were now only thirty accused named in this new document, picked, it seemed, as the most radical of those originally arrested. Liberals and Christians had been excluded as no longer suiting a case now firmly tied to a key proposition: that the ANC was a Communist organisation and the thirty accused were committed Communists who had conspired with the object, as the indictment now boldly averred, of 'advocating, propagating or promoting the adoption and implementation in the Union of South Africa of the Marxist–Leninist doctrine in which there is inherent the establishing of a Communist state by violence'.

Charges against the remaining sixty-one would await another day.[23] Further procedural skirmishing ground out the months of 1959. The *Rand Daily Mail* noted that the case had broken another record – the longest legal argument on the terms of a criminal indictment in South African history. The attempt to quash the new indictment failed, as did the defence's appeal from that refusal, and it was not until 4 August 1959 – almost three years after their original arrests and a year and three days after the trial had been due to begin – that the thirty remaining accused finally had the opportunity to enter their pleas of not guilty on all charges.

The Crown's case was now opened with lurid ferocity. The judges were told that the aspirations of the Freedom Charter involved 'the complete smashing of the entire State apparatus in its present form'. It was a 'revolutionary document' replete with political demands which could only be achieved, as the accused must have known, by violence. The accused, it was claimed, were part of an international Communist-inspired movement 'pledged to overthrow by violence all Governments in non-Communist countries where sections of the population did not have equal political and economic rights'. Their speeches, thundered Pirow, 'bristled with references to the spilling of blood . . . Insistence upon violence runs through this case in an unbroken thread'.

A matter of weeks later, during which various prosecutors had in a prolonged lather of outrage read out various leaflets and minutes of ANC meetings seized by the police, the trial claimed its first – but not its last – victim. On a Monday in October the court was told in solemn terms that Pirow had died during the weekend of heart failure; overwhelmed perhaps by the fury of his indignation. The Union flag was lowered to half-mast outside the court as unctuous tributes were paid to the former Nazi. Pirow's immediate understudy, Jacob de Vos QC of the Cape Bar, was now propelled to the forefront.[24] Pirow's demise benefited the accused, for de Vos would prove to be a man hopelessly out of his depth, overwhelmed by the ungainly scale of the prosecution's case and the deftness of the defence team.

The Crown battleship ploughed on, now with de Vos as its unsteady helmsman. Documents supposedly proving the sanguinary revolutionary intent of the accused were ponderously read out (by mid-October the tally had reached 6,000 documents, comprising, it was estimated, over one and a half million words). Scores of witnesses paraded into the witness box to relay the contents of speeches they had heard at political meetings around the country. Months passed and the judges could barely hide their despair at the slow pace of the proceedings – 'at this rate we will sit forever', lamented Mr Justice Kennedy.

The team of defence advocates divided the work of representing the defendants in the dock, with each accused assigned to one of them as their main contact. Nelson Mandela was assigned to Kentridge, and for many weeks Accused Number Six was spared the treason bus and got a lift to court in his advocate's car (a dark grey Austin A10 with a dashing red stripe down the side) so that they could discuss the shape of Mandela's evidence when he eventually came to enter the witness box. Kentridge remembers picking up the future president of the republic in the dismal early morning at Joubert Park, close to Johannesburg's railway station, and engrossing discussions on the road to Pretoria in which Mandela expounded his political philosophy. If those long talks were useful for Mandela, for Kentridge they were an invaluable insight into one of the ANC's rising stars. Although Kentridge had been given a few briefs from the law firm run by Mandela and Oliver Tambo, he had not really known Mandela before he started representing him in 1958. Mandela's 'full stature as a leader was brought out in the Treason Trial', Kentridge told a British Library interviewer in 2008.

> There's no doubt at all that he had a natural quality of leadership. Quiet, never a demagogue . . . he spoke always with immense authority . . . He never said things in the hope that he'd be liked for it. Even in the witness box, he knew that there were things the judges didn't want to hear, but he spoke them out.

*

The prosecution's star witness was to be Andrew Murray, a philosophy professor at the University of Cape Town. On 15 October 1959 he was called to the witness box amid what the *Star* newspaper described as 'an atmosphere of suppressed excitement and tension'. After the months of formal document reading, it was as if the phoney war was now at an end and the trial was getting down to business. Murray's task as a witness was to expound to the court the theory and practice of communism and explain why, in their essence, the policies of the ANC were Marxism–Leninism incarnate. If the Crown could prove that the ANC was a Communist organisation then, so it contended, it could prove that its purpose *ipso facto* was the violent overthrow of the state. Like the recently deceased Senator McCarthy, the fervent Professor Murray saw Reds under every bed; and during the turgid weeks that led up to Murray's arrival in court Kentridge had been busy preparing a cross-examination designed to explode the professor's general thesis that all anti-government critique was saturated in the taint of communism. Kentridge recalls wading through the works of Marx, Lenin, Stalin, Nehru, General Smuts and a host of other political thinkers to prepare the ground for the destruction of Murray's testimony. For three whole weeks Maisels, followed by Kentridge, cross-examined Murray.

Q: Do you not think that the African may well regard himself as oppressed and exploited by the White man?

A: Yes, in certain spheres of life.

Q: And this is so whether he is a Communist or non-Communist?

A: Yes.

Q: The Black man might well regard the Government as reactionary?

A: He could.

Q: Nazi?

A: Yes.

Q: Fascist?

A: Yes.

Q: Undemocratic?

A: Yes.

Q: Having regard to the restrictions on his movement, on his right of privacy in his own home, the powers of the police over him, he might be tempted to describe South Africa as a police state without being a Communist?

A: There might be justification.

Q: So words like oppression, reactionary, exploitation, fascist, undemocratic, which you have so far stamped as Communist, can equally in the eyes of the African non-Communist be considered as applicable.

A: Possibly.

The transcript of Murray's evidence offers a fascinating insight into the political preoccupations of the 1950s. The questioning ranges across Stalin's political philosophy, Soviet influence in Africa, the People's Republic of China's application to join the United Nations, the African independence movements, the Mau Mau insurrection in colonial Kenya, the social and economic policies of the British Labour Party and opposition to the testing of the atom bomb. At times the questioning takes on the urbane tone of the university senior common room, the advocate reassuringly playing to the academic *amour propre* of the witness:

Q: Professor, one of the difficulties, of course – one of the added difficulties is, as you have told us, that many of the ideas of Marxism–Leninism are not even original to Marx or Lenin; for instance, the idea that everything is in a state of flux is a very old idea in philosophy?

A: Yes.

Q: The philosophy of materialism, of course, is not an invention of Marx?

A: No. The dialectical form, the special form is Engels, of course, but materialism generally is not.

Q: The idea of the dialectic was derived from Hegel?

A: Yes, but dialectic materialism is Marx–Engels, of course.

Q: The labour theory of value, for instance, was derived from Ricardo probably?

A: Yes, I think Marx gave some twists to it.

Q: Lenin drew on Hilferding and Hobson for his theory of Imperialism?

A: I think Lenin drew on Hobson and Hilferding for information, which was then squeezed into the principles contained in *Das Kapital*, you see.

Q: What about the idea of the importance of economic classes; that is as old as Aristotle, isn't it?

A: Yes . . .

Q: Let's take another idea that you've mentioned, the idea that those who hold economic power in society are the effective rulers of it. That didn't originate with Marx, did it?

A: Yes, that is not Marx.

Q: One can take that back to Harrington's *Oceana*?

A: Yes. In the seventeenth century.

ANC meetings at the time always started with Christian prayers. Kentridge was interested in the extent to which that was compatible with the teachings of Lenin.

Q: Professor Murray, have you got volume II of Lenin's *Selected Works* there? Please turn to page 658, *Socialism and Religion*. Let us just see how strong the views are in order to assess the extent to which religion might be tolerated by a Marxist–Leninist. In the middle of the page you find, in the middle of the second paragraph, Lenin says: 'Religion is one of the forms of spiritual oppression that everywhere weighs on the masses of the people who are crushed by perpetual toil for the benefit of others and by want and isolation' . . . and then if you look at the last three lines of that paragraph he says: 'Religion is the opium of the people. Religion is a kind of spiritual gin in which the slaves of capital drown their human shape and their claims to any decent human life.' That is pretty strong language, isn't it?

A: Yes.

Q: You find, in the same volume, at page 675 at the bottom of the page as part of a letter to Gorki, Lenin writes: 'Every religious idea, every idea of God, even every flirtation with the idea of God is unutterable vileness' . . . at the top of the next page he says: 'It is contagion of the most abominable kind.' One could really hardly find anything more strongly against the idea of religion? Isn't this the classical communist approach to religion?

A: Not in policy and in practice, that is the issue . . .

Q: Supposing a Marxist–Leninist was taking it upon himself to analyse the political situation in any country. Could or would he ever do so in terms, for instance, of saying that Christian principles must be applied, invoking the name of God, dealing with the matter in the light of religious and not Marxist–Leninist principles?

A: Not the advanced Marxist–Leninist. But the baby Marxist–Leninist may be well – may well be allowed to do that, because in the last war, the Church supported the war, in terms of religion and in terms of Marxist–Leninist analysis of capitalism . . .

Q: [*With irony*] What is a baby Marxist–Leninist?

A: A person who has perhaps not climbed to the top of the organisation and so on, where I presume his religious views might be
more controlled.

Murray's cross-examination resulted in his slow, inexorable dismantling as a credible witness. A central tenet of the prosecution case was
that the Freedom Charter was a communist-inspired blueprint for the
destruction of the existing state. And yet its demands, the professor
meekly agreed, were consistent with the American Declaration of
Independence and the constitutions of most western nations. A
favourite game of the defence was to read out to Murray unattributed
quotations from the likes of William Pitt, Milton, Voltaire and the
American presidents Lincoln and Wilson – and then to ask him
whether they were communistical. When the professor emphatically
confirmed that they were, the identity of the author was gleefully
revealed. At one point the defence even read out, anonymously of
course, a passage from Murray's own writings – in an Afrikaans family
magazine called *Die Huisgenoot* (*The Home Companion*) – which the
learned professor, forgetting his authorship, also judged, with particular certainty, to be communist in intent. There must have been some
chortling in the café that day. What Kentridge did not reveal was that
there was a personal element to the cross-examination. As an undergraduate at Wits twenty years earlier one of Kentridge's papers had
been marked by Murray as an external examiner. Murray had defied
Kentridge's tutor's confident prediction that he would gain a high first
and given the paper a second. In this case revenge was a dish best
served cold.

Murray's evidence was a disaster for the prosecution. One detects
that in the first few weeks of 1960 it began to shift its ground before
it closed its case on 10 March. The Crown's argument was no longer
that the accused had advocated violent revolution, but the rather
more subtle charge that, as befitted students of wily Leninist ju-jitsu,
they had advocated *non-violent* action calculated to provoke the state
to respond with brutal repression, thereby leading to what was termed
'contingent retaliation': a spontaneous violent reaction by the black
population resulting in the overthrow of the state.

★

On 14 March 1960 Kentridge opened the defence case by calling its first witness, Dr Zamie Conco, Accused Number Thirty. Conco was a doctor in his late thirties and a member of the National Executive Committee of the ANC. In answer to Kentridge's questions he explained the circumstances of his politicisation with quiet dignity.

> Q: Now, Dr Conco, I want you to take your mind back to 1943 when you were a student at the University of the Witwatersrand. Were you at that time appointed a demonstrator in Anatomy?
>
> A: Yes, I was appointed demonstrator in Anatomy as I had done an extra year in Anatomy and Physiology, and when the second-year students came I had to demonstrate to them Microscopic Anatomy.
>
> Q: Did this appointment of yours bring about any reaction?
>
> A: There was a terrific reaction amongst some of the students, a certain section of the students was definitely opposed to my demonstration, though the majority of the students came to me and asked me to continue demonstrating to them.
>
> Q: And in fact you did continue as a demonstrator in Anatomy?
>
> A: Yes, I continued doing so.
>
> Q: But did this opposition which came from some quarters to your appointment have any effect on your thinking?
>
> A: It did; it had quite a considerable effect on my thinking.
>
> Q: What did it lead you to do?
>
> A: Well, here was a situation in a University where race counted so much and one thought of . . . I then aligned myself to a political movement.

Kentridge showed Dr Conco the indictment:

> Q: You'll see it says 'It was the policy of the ANC to overthrow the State by violence.' Is that true or not?
>
> A: No, that's untrue.

For more than three days Dr Conco was cross-examined by the relentless John Trengove, the most effective member of the prosecution team, on his political philosophy and the ANC's policies. There were moments of discomfort as the witness was shown documents prepared for various political conferences.

> Q: Now, doctor, there is another resolution here. Resolution 13: 'Conference, on behalf of the youth of South Africa, expresses its deepest sympathy with the peoples of the Soviet Union who lost a leader and father through the death of Marshal J. V. Stalin.' Now, would that be consistent with ANC policy?
>
> A: That's a resolution of condolence, My lords; I would not have anything against it.
>
> Q: Now it goes on: 'J. V. Stalin was not only the architect of the Soviet Union, but he pledged himself to the cause of world peace and national liberation of the oppressed people throughout the world. In this regard the death of Stalin is a blow to all peaceful and freedom-loving peoples of the world. The youth of South Africa hopes that the noble ideals of Stalin have been left as a heritage to the Soviet Union and the world, and the greatest memorial to him would be to strive so that peace and freedom ultimately dominate the world.' Would that part of the resolution be consistent with the ANC attitude towards international affairs?
>
> A: I think, some people, when a great leader in a state dies, would express that opinion, but I wouldn't say that it is ANC policy. Whenever a great statesman dies condolence is usually expressed.

But Conco resisted the repeated suggestion that the ANC advocated a policy of violence. Trengove put an ANC policy document to him which contained the words 'ultimately the people will be brought together by inspired leadership and courage and boldness, even to the extent of suffering imprisonment and death for the cause'.

> Q: Dr Conco, do you hold the view that people who undertake to implement the ANC Programme of Action, that people who undertake that duty, must be prepared to face death?
>
> A: We have warned our people that if they take part in a demonstration, for instance, there is the possibility of having to suffer or being shot at.

68

On Monday, 21 March 1960 Dr Conco stepped out of the witness box. Nelson Mandela, watching from the dock, was relieved. Conco had been a calm and articulate witness. He also proved to be a prescient one. At lunchtime on the same day one of the cataclysmic events in South African history occurred. In a township known as Sharpeville, some seventy-five miles from Pretoria, policemen opened fire on a large but peaceful crowd protesting against apartheid pass laws. The Sharpeville massacre – as it soon became known – resulted in at least 69 black civilians being killed and over 187 wounded, most of them shot in the back as they fled an indiscriminate barrage of automatic and rifle fire.

As news of the terrible events at Sharpeville reached them, shock descended on the accused and their lawyers. The massacre seemed to imbue the Treason Trial with an even greater historical import. Its light-hearted moments became fewer; Maisels's 'customary nonchalance has gone', Helen Joseph noted in her diary. Dr Conco had been replaced in the witness box by Chief Albert Luthuli, president of the ANC, no longer a defendant but come to give evidence on behalf of his comrades. Each day, as the full enormity of the tragedy at Sharpeville unfolded, Luthuli had to withstand an onslaught of questions in a Pretoria courthouse. In Johannesburg on 26 March he symbolically burned his pass, as did many others, including Mandela. After a huge march by 30,000 people on the parliament building in Cape Town took place on 29 March, the government panicked and a draconian state of emergency was declared. South Africa was in full-blown crisis.

When Kentridge arrived at court on the morning of 30 March the witness box was empty and most of his clients were nowhere to be seen. Only twelve of the thirty were present. Urgent phone calls were made and Kentridge was able to speak to the head of the security branch, Colonel Prinsloo. After the judges had taken their seats on the bench, Kentridge, his agitation barely concealed, told them the position:

My Lords, we have certain information. The Accused who are not present were arrested by the Security Branch in the early hours of this morning according to my information. My Lords, the witness Mr Luthuli was arrested at three o'clock this morning by members of the

Security Branch . . . we have had certain information which we have found rather disquieting about the treatment which he has received while in custody, which I personally hope turns out to be incorrect. However, My Lords, in the circumstances, I wish to make an application to Your Lordships under Section 216 of the Code to order the police forthwith to produce the witness in Court.

Not only had Chief Luthuli and eighteen of the accused been arrested that night; under the auspices of the so-called Public Safety Act 1953, thousands of others had been rounded up across South Africa and were now detained in prison. For Nelson Mandela the pounding at the door had come at one thirty in the morning; six armed security police had ransacked his house, seized him and thrown him into a crowded cell with a single hole in the floor serving as the communal lavatory. Luthuli was eventually brought to court later that day and Kentridge was shocked to see that he, an ill man of sixty-two, had been assaulted by prison staff earlier that morning.[25] The remaining accused, who had somehow evaded the previous night's mass arrests, were taken away by the police as the court adjourned.

Emergency regulations were swiftly issued by the government to establish a form of martial law. One provision now made it an offence to utter any 'subversive statement' – defined as a statement which was likely to have the effect of

inciting the public or any section of the public . . . to resist or oppose the government or any Minister of State or administrator or official . . . or of engendering or aggravating feelings of hostility in the public or any section of the public . . . towards any section of the public or person or class of persons.

Thus all public criticism of the government was now punishable by law. No exception was made for statements made on oath in a courtroom. How, then, could a defence witness safely give evidence – for instance justifying ANC policy – knowing that anything they said in the witness box could lead to a prosecution or indefinite detention without trial? The judges expressed their concern and a stuttering de Vos was unable to provide any reassurances. On 1 April the court adjourned the trial until 19 April to give the prosecution an opportunity to try to break the impasse.

Having enjoyed a semblance of freedom since their original arrests back in December 1956, all of the trialists were now back in detention, held without charge in conditions of utter squalor in Pretoria Central Prison. Meanwhile, the world outside their prison walls was in turmoil. Kentridge recalls a South Africa which seemed to be teetering on the brink. Military units were called up; the mass arrests and incarcerations continued; protests were brutally suppressed. 'It was a staggering two weeks, when revolution appeared to be imminent, and though turned back, its threat still quivered in the air,' writes Stephen Clingman.[26] On 8 April both the ANC and the more militant Pan Africanist Congress were declared illegal. On 9 April a white farmer called David Pratt fired two shots, from point-blank range, into the head of Prime Minister Hendrik Verwoerd. The doctors who treated him described his survival as 'absolutely miraculous'. Many Nationalists saw the prime minister's rapid recovery as a sign that he – and apartheid – had divine providence on their side.[27]

The trial resumed on 19 April 1960. This time the accused arrived not on the jolting, song-filled treason bus from Johannesburg but in Black Marias from prison. The prosecution offered ministerial assurances that witnesses called by the defence would not be prosecuted or detained for anything they said in court. Surely that was good enough, the judges – anxious to resume the trial – suggested to Kentridge. The advocate stood his ground:

> My Lord, one must remember also that there is nothing sacrosanct about the Minister of Justice. But as far as my clients are concerned, or witnesses for that matter, I am afraid that we cannot assume that they will simply accept an assurance . . . After all, My Lord, if one considers certain things which have recently been said by the Minister about the African National Congress, my clients and other members of the African National Congress obviously do not accept their bona fides. It is not a matter which we can discuss here, who is right or who is wrong. But I don't know that a witness should be called into the box and asked, do you accept the bona fides of the Minister of Justice, and,

on this assurance, do you accept its value or validity, and then if he says
no, Your Lordship suggests that he might be asked why. Must he then
go into the question of why he takes a certain view about the Minister
of Justice. I wouldn't like to do it in his position, certainly not under
present circumstances. But, My Lord, as I have said, if this case must
go on, it must go on in the face of all the difficulties stated in Your
Lordships' Judgment, but at present we cannot say that it can go on on
the basis of any Ministerial assurance.

And he concluded with a clear warning as to the consequences of
permitting the trial to proceed:

> My Lord, if the case does go on in spite of the difficulties, naturally the
> legal representatives of the Accused will have to consider whether in
> those circumstances they can really be of any value to their clients and
> whether it is really worth the expenditure on legal fees to have con-
> tinued legal representation. But that, My Lord, is another matter.

Kentridge's submissions clearly hit home. Desperate to persuade
the court to allow the trial to continue, the government swiftly
amended the emergency regulations. Surely no advocate has ever
managed to effect a change in the law so quickly simply by the force
of their submissions? Within days a new clause was introduced,
providing that no evidence given by a witness in a criminal trial
commenced before the declaration of the state of emergency could
be used in evidence against them; nor could that evidence be taken
into account by the minister of justice or any police officer. Kentridge
and Maisels consulted with Mandela and the other accused. There
was general agreement that this new provision was a nonsense: the
minister might order the detention of a witness and simply say that he
had done so for some reason – which he could decline to specify –
other than the witness's evidence, and that would be the end of the
matter. Nevertheless, on 26 April the court decided that the amendment to the regulations was sufficient for the trial to continue.

Duma Nokwe, Accused Number Sixteen, and the first black advocate to practise at the Johannesburg Bar, stood up in the dock to
address the court directly.

May it please Your Lordships. I have been asked by the Accused to represent them and to express their views to the Court in relation to the Judgment that this trial should continue despite the difficulties contained in Your Lordships' previous Judgment, as stressed by Counsel in argument. In the light of these difficulties, Your Lordships, all the Accused in this case cancel the instructions to Counsel and have instructed them to withdraw from this case.

The judges looked astonished. 'Do you realise what that entails, Mr Nokwe?' gasped Bekker from the bench. The accused knew precisely what it entailed. They were now on their own. But they had also made a point about the iniquities of the state of emergency which would be broadcast around the world. Maisels, Kentridge and the other defence lawyers stood up and theatrically gathered together their papers. Before he led his team out of the courtroom, Maisels announced their departure with terse formality: 'We have no further mandate and we will consequently not trouble Your Lordships any further.' With that, the accuseds' lawyers trooped out. Kentridge drove back to Johannesburg, wracked with anxiety at how his now former clients would fare. The next three months of his life would be devoted to the Sharpeville inquiry (see Chapter 4).

The defence was now conducted by the two qualified lawyers among the accused: Duma Nokwe and Nelson Mandela. Their detention continued throughout the spring and summer, their lives divided between days in court and evenings and nights in the hellish conditions of Pretoria Central Prison. Mandela was held with four others in a cell measuring nine feet by seven (approximately three by two metres). A single sanitary pail served them all; for bedding they had vermin-infested blankets and mats. Albert Luthuli, also held in prison and in increasingly poor health, would spend the whole of May being mercilessly cross-examined by Trengove. Helen Joseph recorded her increasing feelings of hatred towards the advocate. But Luthuli emerged well from the ordeal. When Trengove put it to Luthuli that he never expected the white government to accede peacefully to the ANC's demands and dismantle the apartheid system, the disarming answer came back: 'My Lords, I wouldn't be in Congress if I didn't expect that white South Africa would someday reconsider. That is my honest belief. When, My Lords, I cannot say.' Kentridge would later describe Luthuli as one of the few truly great men he had ever met. The next year, to the disgust of Afrikanerdom, he would be awarded the Nobel Peace Prize.

By mid-July 1960 some of the regulations introduced in March under the state of emergency had been relaxed. In consultation with his co-accused, Nelson Mandela decided that the time had come to recall the defence advocates. And so Kentridge resumed the routine of the early morning drive to Pretoria. He and his fellow counsel were given a warm welcome by their clients. Kentridge's first task was to complain to the judges about the wretched prison food that the accused – still incarcerated – were receiving. It was, he said, 'completely unfit for human consumption'. Rumpff ordered a five-minute adjournment so that he and the other two judges could sample the cold cornmeal porridge, known as *mealie pap*, that Kentridge had had brought to the courthouse from the prison kitchens. 'We sat entranced at the spectacle of policemen solemnly marching through the court to the judges' chambers bearing dishes of cold porridge sprinkled with beans and chips of coarse meat, and rusty mugs of gaol coffee,' Helen Joseph recalled.[28] Rumpff came back into court and solemnly told Kentridge that he had tried a spoonful of the slop and found it 'cold and unappetising': he ordered the prison authorities to improve the food's presentation and ensure it was served hot, not cold. It was a small but morale-boosting victory.

The time was approaching when it would be Nelson Mandela's turn to enter the witness box. As one of Kentridge's designated clients, it would be for the young advocate to lead out Mandela's evidence through what is known as 'examination in chief', the process whereby a witness presents their evidence to the court before they are subject to cross-examination by opposing counsel. Many criminal barristers view examination in chief as the most challenging form of advocacy. It is at this moment that the court is first introduced to the witness. Leading questions are forbidden. The witness must speak in their own words, guided but not prompted by counsel. It would be Kentridge's task over a number of days to create the platform for Mandela, the acknowledged star in the ranks of the accused, to state his political philosophy to the judges, and to the nation as a whole. His shoulders thrown back, his magnificent physique and princely bearing undiminished by four months of prison hardship and squalor, Mandela strode into the witness box. His co-accused Helen Joseph noted in her diary Mandela's importance:

> Seven years he had been banned now, and restricted to Johannesburg, but he was still a leader of his people. Among the accused, he was *our* leader, accepted by all of us. As our spokesman he had challenged the Court on several occasions already. I thought of the Crown witnesses and took pride in this man of integrity and courage.[29]

First Kentridge led out Mandela's background, education and profession. He then moved on to his membership of the ANC, the foundation of the ANC Youth League and his drafting of the Youth League's Basic Policy document.

Q: Now if you can state one basic idea as being contained in that policy, what is that idea?
A: Well, the cornerstone . . . is the policy of African nationalism.
Q: Do you think that the idea of African nationalism was a new idea in the African National Congress at that time?
A: No, My Lord, it was not a new idea, but for the first time it was set out in a document in a clear and connected fashion.
. . .
Q: The Policy says there that the African people in South Africa are oppressed as a group with a particular colour. They suffer national oppression in common with thousands and millions of oppressed colonial peoples in other parts of the world?
A: That is correct.
Q: And then it gives the fundamental aims of African Nationalism as being (1) the creation of a united nation out of the heterogeneous tribes and (2) the freeing of Africans from foreign domination and foreign leadership. What was understood by foreign domination and foreign leadership?
A: Well, foreign domination and foreign leadership referred to imperialism.

Q: And as far as the Union of South Africa was concerned did you
   regard it as a country which is subject to foreign domination?
A: Yes, we regarded it as a country subject to White supremacy.

A critical question had to be asked: 'Did you in the African
National Congress Youth League regard White people in South
Africa as foreigners?'

Mandela explained that there were two streams of African
Nationalism. The more radical one was summed up by the cry 'Hurl
the White Man to the sea', but he had prevailed on the Youth League
to adopt the more moderate one of coexistence.

Q: Have you ever heard it suggested that perhaps the Congress
   should go over to a policy of violence?
A: Never, My Lord.
Q: Have you ever understood the Congress ever to entertain the idea
   of using violence?
A: No.
Q: When you joined it, was it a non-violent or a violent
   organisation?
A: It was a non-violent organisation.
Q: And while you were a member of it, did it ever change that policy?
A: No, My Lord.

Kentridge moved on to the ANC's 1949 Programme of Action, a
reaction to the National Party's election victory the previous year.
This was the document that had guided the ANC's political activities
throughout the 1950s.

Q: Was the Programme of Action a change to violence?
A: Never, My Lord.
Q: Now again, speak for yourself, Mr Mandela. How did you
   understand this new Programme of Action? What was the essential difference that this Programme of Action was to bring about
   in the work of the ANC?
A: My Lord, up to 1949 the leaders of the ANC had always acted in
   the hope that by merely pleading their case, placing it before the

authorities, they, the authorities, would change their hearts and extend to them all the rights that they were demanding. But the forms of political action which are set out in the Programme of Action meant that the African National Congress was now going to rely not on a change of heart, a mere change of heart on the part of the authorities. It was going to exert pressure in order to compel the authorities to grant its demands.

Q: As you understand the methods contained in the Programme of Action, the methods of pressure, do you understand that as excluding the idea of negotiation?

A: No. They do not exclude the idea of negotiation.

Q: How does negotiation fit in with a method of pressure as distinct from pleading?

A: Well, obviously negotiation can only take place where both parties have something to give. If I launch a strike in order to attain certain objectives, and assuming the authorities ask for discussions, it may be necessary for me to call off the strike. I negotiate on the basis that I have something to offer. I offer to call off a strike if and when my aspirations are realised.

These were brave words to utter when facing a capital charge of treason, and Kentridge looks back on Mandela's demeanour in the witness box with admiration. 'The case taught me something about the character and calibre of the ANC leaders: their principles and their moral strength.' His client was in the witness box for six days. Prosecution counsel's questions seemed to bounce off him like paper darts. Only once did he lose his patience, when Rumpff challenged the idea of a universal franchise and asked Mandela: 'What is the value of participation in the government of a state of people who know nothing?'

Throughout the months of the defence evidence, Rumpff's interventions had increasingly worried defence counsel. Kentridge felt that he was 'very, very hostile' to many of their witnesses. In August 1960, alongside Bram Fischer, Kentridge made a delicate submission: that Rumpff, the senior judge of the court, should recuse himself from presiding further because of his perceived bias. As we have seen this was the second such application that had been made and the first had hardly fared well. Kentridge took the judge through all his hostile interventions during the cross-examination of the defence witnesses. In particular, when Nelson Mandela had explained the ANC's policy that South Africa should have universal franchise, regardless of race or qualification, Rumpff had openly scoffed at a policy which allowed the 'uneducated' the vote.

> My Lord, we do submit, with respect, that these particular questions were from the point of view of the accused unfortunate; they suggest that allowing uneducated people to vote is really no different from allowing children to vote, that uneducated people, like children, would simply be led where their leaders would want to lead them. Now, My Lords, I'm sure that when Your Lordship asked those questions, Your Lordship did not realise just how hurtful those questions would be to the accused. Your Lordship, I'm sure, will on reflection understand that not only are many of the followers of the accused not educated persons, but a number of the accused themselves, by reason of the poverty of their parents, have not enjoyed the advantages of education, but none the less they are grown men, they have their self-respect, they are respected by their associates, they are regarded as mature and adult men, and this comparison between their capacity to exercise a vote, and the capacity of children, I'm sure Your Lordship will realise when I put it now, must have been and was indeed most hurtful and humiliating to them.

There was no getting around the fact that Kentridge was making a direct criticism of a senior judge and he had to choose his words with care. His measured submission contrasted with the prosecution's hysterical response to it. The increasingly preposterous de Vos stood up to castigate the application to recuse Rumpff as 'disgraceful' and a 'contempt of court' which 'represented a wilful insult to the Presiding Judge'. This was a serious and unwarranted attack on Fischer's and Kentridge's professional integrity; and it was interesting that Rumpff, rather than embracing the prosecution's unctuous show of support, expressed irritation at de Vos's shrill display. Rumpff inevitably rejected the recusal application but in listening to Kentridge's submissions he had shown considerable circumspection. Perhaps the application would serve a deeper purpose: to keep the judge intellectually honest in the months to come.

On 31 August, after five months of detention under the state of emergency, the twenty-nine remaining defendants were finally released (the thirtieth, Wilton Mkwayi, had disappeared abroad before he could be arrested in March). As had long been rumoured, the state of emergency imposed after the Sharpeville massacre was lifted shortly afterwards. On 1 September, Helen Joseph was able to drive herself from her home in Johannesburg to court for the first time, rather than being bussed in from prison. That evening she found two parking tickets on the windscreen; it seemed a price worth paying. For all the joy of newly gifted liberty, the defence case was now at its most vulnerable point: Robert Resha, Accused Number Seventeen, a journalist and member of the ANC National Executive, was a firebrand smouldering with righteous anger at the injustices of apartheid. In his examination in chief he told the court of his recent circumstances; a horrifying everyday story of life under the system:

Q: You are a married man with two children and you lived for a
   number of years in Sophiatown [a predominantly black suburb of
   Johannesburg]?
A: That is correct.
Q: During approximately what period did you live in Sophiatown?
A: I think from 1940 to 1959.
Q: What happened in 1959?
A: In 1959 while I was in this place [i.e. on trial in the Old
   Synagogue], the Re-Settlement Board demolished the house in
   which I lived, throwing my property outside the house whilst my
   wife was away at work and my children were at school.
Q: When you arrived home that evening you found your property
   on the pavement?
A: Fortunately there are still good people in this country who looked
   after my belongings until I came back from this case . . .
Q: Did you receive any notice about this demolition of the house?
A: I did not receive any notice.[30]

Resha was cross-examined for many days about his more inflammatory speeches. In one, which had been secretly recorded by a government spy, he was heard to tell his audience:

A volunteer is a person who is disciplined. This is the key of the volunteer – discipline. When you are disciplined and you are told by your organisation not to be violent you must not be violent; if you are a true volunteer and you are called upon to be violent, you must be absolutely violent, you must murder, murder, that is all.

Trengove put to him the prosecution's new theory of 'contingent retaliation': that the ANC had sought through its resistance activities to provoke governmental force in order, in turn, to create violent revolution.

Now, Mr Resha, I want to put it to you that you know that in all these campaigns that have been organised as far back as the 1946 Mineworkers Strike, that if it had not been for the restraint and tact of the police you would have succeeded long ago in involving the whole country in bloodshed?

That Trengove could put that question after the events of Sharpeville provides an uncomfortable insight into the mask that an advocate has to adopt when he comes into court. Resha maintained his calm:

My Lords, it has never been the policy of the African National Congress to involve this country in bloodshed. What the African National Congress has done, to the benefit of South Africa, and I think many right-thinking people owe that to Congress, is that we have avoided bloodshed right through all these instances you have quoted.

On 3 October 1960 Kentridge started examining the last witness called by the defence, Professor Z. K. Matthews. Matthews, then fifty-nine, was the leading black academic in South Africa, a committed Christian, and a man of immense moral stature. Kentridge led out his achievements. He had been the first black person to graduate from a South African university and the first black headmaster in South Africa. He had obtained post-graduate degrees at Yale University and the London School of Economics. He had been appointed professor of African studies and principal at the University College of Fort Hare. Various American universities had appointed Matthews as a visiting professor; but the South African authorities had refused to extend his passport to allow him to leave the country to take up the invitations. During the state of emergency he had been detained without charge for 135 days. The judges on the bench seemed to visibly diminish before this man, who answered Kentridge's questions with quiet authority. A long-standing member of the ANC, he – as Mandela had done a few weeks earlier – explained its decision, after the 1948 election, to set out a Programme of Action which embraced new methods of civil disobedience, economic boycotts and industrial action against the institution of apartheid.

Q: Did you believe that you could use the methods in the 1949 Programme without the danger of your followers resorting to violence?

A: Yes, we very definitely believed that these methods could be used without leading to any violence on the part of our members.

Q: Did you bear in mind the possible reaction of the government to your methods as set out in your Programme of Action?

A: Yes, we did.

Q: What did you think the government's reaction might possibly be?

A: Well, there was always the possibility that the government might react towards the use of these methods by the application of force.

Q: Were you prepared to face that?

A: We were prepared to face that, yes.

Q: What was the alternative as you saw it?

A: Well as we saw it, the alternative was for the members of the African National Congress and the African people generally merely to resign themselves to the position in this country, to fold their arms and do nothing, and that seemed to us unthinkable . . .

Q: Professor, what did the African National Congress hope to achieve by the methods set out in the Programme of Action?

A: We hoped by the use of these methods, if they were supported by a sufficiently large number of people, and were sustained over a sufficiently long period of time – we hoped that we would influence both the government and the White electorate by drawing their attention to what we considered to be our unsatisfactory position in this country.

Sixty years on, Kentridge recalls Matthews's extraordinary restraint in the witness stand. For two days the advocate asked him about ANC policy and its actions over the previous ten years. This was a man whose health had been ruined during his four months' imprisonment, from which he had emerged just weeks earlier. Yet he could still speak simply about his people's 'unsatisfactory position'. Could any sentient being in court not have felt a tide of sympathy for this evidence?

After Matthews left the witness stand, unscathed by cross-examination, the defence closed its case. De Vos, leading a team of seven prosecution counsel, seemed taken unawares. He sheepishly stood up to request an adjournment of a month to allow the prosecution to prepare its closing submissions. The judges could not conceal their disdain – his request was 'extraordinary' – but they wearily acceded to it. The atmosphere of the courtroom had shifted over the months. The judges, supposed men of the establishment, had, perhaps for the first time in their lives, been confronted by articulate black men and women talking to them directly about their ideals, motivations and values. Far from being advocates of Marxist–Leninist revolution, the defence witnesses as a whole had spoken with honesty and coherence about the restraint of the ANC in the face of government brutality. They seemed to have occupied a moral high ground far removed from the grubbiness of the prosecution witnesses.

This was a case whose capacity to do things on the grand scale was not flagging. There were still months of legal submissions from the Crown and then the defence to come. The prosecution expounded its case on conspiracy, on the meaning of high treason, on communism, on the roles of each of the accused. The judges heard their submissions with increasing shows of annoyance. A case can be lost if the court loses confidence in the advocates advancing it: here the court's contempt for de Vos was liable to colour its response to the substance of his argument. Kentridge recalled that he had never heard a judge being ruder to an advocate than Rumpff was to de Vos. Undaunted, the prosecution submitted that

The Crown has proved beyond all reasonable doubt that each and every one of the Accused were engaged in the prosecution of a plot against the State, and it was a plot, My Lords, of such a nature that if it had been allowed to follow its course unchecked, it would have ended without any doubt, My Lords, in bloodshed, death, disaster to the citizens of this country, whether they be Black or White . . .

This was hopelessly hyperbolic rhetoric in the face of the months of measured and clearly persuasive defence evidence. Rather than offering the court some at least technically attractive way to reconcile guilty verdicts with that evidence, the prosecution was, in effect, defying the judges to disregard it entirely; in other words, to display shameless complicity in order to further the political interests of the government which had launched the prosecution.

When the defence commenced its submissions, in March 1961, it met with a much warmer reception. For several days Kentridge explained the meaning and limits of the concept of treason, an analysis described by Stephen Clingman as 'devastating'.[31] He demonstrated that the prosecution's definition of that word had become so expansive that it would stigmatise virtually any campaign to effect a change in the law other than through the ballot box (a route of course denied to the non-white population) as treasonous. Throughout the 1950s the ANC had tried, on behalf of sections of the population denied the vote, to influence public policy through boycotts, demonstrations and strikes. These means may have been illegal under the laws of South Africa at the time, but they could hardly be equated with the legal definition of treason. The critical element of the crime of treason was the use of violence to effect a change in government. Kentridge continued:

The suffragette movement might have been considered dangerous to the state by some, the Chartist movement in England was no doubt considered by some dangerous to the state. We submit that the law of treason has fixed the dividing line at force, and when one speaks of extra-parliamentary activity, which falls short of force, one is really considering methods of pressure brought to bear on the electorate and parliament and therefore working essentially through the ballot box. And that is why, My Lord, we submit that a non-violent extra-parliamentary activity, aimed at a change of the law, even if that part of the law be called the Constitution, is not treason and is no evidence of an intention to use treasonable means.

The prosecution had alleged that the ambitions of the Freedom Charter were so extensive in their challenge to the status quo – universal suffrage, wholesale redistribution of wealth, nationalisation of certain industries – that the ANC and the accused could never have believed that they could be achieved other than by violent insurrection. Kentridge, scarred by his recent experiences of the Sharpeville inquiry, responded in an impassioned submission extolling the power of collective action against the might of the state:

But, My Lord, supposing one believes that one has a tough, brutal government and an electorate which is at present most unwilling and likely to continue to be unwilling voluntarily to make the concessions which are demanded in the Freedom Charter. My Lord, one asks, what follows from that. Can one say that because of that one believes that a nationwide general strike cannot succeed? My Lord, one asks why one can't believe that the tyrannical government which won't succumb to mere persuasion, will succumb to economic pressure. My Lord, one may believe a government is brutal, and it is ready to use force, even eager to use force, and yet one may believe that although it may shoot down a mob without compunction, that although it may disperse processions brutally without compunction, that although it may not hesitate to use machine guns, yet one may believe that even such a government would not be able to go into a million or two million households and break up a stay at home strike by force.

*

On his release from detention at the end of August 1960 Nelson Mandela knew that were he to be convicted of treason, even if he escaped a death sentence he would likely go back to prison for a very long time. This might well be his last brief window of freedom and he filled it with intense activity. When he was not in court in Pretoria Mandela revived his legal practice and laid plans for an ANC which, having now been officially proscribed, would in future have to operate covertly. The frenetic work took its toll on his family life: when his second child with Winnie was born in December 1960, he was again, as he later lamented, not able to be present at the birth.

The trial encompassed deaths as well as births. Just as it was within touching distance of a conclusion it was, for a second time,

interrupted by an unexpected death, this time of the oldest defendant, Elias Moretsele, who succumbed to a heart attack on 10 March
1961. Born in 1897 and a member of the ANC and its predecessor
since 1917, Moretsele was a former president of the ANC in the
Transvaal and had been a phlegmatic presence during the long trial.
'We used to tease him and be teased by him; often he slept in court,
a weary old man, but with an indomitable spirit,' wrote Joseph. 'I
used to hear his rumbling comments behind me, and his deep chuckle
at some of the absurdity of the evidence.'

On 23 March 1961 the three judges cut short the defence submissions, announcing that they wished to consider the overall position
the trial had reached and would reconvene the next week. 'We don't
at first understand what this means,' wrote Helen Joseph in her diary,
'and then our counsel tell us that it can have only one meaning –
victory, acquittal. It is all so sudden that we are stunned and we don't
dare to believe it.' The suddenness of the halt to proceedings surprised
everyone: Kentridge had fully expected the case to carry on until
June.

The treason bus sets off one last time from Johannesburg on the
morning of Wednesday, 29 March 1961. This time the mood is reso-
lutely optimistic, and songs of hope and defiance are sung. On arrival
in Pretoria the trialists – now reduced in number to twenty-eight –
are met by cameras and reporters. The judges process into the Old
Synagogue for a final time. The public gallery reserved for
'Non-Europeans' has always been full throughout the months and
years of the trial. Today the gallery reserved for 'Europeans' is also
crowded. Rumpff, whom the defence had twice tried to have recused,
reads out the court's short reasons:

> It is impossible for the court to come to the conclusion that the ANC
> acquired or adopted a policy to overthrow the State by violence – that
> is in the sense that the masses had to be prepared or conditioned to
> commit direct acts of violence against the State . . . While the prosecu-
> tion has succeeded in showing that the Programme of Action contem-
> plated the use of illegal methods (e.g. strikes, boycotts, etc.) . . . for the
> achievement of a fundamentally different State from the present, it has

failed to show that the ANC as a matter of policy, intended to achieve this new State by violent means.

The court remains silent. As if to help the accused grasp the momentous import of what has just happened, Rumpff adds: 'You are found not guilty and are discharged and you may go.' The accused are stunned; the smiles of Kentridge, Maisels and Fischer, turning round to their clients, convince them that they are not dreaming. Nelson Mandela and his co-accused leap to their feet; friends and relations flock around them. Winnie embraces Nelson. As they leave, the crowd outside begins to sing 'Nkosi Sikelel' iAfrika' ('Lord Bless Africa'), the ANC's anthem. Maisels is carried out in triumph on the shoulders of the accused.

News of the acquittals reverberates around the world. The following day the *Guardian* devotes a leader to the outcome:

> Jubilation must be the first reaction to the news that the accused in the South African treason trial have been found not guilty of high treason. The decision of the Special Criminal Court of three judges demonstrates that the rule of law is alive in the Union, even if it appears now only in attenuated form. But this sense of delight that the accused are free – permanently one hopes – should be tempered when viewed against the history of this disgraceful persecution of South Africans whose only aim (so the Court found) was to advocate the substitution of the present Government by a democratic form of government . . .

Kentridge's realisation that the accused might actually be acquitted had dawned on him by slow degrees. 'If you'd asked me at the beginning of the trial, I'd have said it was very unlikely that they were all going to be acquitted,' he later recalled. Still, hearing Rumpff formally acquitting his clients was an emotional moment for him. Kentridge had been the backbone of the defence, and its intellectual engine room; a constant daily presence in court while the older QCs Maisels and Fischer dropped in and out. The defence of the trialists had been a mammoth collective effort, and had involved an extraordinary level of collaboration between lawyers and clients. However, although with his usual modesty he denies it, the acquittal of the twenty-eight who ran the full course of the trial was Kentridge's achievement above everyone else's.

There was a party that night at Bram Fischer's home, at 12 Beaumont Street, a regular meeting place for the accused and their lawyers during the trial. Amidst the celebrations – watched over, as usual, by the security police – Kentridge, so precise in his courtroom demeanour and so restrained in his persona, allowed himself a moment of release. Fischer's wife later recounted how Kentridge, the 'staid, soft-spoken, oh-so-correct lawyer', put some ice down Michael Parkington's shirt and placed a champagne cork in his ear. Then, Molly Fischer wrote to her daughter, he 'danced a little jig and was heard to use bad words'.

One person missing from the party was Nelson Mandela. He knew that the response of the government to his acquittal would not be that hoped for by the *Guardian*. In his autobiography Mandela explained that the result in the Treason Trial could only make the state more bitter and ruthless in its response to political challenge.[32] He had made a decision to go underground and to devote his life to keeping the ANC alive as a now clandestine organisation. That night he was neither celebrating with his comrades nor at home with his family, but sequestered in a safe house in Johannesburg. For the next eighteen months, until his final arrest in August 1962, he lived a life in the shadows.

At the time the Treason Trial was frequently described as one of the most important in modern legal history. A conviction would have rendered political activity by non-whites essentially impossible, as well as resulting in the incarceration, or worse, of the leaders of the anti-apartheid movement. But even as the acquittals were pronounced it seemed as if they belonged to an earlier age. The government had already pre-empted the result: the ANC and other anti-apartheid organisations had been banned the year before. The ANC would remain proscribed for almost thirty years. This would be the last major political trial conducted according to normal rules: as we will see, in response the government swiftly instituted new legislation to facilitate the conviction of its perceived enemies.[33] As Mandela had predicted, the state went on to treat many of the treason trialists with vindictive cruelty. After his acquittal Ahmed Kathrada was subsequently jailed for six months for breaking a banning order by visiting his sick mother while the trial was under way. Despite winning the Nobel Peace Prize in 1961, Albert Luthuli would be confined for the rest of his life in a form of internal exile. By the time Helen Joseph's account of the trial, *If This Be Treason*, was published in 1963,[34] several of the accused, including Mandela, were again under detention, and two had been deported. The anti-apartheid struggle was entering a new phase. The government was now resorting to naked force in its suppression of non-violent resistance and the ANC was, in turn, moving towards a new policy of sabotage and militancy. As Nelson Mandela later put it: 'the attacks of the wild beast cannot be averted with only bare hands'. Yet the Treason Trial had succeeded in projecting to the world the sincerity and idealism of the black leaders who were on trial and the moral bankruptcy of the state which had sought their conviction. It would become one of the key events of the anti-apartheid struggle, looked back upon by Mandela and his co-accused with justified pride.

In its malevolent immensity the Treason Trial seemed like a Kafkaesque version of *Jarndyce v Jarndyce*. Isie Maisels recalled the case as 'absolutely endless . . . I can't tell you how terrible it was.'[35] The full transcript of the court proceedings runs to over 25,000 pages.[36] The prosecution exhibits included some 12,000 documents, mostly seized in police searches in the months leading up to the final arrests. They ranged from the expected – a copy of the Freedom Charter and ANC membership lists – to the absurd: notes on eighteenth- and nineteenth-century historical questions such as the foreign policy of Lord Castlereagh; the slave trade and the Vienna Settlement of 1815; two years of back numbers of a magazine called *Fighting Talk*; a Russian recipe book; a pamphlet enticingly entitled 'Why Is the Cult of the Individual Alien to the Spirit of Marxism–Leninism.'

By the time the case finished, the prosecution of the accused – who had irremediably lost so many years of their lives to it – appeared shameful to almost everyone involved. Even the judges seemed disgusted by it. Mr Justice Kennedy had previously sentenced twenty-two Africans to death in an unrelated trial. Yet, according to Mandela, after Professor Matthews had given evidence the judge shook hands with him, wishing that they could meet again under better circumstances.[37] Kentridge recounts that after the trial was over even Advocate Trengove, the most remorseless of the prosecution counsel, paid a visit to Matthews's home in an act of contrition, though apparently Matthews declined to grant him the absolution he perhaps sought. Still, Trengove went on to become a notably fair judge and in retirement helped out at the Legal Resources Centre co-founded by Felicia Kentridge.[38] One of the original Treason Trial accused, Alfred Hutchinson, once asked: 'What treason was there? Is it treason to ask that Black and White should live together, as brothers, countrymen, equals? Is it treason to ask for food? Is it treason to ask that passes be abolished? And that we might walk freely in the land of our birth?' By the end of the trial it seemed that only Advocate de Vos disagreed with those sentiments. In a biting satirical poem written at the trial's conclusion, Kentridge's wife Felicia lampooned the prosecution's leading counsel:

> When in disgrace with fortune and men's eyes
> He all alone beweeps his outcast state
> He thinks of old indictments squashed like flies
> And 91 reduced to 28.
> With bootless cries to Rumpff he curses fate
> And sadly thinks how sadly he has failed
> That 91 reduced to 28
> And no one hanged or even flogged or jailed.
> But one small laurel crowns that lofty brow,
> For after all it's only 28.
> He wanly smiles and softly says 'Here's how'
> And chalks old Moretsele on his slate.
> This QC screeches treason to the skies
> To gain a cheap conviction, twists and lies
> He founds upon allegiance to the Crown
> And stands a traitor to his silken gown.

The Trial lodged itself in the wider public and literary imagination. Many memoirs of the time reference it. In 1981 Mongane

Serote published his famous novel *To Every Birth Its Blood*. In it he depicts a trial at the Old Synagogue and captures the collective resilience of the accused:

> Every day, when the twenty-five came in, walking up the stairs, a freedom song broke loose, climbing the stairs slowly, heavily, through the two huge doors of the Pretoria Synagogue. In there, it rose, above the floor, above the many, many benches, above the judges' bench, to the ceiling and out of the building to the sky. Every day at this time when the twenty-five came in, crowds and crowds of black faces, white faces, crowded the streets before going to work to see the men and women, singing, fists clenched and raised high, go up the stairs slowly, into the court.[39]

The case had consumed Kentridge's almost every waking moment for three gruelling years. It had been an exhausting experience but also, in the end, an uplifting one. The bond between the lawyers working on it became exceptionally strong and lifelong friendships were forged. Kentridge experienced the privilege of spending months in the company of the greatest figures in the struggle against apartheid. He also made wider connections. Erwin Griswold, dean of Harvard Law School and later the United States Solicitor General, was an observer at the trial and would invite Kentridge as a visiting reader at Harvard some years later.[40] Rebecca West, then one of the most famous writers in the world and author of the ground-breaking work on treachery in the twentieth century, *The Meaning of Treason* (1947), came out to South Africa on a journalistic assignment in early 1960 and spent several days at the Old Synagogue. One of her articles for the English *Sunday Times* misattributed certain judicial comments to Mr Justice Kennedy, who took the unprecedented step of suing her for libel. West, who had become friendly with Kentridge, sought his informal advice.[41]

Kentridge's eldest son William was three when the trial started, and six when it finished: for as long as he could remember, his father had always been preoccupied with what he thought of as the 'trees and tile', which he somehow linked to pine trees growing in his parents' garden and a tiled table outside the house.[42] As he returned to

Johannesburg after the acquittals, Kentridge knew that he needed a period away from the law. A few days later he and Felicia embarked with their two children on a protracted trip to Europe. In July 1961 the full written judgment of the court was handed down, explaining its reasons for acquitting all the accused. It extended to hundreds of pages. Kentridge could hardly bear to read it.

Forty years later Mandela and Kentridge met again at a dinner held to inaugurate the Sydney and Felicia Kentridge Award.[43] Mandela was now the ex-president of South Africa. Seeing his former counsel across the room, he walked up to cheerily greet him: 'Sydney, do you remember me?' In a speech later in the evening, Mandela recalled

the brilliance and courage of Sydney Kentridge, which I witnessed day after day in the Old Synagogue here in Pretoria . . . his brilliance shone out and with it, the promise of the career to come. His manner was always understated, controlled and relentlessly rational. His cross-examination was devastating.[44]

4

The Sharpeville Inquiry (1960)

IN MARCH 1960, three-quarters of the way through the long and wearisome Treason Trial, a cataclysmic event took place seventy-five miles from the converted synagogue in Pretoria where Sydney Kentridge had been defending Nelson Mandela and his co-trialists. The mass shooting by police on Monday, 21 March at Sharpeville, a black township outside Vereeniging, some forty miles south of Johannesburg, would prove to be one of the seminal world events of the second half of the twentieth century. The photographs of protestors fleeing the fusillades provided enduring images that are now indelibly associated with the barbarism of the apartheid regime. At least sixty-nine people were killed, all of them black and many of them children, and another 187 or more were wounded, some sustaining terrible injuries.

Huge protests ensued. Nelson Mandela and Chief Luthuli publicly burned their passbooks before hundreds of supporters (Kentridge would later represent Luthuli on charges connected with the destruction of his pass). The implacable violence inherent in the apartheid state had been starkly revealed, leading Mandela and other key decision-makers within the ANC to the realisation that political change would never come through peaceful negotiation. In panic, the government declared a state of emergency, which led to the imposition of a form of martial law. Kentridge vividly recalls the arrival of the news of the massacre at the Old Synagogue and the sense of desolation that descended on the trialists and their lawyers. There followed the stark reality of incarceration: all twenty-nine remaining Treason Trial defendants, previously on bail, were shortly afterwards interned, as were thousands of others across South Africa, as the state acted to avert a mass uprising.

The ensuing judicial inquiry into the massacre saw Kentridge – finding himself at a loose end for a few months after the Treason Trialists disinstructed their legal team – retained to represent Ambrose Reeves, the bishop of Johannesburg, and some of the bereaved families of Sharpeville. The inquiry resulted in a report that, almost inevitably, largely exonerated the police of wrongdoing. However, the law can sometimes effect change not through its outcome but in its process. The schizophrenic character of the South African polity in the apartheid era, with its obsessive adherence to a legitimising semblance of legal form, meant that for several weeks public hearings took place (attended by observers from across the globe, including Elwyn Jones QC MP, later a Labour Lord Chancellor),[1] at which dozens of witnesses gave testimony of the events of that fatal day. The mendacity of some of the police witnesses – exposed by the cross-examination of Kentridge and his colleagues – and the poignancy of the evidence of the bereaved and maimed inhabitants of Sharpeville were reported around the world. In the formal setting of a courtroom the voices were heard of people who were otherwise voiceless; and those unaccustomed to having their word contradicted were exposed as liars.

Kentridge saw his role at the inquiry as a form of truth-telling: the creation of a formal and public record both for the contemporary world and for posterity. The result was a kind of legal cleansing; an early form of a truth, if not a reconciliation, commission. The miasma of propaganda and lies that the South African state had moved swiftly to wrap around the terrible events of that day was expunged. The Sharpeville shooting was revealed for what it was: one of the most heinous episodes in the history of South Africa.

Sharpeville (originally Sharpe Native Township) dated back to 1935, when it was created to relocate the inhabitants of an overcrowded earlier settlement for black workers on the outskirts of the Afrikaner town of Vereeniging to a larger and more distant site. Laid out on a grid of wide, dead-straight streets punctuated by open spaces, it was, by the standards of the day, something of a model township. The first wave of homes were relatively spacious and it could boast an unusually wide range of amenities: a clinic, sports stadium, crèche, beer hall and even a public library. A new red-brick police station, opened in October 1959, was one of the few to be built in the centre of a township rather than on its periphery. A second phase of housing put up in the 1950s – temporary huts on concrete platforms – was much less inviting, and as the decade wore on tensions increased. Local bus fares doubled and rents were raised, forcing many families into financial difficulties. By 1960 unemployment in Sharpeville was heading up as employers increasingly chose to hire migrants willing to do menial work for less pay. The township's 'Native Advisory Board' was just that – advisory – and could do no more than present grievances to the white-led local administration, which normally ignored them.

The inhabitants of Sharpeville were also affected by national developments. The much hated 'pass laws', which had applied to all black men since 1952, were being extended to black women in 1960. Passes (officially called 'reference books', but universally and contemptuously dubbed *dompas*, Afrikaans for 'stupid pass') functioned as internal passports, enabling the authorities to rigidly enforce the legal restrictions on where black people could travel or work. Those restrictions could be, and often were, tightened arbitrarily, rendering families destitute if a breadwinner was no longer permitted to travel to his or her workplace. Black people had to join tedious queues to present their passes to officious police officers. Not carrying a pass was a serious offence, and could lead to a humiliating personal search. The extension of such searches to black women was, for many, the final straw. By 1960 black people had started burning their passes, or symbolically handing them back to the authorities at organised protests.

The ANC had initiated a Programme of Action – strikes, boycotts and mass civil disobedience – as soon as the foundations of the apartheid state began to be constructed in 1948. But by the late 1950s some within the ANC saw its leadership as out of touch, 'genteel and middle-aged'.[2] In 1959 the Pan Africanist Congress (PAC) was formed by a breakaway group of militant younger ANC members who espoused a form of black nationalism – Pan Africanism – in contrast to the avowed multiracialism of the ANC. Most Pan Africanists deplored the ANC's commitment to passive, non-violent resistance for being ineffective. Some saw the ANC as 'captured' by white liberals and Communists, and its Freedom Charter as an unambitious, vacuous statement designed to mollify whites, not secure black liberation. As we have seen, this was of course a very different interpretation from that which was being placed on the charter by the prosecution in the Treason Trial.

The fact that many ANC leaders were defendants at the Treason Trial and the proceedings preparatory to it from 1956 onwards only helped the rise of the Pan Africanists. Trapped in the maw of the seemingly never-ending legal process, the accuseds' main priority for several years was avoiding the gallows or a long jail sentence, not planning the next steps in the anti-apartheid struggle. It was against that backdrop that PAC was launched by Robert Sobukwe in Orlando, Soweto, with near religious fervour (at its first meeting there was much talk of Simon of Arabia, the black man who had supposedly carried Jesus from the cross). PAC's official manifesto stopped short of calling for whites to be ejected from South Africa and 'driven into the sea', as the most militant Pan Africanists demanded. Instead it included a long homily about 'personal habits', demanding that PAC members 'maintain an exemplary standard of cleanliness'. But at meetings the rhetoric was much more fiery: at one rally one of PAC's leaders, Potlako Leballo, castigated 'white foreign dogs in our continent [who] must surrender to the rule of Africa by Africans'. Such talk alienated liberal whites but was well received in the black townships, particularly by young unemployed men who had no stake in society and little to lose. It is estimated that within four months of its founding PAC had gathered 25,000 members, many living in the townships around Johannesburg. Sharpeville itself had an unusually young populace: by 1960, 21,000 of its population of 37,000 were under the age of eighteen. This was fertile ground for the more militant-minded PAC.

By the end of 1959 PAC was preparing to steal a march by starting an anti-pass campaign ahead of the ANC's own, due to begin on 31 March 1960.[3] PAC rejected the ANC's tactic of publicly burning passes, which they saw as ineffective posturing. Instead, their plan was for black men to leave their passes at home and then present themselves en masse at police stations, demanding to be arrested. They knew that in the short term there might be bloodshed: 'The tree of freedom is watered with blood,' one Pan Africanist told the bishop of Johannesburg a few days before the Sharpeville shooting.

A 'day of action' was planned for Monday, 21 March. Large crowds gathered at several police stations around Cape Town and Johannesburg. Sobukwe had called for 'absolute non-violence' in PAC's anti-pass campaign, but outriders on the ground were not always so peaceable. There is evidence that they threatened to 'lay hands on' Sharpeville residents who tried to defy their strike calls and go to work on the day. Before dawn that morning, local bus drivers were in effect abducted from their homes to prevent them from driving residents to their work-places; at daybreak some passengers waiting in vain at bus stops were threatened with violence if they persisted in trying to get to work by other means, and in some cases assaulted. Roads out of Sharpeville were blocked by PAC operatives, and phone lines were severed. In the early morning church bells were rung, summoning the populace to congregate at the police station. By about 11 a.m. a crowd numbering a few thousand had gathered around the station's northern, southern and western sides. It did not seem to be cowed when, at about 11.15 a.m., a Harvard spotter plane of the South African Air Force made a low pass over it, closely followed by the ear-splitting howl of a Sabre jet fighter. Most had never seen such aircraft at close quarters before, and were more excited than afraid. This was turning into an air show, and their protest was clearly making waves. Some local PAC leaders then presented themselves at the main gate of the police station without passes and demanded that they be placed under arrest. A Sergeant Wessels declined the invitation.

Sharpeville police station's usual complement was fewer than forty. But a steady stream of reinforcements had arrived all morning, and by 1 p.m. there were at least five times the usual number of officers at the station. The official headcount, probably an understatement, would later be given as 130 white policemen, armed with Lee-Enfield .303 rifles, Sten sub-machine guns and revolvers; and 70 black policemen, bearing knobkerries – a form of club.[4] The final contingent had arrived in a fleet of Saracens, six-wheeled armoured personnel carriers which were a ubiquitous part of apartheid policing, three of them with Browning machine guns mounted on top.

Ian Berry, a young British photojournalist then working for the black *Drum* magazine, had followed the Saracens into Sharpeville with his colleague Humphrey Tyler. Berry explains that the two of them had driven in speculatively; they had no sense that something momentous was going to happen.[5] He started walking among the demonstrators, taking photographs in what he recalls as a festive atmosphere. Few were armed with anything other than umbrellas to guard against the hot sun, or walking sticks. People ambled to and fro to fetch food and water. Some were pressed up against the station's perimeter fence, but no attempt was made to storm it. While a number of women were said to have spat at black officers and lifted their skirts at them (a sexual insult), others sang hymns, including 'Abide with Me'. Some elderly protestors – or curious onlookers; it was in many cases hard to tell the difference – sat on fold-up chairs at the edge of the crowd, as if enjoying a family picnic.

Just after 1 o'clock, as the hot sun beat down, two local PAC leaders were arrested when they refused to call off the protest. The police now seemed to be in a state of paralysis, uncertain how to respond to the large crowd that showed no sign of either dispersing or attacking them. In 1960 an estimated one-third of white South African policemen were under the age of twenty-one, and many were poorly trained and trigger-happy. The political scientist Philip Frankel has explained how apartheid had 'encased' such officers with an 'explosive mixture of fear, frustration, rage and isolation'.[6] Many of the reinforcements brought into Sharpeville that morning were young working-class Afrikaners 'accustomed to ready obedience' from blacks, and who heard innocuous cries of 'Afrika!' and 'Iswe Lethu' ('our dream') as threats, not greetings. Such officers often referred indiscriminately to black demonstrators as *tsotsis* – a derogatory term for young criminals, hooligans or vagabonds – even if they were peaceful. Many officers – both from Sharpeville and elsewhere – had been up all night dealing with unrest that had begun on the Sunday. They were tired and tense.

A senior officer, Lieutenant Colonel Pienaar, arrived at the police station from Johannesburg at about 1 p.m. and immediately disagreed with his fellow officers about how best to disperse the crowd, which he was convinced was intent on forcing its way into the station. A vivid insight into his state of mind was provided in his later evidence to the inquiry: 'the native mentality does not allow them to gather for a peaceful demonstration. For them to gather means violence.' As occasional stones started being thrown, the police ordered the crowd pressed against the low chain-link fence around the station compound to move back, an instruction with which it was impossible to comply given the throng behind. The police then decided instead to start 'rounding up the leaders' – arresting those they thought were controlling the crowd. Shortly after 1.30 p.m. a Lieutenant Colonel Spengler was trying to arrest a protestor by the gate on the west side of the enclosure and stumbled, just as a section of fence partially gave way under the pressure of bodies. For the first time that day, Pienaar ordered his men to load their weapons. The police later claimed – falsely – that at about the same time dozens or even hundreds of protestors started breaking through the police station's gates. A few moments later Geelbooi Mofokeng, a local PAC hothead, produced a pistol and fired. Although the crowd instantly restrained him, so his two shots flew harmlessly into the air, police officers lined up by the fence immediately called out 'Skiet!' or 'N'skiet!' ('Shot!' or 'Shoot!'). Even if this was intended as a warning that shots had been heard, most officers interpreted it as a frantic call to open fire. An officer helping Spengler to his feet started firing his sub-machine gun into the crowd, and about seventy-five other white policemen immediately followed suit with revolvers, rifles and automatic weapons, without warning, from three sides of the police station.

The police later admitted that some 700 rounds were fired in at least two sustained volleys; more recent estimates suggest the true number was closer to 1,300. As the fusillade abated, witnesses heard a number of isolated shots, as if the police were taking aim at specific targets instead of shooting indiscriminately into the crowd. Photographs showed officers reloading their weapons and then firing again. Some heard one demonstrator crying out 'You've shot enough' in the brief lull after the initial volley of gunfire, only to be cut down by the second. Ian Berry's colleague, the reporter Humphrey Tyler, saw a policeman standing on top of a Saracen swinging his gun in a wide arc as he fired, 'as if he was panning a movie camera – from the hip . . . One woman was hit about ten yards from our car. Her companion, a young man, went back when she fell. He thought she had stumbled. Then he turned her over and saw that her chest had been shot away.'[7] Another witness said that the crowd fell to the ground 'like a wheat-field that had been hit by a cyclone'. Terrible injuries were sustained: one witness reported seeing a foetus fall out of a pregnant woman's stomach wound. Many were hit below the waist; several survivors had to have their legs amputated. Some of those shot had taken no part whatever in the demonstration. One man who happened to be cycling through Sharpeville had his head blown off; another was hit in the leg while lying on the grass outside his house, several hundred yards from the police station, quietly reading a book.

No white policeman was seen aiding any of the wounded, who lay strewn over the open ground and roads that surrounded the police station. Only civilians and a few non-white policemen tended to them. A pile of spears, swords, sticks and stones was soon assembled outside the police station for the benefit of press photographers, as apparent evidence of the violence and threat of the crowd. Some officers were seen pitching stones in over the police station's fence, to exaggerate the scale of the stone-throwing that had preceded the shooting. Sharpeville was swiftly sealed off from the outside world: no one was to leave or enter. Ambulances took away the wounded and police lorries removed the dead. The government issued a communiqué that the police had been 'forced to fire in self-defence' after a 20,000 strong mob had made a 'deliberate attack on a police station with assorted weapons, including firearms'. The disinformation operation had begun. Shortly afterwards a heavy thunderstorm broke over Sharpeville, washing away the blood that stained its streets.

What is staggering about the aftermath of the massacre is the lack of contrition or sympathy extended to the victims by the Afrikaner community. Instead, its reaction to the atrocity was one of fear: of a backlash by an enraged black community; of a possible race war. The response was even greater repression and a clear narrative for the future: the deaths and injuries at Sharpeville were entirely the fault of the blacks themselves. Just six days after the massacre Prime Minister Verwoerd set what would become the prevailing tone of unapologetic defiance, proclaiming in a speech that 'the white man brought civilisation to this country and all that you see which the Bantu has inherited today was created by the knowledge and diligence of the white man'.[8]

News of the shooting took some time to reach the outside world. Ian Berry instantly knew that his photographs had captured a momentous event; he swiftly departed Sharpeville, anxious that he might be searched and his film confiscated. In the event *Drum* declined to publish his photographs for fear of the government's response. Instead the film was sent to an agency in London and soon dominated the front pages of newspapers around the world. Although several journalists had witnessed the shooting, the shocking stories they filed in the foreign press did not reach South Africa straight away. Even Ambrose Reeves, the Anglican bishop of Johannesburg, in whose diocese Sharpeville lay, was unable to find out exactly what had happened until the following day. Reeves had been born in Britain and spent the first decades of his priesthood there. He had not set foot in South Africa until his ordination as bishop of Johannesburg in 1949. In the 1950s he regularly visited local townships, where his cassock was a common sight, and where he was welcomed by the black population, keen for influential whites to see the conditions they had to live under. Viewed by the regime as a 'radical leftist ecclesiastic', Reeves was an unblinkered outsider who could see apartheid's evils more clearly than most whites who had lived in South Africa all their lives. Moreover, he was unafraid to speak truth to power.

As soon as Reeves heard that there had been a shooting he went to Baragwanath Hospital in Soweto, to which the most seriously wounded had been taken, and spoke to scores of survivors, most fearful of what would happen to them when they were discharged. They had good reason to be: many were subsequently arrested on charges of public violence and taken straight from hospital beds to cells in Boksburg jail, south-east of Johannesburg. Wounded survivors who had stayed away from hospitals were also rounded up by groups of policemen that roamed Sharpeville in the days after the shooting, arresting anyone who showed signs of injury. Survivors were warned off from speaking to the media or giving evidence to the inquiry that was later established. Some were told that if they testified they could be put in detention 'as a precautionary measure'. Once the state of emergency was declared, on 29 March, detainees could be held indefinitely without access to lawyers, making them even more vulnerable to beatings and torture.

By Wednesday, 23 March news of the horrific scale of the shooting was out, and an appalled Reeves told a *Rand Daily Mail* reporter that he thought a judicial inquiry was called for. Later the same day Reeves's attorneys (Routledge, Douglas-Wilson, Auret & Wimble) persuaded a magistrate to allow a sympathetic pathologist, Dr Shapiro, to attend the post-mortems of those killed in Sharpeville – a crucial step that ensured the world later learned that most had been shot in the back as they fled in panic. Survivors consistently told Reeves that there had been no attack on the police before the shooting began: far from being belligerent, even the most militant members of the crowd had begged officers to arrest them. The gates were unlocked and the fence was low – just four and a half feet or so; if the crowd had wanted to storm the police station that could easily have been accomplished. Yet no such attempt had been made. The so-called 'riotous behaviour' described by police amounted to shouts of 'Afrika!', thumbs-up signs and singing.

Once reports emerged of the shooting the reaction across the world was swift. Boycotts of South African goods gathered pace and there were widespread calls for South Africa to be expelled from the Commonwealth. In London, the normally conservative *Times* ran a strongly critical editorial. The British Liberal leader Jo Grimond, speaking in the House of Commons, called the shooting a 'dividing line in history'. Within ten days of the massacre the British Labour Party organised a rally of 15,000 people in Trafalgar Square, said to be one of the largest gatherings in central London since VE Day, in 1945.

But the South African state refused to concede that the police had done anything wrong in Sharpeville. South Africa's ambassador to the UN, Brand Fourie, insisted that the police had fired in self-defence, having been attacked with 'Pangas [machetes], axes, iron bars, knives, sticks and firearms'. Its high commissioner in London said that the shooting had been a response to a 'planned demonstration of about 20,000 natives in which demonstrators attacked the police with assorted weapons including firearms. The demonstrators shot first, and the police were forced to fire in self-defence and [to] avoid even more tragic results.' The concerns expressed by Western governments were dismissed, Dr Verwoerd warning that South Africa should not be 'thrown to the wolves. If we are swallowed up in the sea of the black masses of Africa, they will lose their best friend and most faithful ally on the African Continent.' South Africa's diplomatic offensive appeared to have worked. The UN Security Council adopted a resolution deploring 'that the recent disturbances . . . should have led to the loss of life of so many Africans' and calling on South Africa to abandon apartheid; but the Nationalists drew comfort from the pointed abstention of the United Kingdom, along with France. On the whole, there was a muted response to the shooting from those foreign governments that really mattered to South Africa.

But the South African government did make one concession to international opinion, albeit a strategic one. On 1 April, eleven days after the shooting, the governor general, Charles Swart, announced the establishment of a commission of inquiry into the shooting, which would hold public hearings and produce a report. Bearing the anodyne title 'Commission of Inquiry into the occurrences at Sharpeville (and other places) on the 21st March 1960', it had been agreed at an emergency cabinet meeting as a damage limitation exercise: a message to an uneasy world that the rule of law still existed in South Africa. As one writer put it, the 'mailed fist [had to] be encased in a velvet glove'.[9] For diplomatic and economic reasons the government had to be seen to permit an objective examination of what had happened at Sharpeville, while ensuring that the inquiry's conclusions vindicated the state and its security apparatus. It was vital for the police to be exonerated and for Sharpeville to be turned from a national crisis to a political opportunity. There was never to be a public apology for what happened at Sharpeville: from the start, the inquiry's job was to allocate the blame to PAC for provoking a violent demonstration on which the police were fully justified in opening fire.

The Commission of Inquiry was to be chaired by a high court judge called Mr Justice P. J. Wessels, of the Natal division of the Supreme Court in Pietermaritzburg. Wessels was a shrewd choice. He was not regarded as an entirely partisan judge, and so would lend a veneer of credibility to the proceedings; but he was considered sufficiently pliant to deliver the conclusion the government wanted. Witnesses were to be called by Advocate P. S. Claassen QC, attorney general of the Orange Free State, who was ostensibly there not to promote a particular viewpoint but to present the evidence dispassionately with a view to arriving at the truth. In practice he represented the interests of the state, cross-examining witnesses who put forward accounts of events which contradicted the government's preferred version while police witnesses were gently led through their self-exculpatory testimony.

Had Ambrose Reeves not ensured that his own legal team participated in the inquiry, no alternative view of events would have been presented. After Kentridge was stood down from the Treason Trial he plunged straight into preparations for the inquiry, which was to commence at speed, on 12 April, at the Vereeniging Magistrates Court. Although Kentridge nominally had as his leaders Isie Maisels QC, George Colman QC and Rex Welsh QC, it is evident from the transcript that Kentridge and his junior Chris Plewman did the lion's share of the work.[10]

The task for Kentridge and his fellow lawyers was not just to draw out the testimony of the black victims of and witnesses to the shooting; it was also to cross-examine the many police officers whose evidence would seek to build a picture of a violent crowd about to storm the police station, on whom there had been no option but to open fire. Those officers were effectively immune from adverse consequences: they could be confident that any evidence they gave would not lead to prosecution or loss of their job. Frankel comments that the police witnesses 'had no compunction whatsoever in fabricating and concealing evidence with an audacity that astounded the lawyers'. Yet under the cross-examination of Colman, Kentridge and Plewman their callousness, and racism, was laid bare.

The political atmosphere in which the inquiry got under way was poisoned by the pronouncements of government ministers. The *Rand Daily Mail* reported on the first day that the minister of external affairs had told a press conference the day before: 'When you are dealing with gangsters, you cannot handle them with kid-gloves.' Kentridge complained to Wessels:

[I]f members of the Executive themselves prejudge the very issues which this Commission has to decide – it is not simply a question of the undesirability of general comment, Sir – but if the members of the very Executive at an official Government Press Conference, members of the Executive to whom you have to report – who have asked for your report – if they prejudge the very issues on which you must report, then the question arises, Sir, whether this whole Commission is not an essay in futility; if notwithstanding anything said or done here, the Executive to whom you must report, have taken the view expressed of where the blame lies, where no blame lies . . . from our point of view we carefully have to consider our position in a Commission where, whatever you do Sir, the persons to whom you must report appear to have prejudged the issue.

Kentridge faced a number of other difficulties in properly presenting his clients' case. It was almost unheard of for a police officer's word to be disbelieved by a South African court, especially when the contradiction came from black witnesses. But without such witnesses it would be impossible; and finding black witnesses willing to give evidence was no easy matter. Kentridge recalls the anxiety of those who had been present at Sharpeville on the fatal day. With a state of emergency in force, and mass arrests of anyone deemed a subversive, testifying on oath to having witnessed the shooting – and therefore to being in the crowd around the police station – was a dangerous thing to do. It was widely known that the injured had been carted from hospital to prison on the pretext that anyone there that day must have been engaged in illegal activity. Despite Wessels's soothing assurance that nobody who testified before him would suffer any detriment, Kentridge and his fellow lawyers could, according to one historian, only 'garner a few bit players, the black marginals to the massacre, who were willing to face the rigours of public interrogation'.[11] Many black witnesses were simply too terrified of the personal consequences if they appeared at the inquiry to speak the truth.

Kentridge recalls the bravery of those who did give evidence. Not only were they putting their liberty at risk, but as they testified they were subjected to the contemptuous smirking and gurning of the white police officers who seemed to dominate the courtroom, lolling in the public gallery or behind Advocate Claassen, as if flaunting their untouchability. These witnesses spoke of the peaceable, indeed festive, nature of the crowd; the absence of weapons; that the only stone-throwing was by overexcited children. Here is part of Kentridge's examination of Reverend Robert Maja, a Presbyterian minister at Sharpeville. In the morning before the shooting Maja had paid a visit to the Anglican vicar of Sharpeville, Reverend Boye. Finding Boye not at home, Maja had gone to look for him in the crowd around the police station.

Q: Can you tell us what the mood of the crowd was at that time?
A: They were happy.
Q: Did the crowd seem to you to be aggressive?
A: No.
Q: Or hostile towards the police?
A: There was nothing indicating fighting.
Q: You did not see any weapons carried by members of the crowd?
A: Not a single one.
Q: At the time you were there at the Police Station amongst the crowd, did you notice any aeroplanes flying over?
A: Yes; they did. A few would come and thereafter a few again and so forth.
Q: Did they dive low over the crowd?
A: Yes; they did. There were youngsters that were throwing their hats at these aeroplanes – 'Horrah! Horrah!' – flinging their hats up.
Q: And how did you interpret that gesture of throwing their hats into the air and shouting 'Hoorah!'
A: They were enjoying it.

Maja had eventually found Boye; they were back at the priest's house drinking tea when the shooting started. He headed straight from a vicars' tea party to a scene of carnage.

Q: Did you cross the field next to the Police Station?
A: I did.
Q: Did you see anything there . . .?
A: There were many people lying there; some of them were dead; some of them . . . their intestines were protruding.

Q: Did you go right up to the Police Station?

A: No. I did not then, having seen that, go to the Police Station. I tried to render assistance to those injured people.

Q: But how far did you go, when you were going to render assistance?

A: From body to body . . . I passed every one of them and I gave some of them water . . . They called me by my name. They said 'Minister Maja, I am thirsty, I want some water.' Some of them said 'Minister Maja, I have been burnt terribly by the sun.' I tried by taking their shoes to make a pillow for them to lie on . . . what I could pick up there as far as the clothing was concerned, I tried to cover them with that to protect them against the burning of the sun . . .

Q: Did you spend some time among the wounded?

A: I was the last one to leave after the dead had been removed, and the wounded.

Q: I just wanted to show you a photograph that was taken after the shooting. Do you see it?

A: That is me, assisting there.

Q: Now, here is another photograph, taken by the photographer of the *Star* after the shooting. Is that you on the photograph?

Kentridge handed to Maja a particularly distressing photograph of one of the dead, the man's head half destroyed by gunfire.

A: I am the one in front . . . I went and fetched an officer . . . the brains were lying out.

Q: What did you do about that?

A: Before the ambulance came, I went to all the officers. I said 'I am asking you, if you take that corpse, please remove the brains as well' . . . It then came to my mind that they had left the brains behind. I went back to the captain . . . I said 'I asked you to remove the brains.' It was then that he called this Non-European Policeman and told him to remove the brains from there.

The transcript reads at this point: 'Photograph showing Bantu constable picking up brains with spade, Exh. "UUU" handed in.'

(This was so powerful a moment that it later found expression in Nadine Gordimer's 1979 novel *Burger's Daughter*.)[12] Kentridge paused for a few seconds.

Q: Amongst the people who were dead and injured, did you find anyone who you knew?

A: It is hard to say. I cannot say because at that time I was very busy indeed. I was very energetic to see what was happening, then.

Q: Did you find afterwards, though, when you heard later who had been killed, and who had been wounded, that you knew many of the people?

A: Some of my congregation were shot dead.

Q: What sort of people were they?

A: I remember an old man, Sepanpoere – he was an old man.

Q: Was he killed?

A: Yes; he was killed.

Q: What sort of man was he?

A: A very decent man.

Q: Is he the sort of man you would expect to go fighting the police?

A: No . . .

Q: When you saw that crowd, did you see any aggressive behaviour, anything which looked like fighting or an intention to fight?

A: I have come here to speak and I have said: there was nothing amongst the crowd there, that I saw, they behaved very well. I went to all these people that were injured . . . these people looked at me . . . they were just looking at me. They looked at me in a manner as if they were going to ask what had happened.

Q: Did they appear surprised?

A: Very.

For all Wessels's platitudes about immunity from prosecution or detention for giving evidence before him, reality soon intruded. Lecheal Musibi, a teacher who gave evidence to the inquiry from his sickbed at Baragwanath hospital – and whose photograph had appeared in newspapers – was arrested soon after being discharged. Kentridge could barely contain his rage:

KENTRIDGE: . . . the really scandalous thing [is] that everyone who
was wounded is automatically a suspect on a charge of public
violence – simply because a man is shot. One might have thought
that the people who did the shooting might be suspects, automatically, on that charge.

WESSELS: That is a matter with which I can't concern myself; that is a
police investigation.

There were fractious moments with Claassen, the advocate to the
inquiry. When Kentridge told Wessels that he proposed to call as a
witness Ian Berry, whose photographs were the most vivid and poignant visual record of the massacre, Claassen objected that Kentridge
and his team 'really seem to have taken the organisation of this Inquiry
into their own hands'. Why had a written statement by Berry not
been handed over to him, Claassen complained, so that he, rather
than Kentridge, could lead Berry's evidence? Kentridge responded:

I would be failing in my duty if I did not point out that the impression
that we have, sitting on this side of the table, is that my learned friend
Mr Claassen has been concerned before this Commission to present
what I might call the Police case and nothing else, Sir. That is the
impression we have. We don't object. We think the Police case ought
to be presented . . . I was not for a moment suggesting that it was on
your direction that Mr Claassen has presented the case for the Police.
I am simply explaining that this is the impression we have here, and
that is one of the reasons why, if we have found witnesses we have not,
so to speak, turned them over to Mr Claassen to lead.

★

The police officers all stuck to the same script. Major Willem van Zyl
set the tone when he referred to 'half-naked women dancing frenziedly
in front of the Sharpeville mobs goading them on'. Another claimed he
had heard shouts of 'police dogs, we will kill you'. A noisy, excited
crowd was transmogrified in their telling into a sanguinary mob
whipped up by maenadic ululation. 'Our backs were to the wall,' said
another. This was the language of 'white civilisation' forming a
defensive square to fend off the savage hordes of the dark continent.
It was a narrative which was comprehensively taken apart over days

of cross-examination by Kentridge and his fellow advocates, George Colman and Chris Plewman. The police estimate of a crowd some 20,000 strong was a wild exaggeration. The fence around the station had at no stage been breached. It was established that the onslaught had gone on for about forty-five seconds; the police officers had reloaded and continued firing when all that would have been visible was people fleeing for their lives across the open ground and roads that surrounded the police station. No order to fire appeared to have been given and nobody admitted that they fired first. No warnings of any sort had been issued. Dr Jack Friedman, Vereeniging's district surgeon, told the inquiry he had examined fifty-two of the sixty-nine bodies of the dead and found a total of ninety-six gunshots in them. About seventy per cent of the entry wounds were in the victims' backs.

A Lieutenant Freemantle insisted that officers were trained to fire Sten guns only in 'extreme emergency' as a last resort, and even then to fire only single rounds, not bursts, 'for economy and greater accuracy'. But Kentridge got Freemantle to confirm that there had been at least 150 armed policemen at Sharpeville at the time of the shooting, many with Sten guns, and that they had mostly used those weapons as full automatics, firing in short bursts. A police sergeant admitted that he had emptied his full Sten-gun magazine into the crowd: 'I kept my finger on the trigger all the time.' Kentridge asked Lieutenant Jacobus Claassen about the fearsome firepower of the sub-machine gun, even if fired in 'short bursts':

Q: How long does it take to fire off with a Sten gun? Is it tremendously fast?
A: It is tremendously fast.
Q: I think we had the figures from Mr Freemantle. He says it can fire thirty rounds in 3.2 seconds; and in fact, of course, we have been told that usually only 25 rounds are loaded. So a man could fire off the whole magazine in about three seconds?
A: Yes.
. . .
Q: You said the shooting went on no longer than was necessary. Now, if you are right, one would not expect the majority of people to have been shot in the back. One would have expected

some, perhaps, to have been shot in the back, but the majority
would have been shot in the front?

A: I do not know how many were shot in the back. I do not know
whether the majority were shot in the back.

Q: What would you expect if the shooting continued no longer than
necessary?

A: Perhaps an equal number would have been shot in the back, [and]
an equal number in the front.

Q: Why would an equal number have been shot in the back?

A: Well, that is my impression. That is what I think.

Q: How could that happen, if the shooting stopped as soon as the
danger was over?

A: The shooting, I think, was necessary and I do not think it
continued longer than was absolutely necessary.

Constable Barend Theron told Kentridge that he had fired revolver
shots over the heads of the crowd, apparently to frighten them, from
the top of his Saracen. The advocate wanted to drive home Theron's
recklessness, his indifference to the fate of the people running from
him and his colleagues.

Q: I have a photograph here of a woman lying dead on the open
piece of ground, and I will show you another photograph which
shows where she was shot. Look at this; do you think perhaps
your bullet caused that?

A: No, it is impossible.

Q: Why is it impossible?

A: A revolver's barrel would not make it [the bullet] turn [so that it
created a terrible exit wound].

Q: Do you think a revolver bullet would not make such a dreadful
wound?

A: No.

Q: What sort of wound does it make?

A: That is what a .303 does . . .

Q: What do you think a revolver bullet coming down would do; you
don't think it would have killed that person – you don't suggest it
would not have killed anyone?

A: No.

Q: But you did not observe whether it hit anyone or not?

A: No.

Q: It might have?

A: Yes, it might.

Q: It might have hit some man?

A: It might have hurt someone.

Q: But if the bullet travelled to the other side of the street . . . there might have been a man there who was running away?

A: Yes . . .

Q: So it might perhaps have hit some child who was standing on the other side of the field just looking on to see what was happening?

A: I do not believe there were children there. Everyone stood at the wire.

Q: You don't know, though, do you?

A: No. As far as I am concerned, there were no people who stood so far away.

Q: But you did not look?

A: I watched.

Q: You did not aim anywhere in particular?

A: No.

Q: Don't your standing orders say that you must not fire in the air over the heads of the crowd because you may injure innocent people?

A: Yes; but this case was different.

Q: Why?

A: It was such a confusion, and I also just shot because everyone else was shooting.

Q: That is really the answer? Everyone else was shooting, and you shot, also?

A: Yes.

Q: It is not because you were afraid that the crowd would turn back. There was tremendous confusion. Other people were shooting, so you thought you would also shoot?

A: Well, it occurred to me that they wanted to turn . . .

Q: [Showing Theron another photograph] Look at exhibit B which shows you shooting. [Sarcastic] Where are these people who you regarded as a potential danger to your Saracens and to the rest of you? Are they the young girls in the foreground, or the children on the right of the photograph, or the man on the bicycle or the woman with the umbrella? Where did the danger come from? . . . [A]re you seriously suggesting that you thought that the people near the motor car on the right hand side of the photograph [about 100 yards from Theron] might turn around and come and attack the police?

A: Quite possibly.

And gradually some police witnesses became more candid and forthcoming. Kentridge cross-examined Captain Frederick Coetzee. 'To use firearms in that crowd would have been horrible . . . because from where I stood, they were like fish in a tin, right up to about 75–80 yards. I don't know how far a bullet would travel before it stops.' He said he had not felt provoked by the cries of 'Afrika!' he had heard all day at Sharpeville ('I shouted back at them "Afrika!" . . . because this is my country, too'). Johannes Joubert, a constable who had fired a Sten gun, followed, and was forced to agree that no bodies were found within three or four yards of the police station's gate. Lieutenant Colonel Spengler admitted he had not thought the crowd would attack. The officer in command at the fatal moment was Lieutenant Colonel Pienaar.

Q: I am suggesting, Colonel, that you could have climbed onto a Saracen in your striking uniform, held up your hand for silence . . . And then you could have said, 'Now, go home or you are going to be shot.' You could have done that, couldn't you?

A: The only explanation I can offer is that time did not permit that.

Q: And your only excuse is that you were too busy doing the other things you have told us about?

A: Yes.

Q: Colonel Pienaar, you could have detailed some other officer to make that effort, couldn't you?

A: I could have, I did not think of that.

The final police witness was Constable Pieter Saaiman, a plain-clothes officer based at Johannesburg's central police station. Saaiman had fired six shots from his revolver into the crowd, he claimed at protestors who were throwing stones at the police officers within the station compound. This was of course part of the police narrative of an exercise in self-defence against an aggressive mob. Kentridge asked him about the first occasion he had taken aim at a supposed stone thrower:

Q: How was he standing?
A: He looked at me and took the stone from his left hand to his right, and when he brought it, I . . .
Q: Was he at the fence?
A: Yes.
Q: Well, at that time I take it that the shooting had not begun?
A: Yes.
Q: The shooting had begun?
A: Yes.
Q: Who was shooting?
A: The police.
Q: Do you mean the police with rifles?
A: Yes.
Q: And Sten guns?
A: Yes.
Q: And this man was standing there to throw a stone at you?
A: That is correct.
Q: [*A sudden tone change*] Are you serious?
A: I tell it as it happened; I cannot tell it otherwise.
Q: At any rate, he was not hit by any of the rifle or Sten gun firing, and you drew your revolver?
A: That's right.
Q: And what did you do?
A: I fired one shot at him.
Q: Did you shoot straight at him?
A: Yes . . .
Q: Did you hit him?
A: I cannot say. I suspect he was shot, but I cannot say.
Q: What happened to him?
A: He fell.

Q: At the fence?

A: Yes, he just fell . . .

Q: By this time, then, the shooting had been going on for some seconds, I take it. Can you then tell me, after you shot this man, what the crowd was doing?

A: They still threw stones and shouted, and then they fell backwards; it bothered me. Then they just started shooting the Sten guns . . . I heard a few revolvers and then I heard the .303s, and then more Sten guns . . .

Q: And you went on firing with your revolver?

A: I still shot at one person, shot at one person.

Q: Why?

A: He had a stick in his hand, and he turned towards Head Constable Malan.

Q: Do you mean he was rushing up at the fence from outside?

A: That is correct.

Q: In the face of all this shooting?

A: Yes.

Saaiman was straight-facedly telling the inquiry that even after a fusillade of hundreds of bullets had erupted, members of the crowd were still advancing on the police with murderous intent.

Q: You . . . are saying that after the shooting had begun, the crowd or people in the crowd made a rush at the fence?

A: Yes.

Q: With what object, do you think?

A: I would say they wanted to assault and humiliate us. That is what their mission was.

Q: Not to commit suicide?

A: No, to humiliate us . . .

Q: Do you think they were coming to jump over the fence?

A: [No answer.]

Q: You see, no one apparently jumped over the fence before that, according to the evidence we have had. You did not see anyone jump over the fence?

A: No.

Q: But although there were people running away, these people came forward in the face of all the fire, you thought to come over the fence and attack the police?

A: It seemed so to me.

Q: That is all you have to say?

A: What else can I say? It bothered me so much.

Q: You know, there was a long time before the police lined up when the crowd was standing at the fence?

A: That is correct.

Q: They did not jump over the fence?

A: I saw that they were close enough . . .

Q: [*With urgency*] Just a moment; they did not jump over the fence?

A: No.

Q: They did not come through the gate?

A: They were close enough to the southern gate, the small gate, and a few crept up to the porch. Then I saw a young Bantu . . .

Q: Let's be serious, Constable Saaiman. They did not come through the gate to attack the police?

A: No.

Q: [*Incredulous*] It was only after the firing started that they did this foolhardy thing?

A: That is correct.

Q: I don't really think there is any point in taking it further. Just let's go back to your state of mind when you first shot at this man with the stone in his hand. Did you shoot him to stop him throwing a stone at you?

A: Yes.

Q: Is that legitimate?

A: Yes, because he knew he was throwing a stone at me.

Q: That is what you felt?

A: Yes.

Q: Can we take it that is the only reason you fired?

A: At that person, yes . . .

Q: Do you know any of the policemen there who were badly injured by stones?

A: I know of some – not seriously, but who were injured.

Q: Anyone wounded so seriously that he had to have medical treatment?

A: No; I do not know of any person receiving medical treatment.

Q: Do you know what happened to the policemen; what sort of injuries did they have – scratches?

A: I saw a person, I think, who had a slightly broken mark on his chest.

Q: How did you happen to see that?

A: I'm talking about after the shooting, in the courtyard.

Q: He took off his shirt?

A: Yes.

Q: And you all had a look at that. You see, let's be serious about this. None of the policemen there were seriously injured by stones. Correct?

A: That is correct . . .

Q: There were very few who were hit at all?

A: There were only a few that were hurt.

Q: You don't seriously suggest that the throwing of stones from the crowd was such a serious danger that the police had to open fire on the crowd to stop it?

A: If we had not acted at that moment, I believe I would not have been at the police station on Friday to tell the story.

Q: Really?

A: I believe it.

Q: That is what you believe?

A: Yes.

Q: And it may be that if there were people who took a somewhat different view from you on the police side, there would not be 70 Africans killed and 180 wounded?

A: If we had not shot . . .

Q: If you had not shot, there would have been a lot of people alive today who are now dead?

A: And there would have been many, who are now alive.

Q: What would these people have done if you had not shot?

A: If they had come over the fence, and they would have done so . . . we would not have been able to use a single firearm.

Q: You say there were some in the gateway?

A: Yes . . .

Q: How many?

A: I do not know; it had been a lot, we were under a whole lot of pressure.

Q: How far did they get in?

A: No, they fell back, again . . . I did not look then either.

Q: You did not see any bodies inside, did you?

A: I saw nothing beyond [the fence].

Saaiman had tried to portray himself as a brave warrior engaged in hand-to-hand combat with a fearsome mob, shooting one advancing stone thrower at almost point-blank range as another threatened Head Constable Malan with a stick. But Kentridge had exposed the truth. His account of a crowd continuing to advance, throwing stones and wielding sticks, even after the police had opened fire, was inherently implausible. It later emerged that, according to police records, Constable Saimaan was twelve rounds down after the shooting; yet he swore that, although he had reloaded after firing off a full cylinder of six cartridges, he had not shot again (the other six cartridges had, he claimed, gone missing from a window sill in Sharpeville police station). Once again, Kentridge had shown that it was likely that the official count of rounds fired came nowhere near the true number.

A journalist with close ties to the police, Harold Sacks, gave evidence of the scene in the aftermath of the killing. He said that a white police officer, surveying the field of slaughter, had found one man lying on the grass who 'pretended to be dead'. 'Harold, come and look at this corpse, we can't find a mark on him,' one officer had joked to him. 'I take it you were not in the mood for humour yourself?' asked Kentridge, with rebuke. 'I was not,' Sacks replied. Sacks claimed to see in the crowd 'absolute loathing, horror, hatred'; prompting Kentridge's sarcastic retort 'I see that you are something of a physiognomist . . . And where did you qualify in physiognomy?' Sacks, whose evidence seemed to be one long justification of the police's conduct, was soon undone in his attempts to classify the facial expressions of the various participants in the aftermath of the massacre:

Q: [*With irony*] Now, I wonder whether you could, seeing that you are so good at describing faces – I don't know whether I should ask you to describe other faces, here, or perhaps in photographs; but have you nothing more to tell, why you thought this was a vicious crowd?

A: Simply from the look on their faces, and the stone throwing in addition; but from the look on their faces; the expression on their faces.

Q: Did you see other people who were not looking vicious? Other Africans?

A: Yes; there were groups that were simply standing there, looking on.

Q: How were they looking?

A: They were just . . .

Q: Were they aghast perhaps?

A: It is difficult to say. My impression was that they were simply passive about the whole thing.

Q: Were the African policemen at Sharpeville Police Station looking aghast?

A: They were looking very sad.

Q: But not aghast?

A: No.

Q: Why weren't they looking aghast?

A: Well, I don't know. I can only say . . . they were looking very sad.

Q: Were any of the white policemen looking sad?

A: Well, they looked absolutely shaken.

Q: But not sad?

A: Well, I . . .

Q: I have no further questions.

On 24 May, towards the end of the evidence, Captain Jan van der Bergh – in charge of the police's own investigation into the shooting – was cross-examined by Kentridge. He was one of the few police witnesses to give evidence in English. Kentridge let the statistics which he disclosed speak for themselves. There was no flamboyance, or sanctimony; simply the eloquence of stark fact. While twelve or thirteen officers had been slightly hurt by stone-throwing, none had been hospitalised. Van der Bergh was – relatively – frank about how many shots had been fired by police, reporting that at least eleven officers had fired their Sten guns and at least forty officers their .303 rifles; one had fired fifty-seven rounds. Some officers had fired twelve revolver rounds, and several who had fired Sten guns – in some cases actually reloading before starting on another fusillade, until they ran out of ammunition – had then taken up their revolvers and used those, until they too were empty. Here was the full enormity of the shooting. To discharge a weapon once in a moment of panic was one thing. To fire, and fire again, until the magazine was empty; reload; and then resume firing into a fleeing crowd was quite another.

A black witness, Elias Lelia, a dress designer, said he had seen many dead and injured people prostrate on the ground, among whom a white policeman had walked and shouted, in Afrikaans, 'Yes, I told you the police would shoot. There you have it; take it; that is your Africa.' A twenty-two-year-old, Agnes Matshoahole, said she had arrived at Sharpeville police station at 1.30, moments before the shooting began. Although not shot, she had been injured in the back after bodies had fallen on top of her. Her monosyllabic replies of 'no' to Kentridge's questions about whether she had wanted to attack the police, heard anyone urging an attack or seen stones thrown, suggest that she was almost as frightened at the inquiry as she had been on 21 March. The last witness of all was Maggie Moteba, a Sharpeville resident who reported that she had been told to expect a speech at 2 p.m., and had been shot through her left knee, fifty yards from the police station, as she fled. 'And can I take it that you did not go there to attack the police and were not attacking the police when the shooting started?' asked Chris Plewman. Moteba's reply, 'No', was the very last word spoken by a witness at the inquiry. In total, 116 witnesses had given evidence over the course of thirty-four days.

Wessels said the inquiry would now be adjourned for ten days ahead of closing submissions, which would start on 13 June. But before the judge formally adjourned proceedings, Kentridge raised one last point. He revealed that, before the shooting started, Lieutenant Colonel Pienaar had shown damage to his car to a United Press reporter fittingly named Henry Scoop. The damage was apparently not serious: Pienaar himself had told the inquiry that there were only 'light marks' on the vehicle. But Scoop had later informed the Bishop of Johannesburg's attorneys that Pienaar had remarked to him, 'If they do this sort of thing, they must learn the hard way.' Unsurprisingly, Pienaar denied making this comment, and Scoop had moved to Europe before he could be subpoenaed to appear at the inquiry. Kentridge asked to submit a memorandum from Scoop as evidence, if necessary sent to him by airmail for signing. Wessels agreed to accept the memorandum unsigned. Thus the inquiry's hearings concluded with the implication that an angry police colonel ordered his officers to load their weapons and prepare to open fire because, half an hour earlier, someone had scratched his car's paintwork. Could the genesis of this atrocity have really been that banal?

In the two weeks between the end of the evidence and the start of closing submissions Kentridge, Plewman and their attorney, the indefatigable Michael Parkington, prepared a 250-page conspectus of the mountain of evidence which had been heard. The preparation of this document involved the most stupendous labour. Kentridge recalls long nights in his study poring over the forty-five volumes of transcripts of oral testimony and writing out in longhand the various sections of submissions. The finished document, running to 227 numbered paragraphs and produced by a legal secretary on an office typewriter of the day, contains not a single correction. One is confronted with the sheer laboriousness of document production in the pre-digital age.

On 15 June 1960 Kentridge stood up to begin almost two days of advocating to Wessels a version of events that starkly contradicted the police narrative. He recalls the immense responsibility he felt. On his shoulders fell the burden not only of presenting an account of state murder but also of acquitting, before the eyes of the world, the thousands of black protestors of all the accusations and insinuations made against them by the police witnesses, the government propaganda machine and the slanders of ministers. This was not a jury speech. Kentridge combined precision with the slow burn of outrage.

What is even more horrifying than the number who fired is the intensity and duration of the firing. The firing was so unnecessarily and unconscionably protracted that one is driven, however reluctantly, to the conclusion that some at least of the men who fired were doing so in order to inflict the maximum possible injury on the crowd . . . It is unnecessary to dwell on the enormity of firing on a fleeing crowd for three-quarters of a minute.

Advocacy is as much about the accumulation of fine detail as grand remonstrance. Kentridge methodically cleared a way through the tangled thickets of evidence of which individual officers had discharged which specific weapons and precisely how many rounds each had fired. The South African police force's meticulous bureaucracy – requiring every round issued to an officer to be accounted for through a return made to the armourer – was now used against it.

The most revealing figures in the returns are those of the men who used two weapons. Thus, two of the men each fired two complete magazines from their Sten guns; then, changing the Sten gun for a revolver, fired 6 rounds with that. One man fired a complete magazine with his Sten gun; he then took his revolver, fired 6 rounds from it, broke it open, reloaded it, and fired two more rounds. Whatever the reason for opening fire, these returns show a deliberation and persistency which can be explained only on the basis of a desire to inflict as much injury as possible . . . Some men who did open fire stopped after firing one or two rounds. They presumably collected themselves, saw that there was no danger and stopped firing. But the men I referred to earlier continued a merciless and inexcusable fire.

The sheer forensic graft at work in Kentridge's submissions is remarkable. He conducted a minute analysis of the positioning of the wounds on the dead and the injured, and of the disposition of the bodies on the fields and roads around the police station. Where the bodies lay told its own story:

The comparative absence of bodies near the fence and the profusion of bodies at distances of 100 yards and more away from the fence also supports the conclusion that the shooting continued for a considerable time into the backs of a crowd that had long before taken to flight.

The submissions moved from the particular to the general problem of the racism endemic in police attitudes.

Sometimes expressed in the police evidence and sometimes implicit in it is an attitude of mind which regards Africans, or at least a crowd of Africans, not as fellow citizens whom it was the duty of the police to protect and help, but as potential enemies. The attitude is not merely one of prejudice against Africans: it is an unhappy mixture of hatred, contempt and fear. The police regarded these people as a 'mob', not as a collection of individuals; and as a mob which understood only the argument of force ... It became clear, in the course of the police evidence, that many members of the police expect unquestioning deference from all the Africans with whom they deal. When they did not find it at Sharpeville, they interpreted the lack of it as riot and rebellion ... Perhaps the most revealing piece of evidence was Lt Col. Pienaar's remarkable statement that the 'Native mentality' (which he claims to know) 'does not allow them to gather for a peaceful demonstration ... For them to gather means violence'. This remarkable combination of ignorance and racial prejudice naturally throws a great deal of light on the acts and omissions of Lt Col. Pienaar himself. But coming as it does from a senior and presumably responsible police officer with over 30 years' experience, it reveals more about the police attitude to the crowd and does more to explain why the police fired upon the crowd than perhaps any other single piece of evidence.

Kentridge made particular use of Ian Berry's extraordinary photographs. Many showed the dead, the dying and the injured lying on the field where they had fallen. In none of those images could any white policeman be seen tending to a victim:

My object in referring to all this evidence is not to show or suggest that all the white policemen were cruel and callous. Many were clearly shocked at the scene before their eyes after the shooting. My object is rather to show that they were cut off from any understanding or sympathy with the individual African human beings with whom they have to deal. It is for the same reason that one must refer to the fact that there has been no official expression of horror, shame or even regret for the tragedy from the police force ... At Sharpeville, the police went on firing into the back of the crowd long after it had turned and begun to flee from the scene. They fired their automatic

weapons in tremendous and devastating bursts . . . The only problem
is to find suitable words of condemnation for conduct of such enormity . . . It was, to quote Winston Churchill, 'a demonstration of the
frightfulness of the strength of civilisation without its mercy.'[13]

Kentridge still has his set of eight-by-ten gloss prints of Berry's harrowing 35mm photographs. Years later, in a public conversation with his
father, Kentridge's son William recalled how, as a boy of six, he went into
his father's empty study and found there a box which, thinking it might
contain chocolates, he opened. In it were those photographs. He sifted
through them in horrified fascination; then closed the box and stole away
as if guilty of some shameful crime. William explained that

> at the age of six one has a sense of children's violence against each
> other in the playground . . . but the sense of adults visiting violence on
> each other was a new and shocking thing; and to see the difference
> between the tiny puncture wound of the entry of a bullet and then the
> same body rolled over where there is just this mass of exploded flesh
> of the exit wound changed my understanding of the world.[14]

He never told his father.

By a strange coincidence, Berry's photographs of men and women
in flight were taken in the same year that Elias Canetti's *Crowds and
Power* was published, in 1960. Canetti's words could be a description
of the scenes Berry captured:

> the flight crowd . . . [is] created by a threat. Everyone flees; everyone
> is drawn along. The danger which threatens is the same for all . . . the
> most striking thing about a mass flight is the force of its direction. The
> crowd has, as it were, become all direction, away from danger. Since
> the goal of safety and the distance from it are the only things which
> matter, all the previously existing distances between men become
> unimportant . . . The flight crowd is the most comprehensive of all
> crowds . . . [it] derives its energy from its coherence.[15]

On 16 June 1960 Wessels's Commission of Inquiry formally ended.
All that now remained was for the judge to produce his report.

Kentridge's work was done, at least so far as it concerned Sharpeville. Within a few weeks he was back in the Old Synagogue for the resumption of his representation of the Treason trialists.

It is extraordinary how much coverage the evidence given at the Sharpeville inquiry received in newspapers, both in South Africa and around the world. Leafing through them now, one gets a vivid sense of the schizophrenic nature of South African life at the time. Sixty-nine people had been killed in one of the worst peacetime massacres in decades; the country was in a state of emergency, effectively under martial law. Yet the coddled life of the white middle classes went on as if nothing had happened. From this parallel world we see, juxtaposed with a report on the massacre, a photograph of a young woman winking to the camera while cradling a dog in her arms. The caption reads: 'Lovely Denise Muir, of Pinelands, Cape, the new "Miss South Africa", hugs her pet boxer dog at her home. And the wink? Well, the boxer couldn't do it, so Denise did.' Pick up another newspaper. It has a full-page report of inquiry evidence in which the question of whether the terrible injuries sustained by some of the dead were inflicted by the use of dum-dum bullets – banned under the 1899 Hague Convention – is debated; on the facing page, an advertisement for Cameo Dubbelife seamless stockings features another recently anointed South African beauty queen, Penny Coelen. 'I've worn one pair for simply ages without a single ladder,' she proclaims, beaming out at the reader. It was as if the country had undergone a sort of cultural lobotomy.

Some commentators have criticised the proceedings for their haste and lack of structure.[16] Undoubtedly the inquiry was not the perfect vehicle in which to undertake a rigorous examination of the events of 21 March and their causes. But it was these public hearings which shaped how that day was to be remembered and understood. It provided the first – and in most cases the last – occasion that some of the key participants spoke about those events in a formal setting. Day after day the testimony of black witnesses, sensitively led by Kentridge and Plewman, was transcribed and published to the world; as was the consistent challenge in Kentridge's cross-examination to the police testimony. Had the Bishop of Johannesburg not taken urgent steps to retain Kentridge and his colleagues, the official record of Sharpeville would have been a very different thing. It would have been a one-sided account of the supposedly justified defensive actions of embattled police surrounded and vastly outnumbered by a murderous horde – a sort of re-enactment of the historical events at Rorke's Drift as, a few years later, depicted (with questionable accuracy) in the British film *Zulu*.[17] Kentridge had debated whether his participation would merely lend credibility to an official exercise in exoneration. In the end he decided that other voices needed to be heard at the inquiry: voices of dissent, of grief and of compassion. In this he was surely right. Without those voices, compellingly refuting the official version, the public memory of Sharpeville would have been very different.

The formal report of the Commission of Inquiry was eventually published in January 1961. On one level, the advocacy that Kentridge and his colleagues had brought to the proceedings had failed. The 204-page report bore out the suspicion that Mr Justice Wessels had, all along, intended the whitewash required of him. It absolved the police of almost all wrongdoing, and it made no recommendations to prevent another such massacre. In a remarkable abdication of responsibility, Wessels decided that it was 'not the task of the commission to report on the liability of persons for their acts and omissions'; it was simply to 'inform'. His report was careful not to read as a simple apologia for police conduct. The credibility of some police witnesses – including Constable Saaiman – was doubted. Wessels concluded that the body of protestors was not intent on launching a general attack on the police station. Nonetheless, he described a discontented crowd pushing against the fence and raining stones down on the police officers within; and, after the Spengler incident, surging through the open gates. This led to a crucial finding: the police officers had reasonably believed that an assault was imminent and had reacted proportionately. The first shots were prompted by what was perceived by the police as an eruption of rioters through the gates.

> It would serve no useful purpose to consider how matters would have developed if no shots had been fired at that moment. Possibly there would have been no loss of life. It is also possible that there would have been a worse bloodbath.

This was a truly outrageous paragraph. Wessels was brushing aside the crucial counterfactual question; yet, in the same breath, he was giving credence to the convenient fiction that, had the officers not fired into the crowd when they did, the station would have been overrun by a frenzied mob bent on spilling blood. The officers were not the merciless killers revealed by Kentridge; they were a disciplined cadre who had responded reasonably to a real, or at any rate a reasonably apprehended, danger. '[T]he men who fired held out in their evidence that they were at that moment of opinion that their lives were in danger . . . I think it can be accepted that this state of mind was probably present in the men who fired.' Consistent with this version, Wessels found that the entire fusillade lasted between twelve and twenty seconds. The proven fact that the great majority of the dead and wounded were shot in the back was casually brushed aside. 'A proposition that the police fired on the rear-guard of a crowd that was fleeing away from them can, in my opinion, in no way be reconciled with the facts,' Wessels intoned.

Kentridge's arguments were addressed several times in Wessels's report. The judge rejected his claim that most of the crowd had not been hostile, and that some had been in a 'happy holiday mood'. He dismissed Ian Berry's evidence that he had walked safely through a non-rowdy crowd at about 1 p.m., forty minutes or so before the shooting, as a 'masterpiece of understatement'. The thumbs-up signs and cries of 'Afrika!' from the crowd were, Wessels considered, not cheerful greetings but threatening gestures. He did not question why several officers were seen reloading their weapons to carry on firing at a terrified crowd in headlong flight. The fact that many of the dead and wounded were found lying more than 100 yards from the fence was ignored. At one point, Wessels concluded uselessly that he 'could neither find that there had not been an attack at the gate, nor . . . that there had in fact been an attack'.

The South African government tried to trumpet Wessels's report as a complete vindication of its policing apparatus. It used it to pour scorn on Bishop Reeves's own recently published book on the massacre as 'blatant lies and fabrications'. Kentridge remembers his disgust at a document so profoundly dishonest. A later commentator has castigated the report as 'so densely unintelligible, so ridden with double-talk, qualifications and refutable logic as to defy both legal reasoning and ordinary comprehension'.[18] Kentridge agrees. But the evidence had spoken independently of Wessels's absurd conclusions. His report was almost immediately forgotten. The tragedy of Sharpeville, as heartbreakingly exposed in the course of the hearings, was not.

Archbishop Ambrose Reeves had left South Africa for London shortly after the massacre, fearing imminent arrest and wishing from a place of safety to tell the world of the enormity of the Sharpeville shooting. Kentridge had a number of consultations with the man who would be his ostensible, but absent, client. On Reeves's return in September 1960 – a brave move in the circumstances – he was immediately deported back to Britain. The government justified his removal by saying, wrongly, that the archbishop had impugned the integrity of its police force by alleging that they had fired dum–dum bullets on 21 March. Reeves's position as Bishop of Johannesburg became untenable, and he reluctantly resigned. He spent the rest of his life in his native Britain, where he never held episcopal office again: it is said that Harold Macmillan vetoed his appointment by Archbishop of Canterbury Michael Ramsey to run a British diocese, for fear that diplomatic relations with South Africa would be further damaged. Later in the same year as Reeves's final return to Britain, Victor Gollancz published his celebrated account of the shooting and its aftermath, entitled simply *Shooting at Sharpeville*. Many of its pages consist of blocks of quotation from Kentridge's submissions and examinations of witnesses, which are left to speak for themselves. The book came out before Wessels's report was published; had it been published afterwards its tone of understated rage would have no doubt been fiercer.

The international outcry over Sharpeville only led to a hardening of the South African government's attitudes. It was in no mood to compromise, and had nothing but contempt for what it viewed as intrusive leftist interference in its affairs by people who had no understanding of what apartheid meant and why it was necessary. The government's position was not notably at odds with that of much of the white population, whose immediate reaction was not sympathy for the massacre's victims, but fear of retaliatory attacks; indeed some opined defiantly that the police had shown not too little, but too much restraint at Sharpeville, and men turned up at police stations to offer their services as vigilantes. For many, even among those prepared to entertain the possibility that the police had overreacted, the force's role as front-line guardians of 'white civilisation' and its privileges still trumped any misgivings about an isolated, if unfortunate, incident. Prime Minister Verwoerd, recovered from an assassination attempt, seemed almost to delight in continuing to outrage global opinion by pushing his apartheid agenda yet further.

In the October 1961 general election – at which the electorate was of course exclusively white – the National Party increased its majority in parliament; and in 1966 there was an even bigger swing to the nationalist right. Following the jailing of the Rivonia defendants in 1964, South Africa entered a decade of relative, albeit insidious, calm: not because the non-white population no longer had grievances, but simply because most anti-apartheid leaders and activists were in jail, and the rest had either gone into exile or been cowed into submission. Not until the Soweto uprising of 1976, and the widespread outrage at the murder of the black consciousness leader Steve Biko a year later (see Chapter 8), did the apartheid state really appear vulnerable again.

The dead of Sharpeville were delivered home in 1960 in sealed coffins, so no one could see their horrific injuries, and the media and political leaders were not allowed to attend the funerals, lest they turned into protest rallies. The cemetery in which most of the victims were buried was repeatedly vandalised and desecrated for years afterwards. Those who had been injured were eventually paid compensation, but this amounted to a paltry 100 rand apiece. Philip Frankel, who revisited Sharpeville at the end of the 1990s while researching his book *An Ordinary Atrocity*, was told by many survivors that a 'palpable sense of disaster' had hung over the township for years afterwards. A pall of suspicion and shame was cast over the community, and for decades afterwards the shooting was rarely discussed openly: in 1980 a visiting journalist could find no one in Sharpeville willing to admit that they had witnessed it.

★

Twenty-four years on, Sharpeville was blighted by black-on-black violence between a new generation of angry youths and perceived 'collaborators' with apartheid. In September 1984 there was renewed unrest over rent increases and allegations of municipal corruption in the much hated, but black-led, community council that now administered Sharpeville.[19] Four councillors were murdered, including the council's deputy mayor Kuzwayo Jacob Dlamini, who was attacked with stones before being burned to death in his car. The violence smouldered on for weeks: by the end of 1984 some 150 people had been killed in and around Sharpeville. Five young black men and a black woman, soon dubbed the Sharpeville Six, were later tried for Dlamini's murder under the so-called 'common purpose' doctrine: a prosecution blatantly brought to seek to impose order on restive townships. None of the accused had been directly involved in killing Dlamini, and one even claimed to have tried to save him from the mob. Nonetheless the single white judge, sitting with two assessors but without a jury, found them all guilty and sentenced each to death simply because they had been part of a crowd of protestors among whom were individuals who had gone on to kill. (On this reasoning, scores of other protestors, never prosecuted, had likewise been guilty of capital murder.) An appeal to the five judges of the Appellate Division of the Supreme Court of South Africa, the country's highest appeal court, failed, the judges deciding that a murder conviction did not require proof of a causal connection between the accuseds' actions and the victim's death – for there was none.[20]

Once again the name of Sharpeville roused world opinion against an apartheid outrage.[21] The hangings of the Six had been set to take place on 18 March 1988. Then on 16 March the United Nations Security Council unanimously passed Resolution 610, in which it pronounced itself 'convinced that these executions, if carried out, will further inflame an already grave situation in South Africa' and called upon 'the South African authorities to stay execution and commute the death sentences imposed on the Sharpeville Six'. On the very same day the issue dominated Prime Minister's Question Time in the UK House of Commons. Mrs Thatcher confirmed that the British ambassador was making representations to P. W. Botha, the South African president. With hours to go before the time fixed for the hangings, a formal application was made on behalf of the Six to stay their execution because new evidence had emerged demonstrating that a key prosecution witness had perjured himself at the trial. A short reprieve was granted pending the full hearing of the application. The case came back before the trial judge, the inaptly named Acting Justice Human, when lawyers representing the Six sought to have the trial reopened. The application was testily rejected, prompting a further condemnatory UN Resolution. The Six launched a further appeal.

In 1988 Kentridge was spending most of his professional life in England, having joined Brick Court Chambers (as it is now known) in London in the late 1970s (see Epilogue). By now in his mid sixties, since the Sharpeville inquiry twenty-eight years earlier Kentridge had become the unrivalled doyen of the Bars of both England and South Africa. It was to him that the Sharpeville Six now turned to present their final appeal at the court of the Appellate Division in Bloemfontein. Kentridge, characterised in a contemporary profile in the *Guardian* as 'the Sir Galahad of the political left',[22] flew to South Africa in August to prepare for a case which had caught the attention of the world and on which six lives depended. He was to lead what was described as the most brilliant legal team South Africa could produce – including the future Chief Justice Ismail Mahomed and a future Justice of the Constitutional Court, Edwin Cameron. One of the accused's sisters, Joyce Mokhesi-Parker, later wrote a book about the Sharpeville Six case. She recalled learning of Kentridge's involvement in the appeal: 'It is hard to exaggerate the impact of the news. Abroad his integrity carried more moral authority than the collective weight of South Africa's judiciary; inevitably and rightly so. There was no advocate as devastating as Mr Kentridge in pursuit of the truth.'[23]

Kentridge visited his clients in prison; 'don't worry, you are coming out', he assured them. Kentridge later recalled the gloomy experience. The Six told him that in the days leading up to the date originally set for their execution they had each had their height and necks measured. It was to ensure the correct rope length was used. They were even required to lie in what were shortly to be their coffins to check that these were of adequate size.[24] Then Kentridge heard a great din among the prisoners in the death-row wing. Prison officers hastily entered the interview room and told Kentridge and his attorney that they had to leave immediately.

> I was later told the reason for the uproar. The Sheriff was coming to tell one of the prisoners that his application for clemency had been rejected and that he would be hanged in five days' time and I was told that whenever that happens there is a tremendous yelling and screaming and wailing from all the other prisoners who are themselves on death row. So, I've always thought that if anyone had any feeling that the death penalty should be reinstituted, they should go and spend an hour on death row.

On the day of the hearing an ITN News report explained that the appellants' hopes 'now rested with Sydney Kentridge QC, South Africa's most distinguished civil rights lawyer'. Television footage showed him striding purposefully towards the courtroom, ignoring the camera, as he always did. The appeal engaged a fundamental legal issue. When invited to reopen the trial on the basis of the new evidence that had emerged, the original trial judge had ruled that the court's jurisdiction had terminated with the dismissal of the original appeal. It was Kentridge's argument before the five judges – which included Judge of Appeal Gustav Hoexter, who as a young advocate had appeared for the prosecution thirty years earlier in the Treason Trial – that the court had inherent jurisdiction 'to regulate its own procedures so as to do justice and to prevent the abuse of its procedures by a dishonest litigant'. The debate, then, was between a narrow legal formalism and an expansive view of the court's power to right a wrong. Kentridge argued that the 'law should not be impotent to protect an innocent man who is in possession of evidence showing that he has been unjustly condemned'. But from where does this power derive, asked Chief Justice Rabie? Kentridge's answer, measured but firm, was noted by many people present in court: 'My Lord, it comes from the heart of the court.'

The *Guardian* described the scene in court that day:

> At 9.50 a.m. yesterday the final legal battle for the lives of the Sharpeville Six began when Sydney Kentridge SC, QC, rose to his

feet in a wood-panelled courtroom in South Africa's judicial capital and delivered the familiar incantation: 'M'Lord I appear for all the applicants with my learned friends . . .' The No. 1 courtroom at the Appellate Division of the Supreme Court was packed with diplomats, press and relatives of the five men and one woman who, some 250 miles away at Pretoria's Central Prison were starting the 999th day of their ordeal on death row . . . The court will give its judgment at a later date. The odds are still against the appeal succeeding, but this three-and-a-half-hour performance by South Africa's greatest lawyer, during which he never once faltered for a word, an answer or an argument, has shortened them.[25]

Here is the account of Charles Crawford, then a young diplomat who attended the court on behalf of the United Kingdom to watch the proceedings:

How, I wondered as a barrister manqué, would Mr Kentridge tackle this one? The eyes of the planet were on him. Every anti-apartheid activist on earth was willing him on to merciless rhetorical demolition of the apartheid regime. He rose to speak. And in a few dramatic sentences he mastered the courtroom completely. Not by attacking apartheid. Rather by describing in appalling heart-wrenching detail what had happened to Mr Dlamini as he was beaten and then burned alive by that Sharpeville crowd.

Then, having confronted the evil horror of the crime in itself, like a priest in an Orthodox church swinging the incense jar he began to sprinkle grains of doubt here and there, to and fro, until he made a powerful case that the convictions were unsupportable on the facts and law and, yes, accordingly unjust. Just terrific technique – it gave the accused their best chance. What he did that day was very subtle. He went out of his way to show respect for the court, treating the issue strictly on its legal merits. And, having established thereby a strong position in the courtroom, he painstakingly went through all the available best arguments one by one, rather than charging at the problem head-on. He seemed to be trying to create less of a clear-cut argument in favour of acquittal, but rather an indefinable but strong mood that to uphold the convictions would be unjust or wrong . . . The wider point of rhetorical technique from that day? Our old favourite: less is (often) more. Especially when a supremely gifted lawyer is on the case.[26]

In the event the court produced a lengthy written judgment which dismissed Kentridge's appeal.[27] But, just as in the Sharpeville inquiry, victory was obtained outside the confines of the courtroom. The day after the judges handed down their judgment it was announced that President Botha had granted the Sharpeville Six clemency. Their death sentences were replaced by lengthy terms of imprisonment. As it turned out, they served just a few more years before being freed by Botha's successor F. W. de Klerk.

The Sharpeville massacre is now seen as a pivotal moment in the history of apartheid and the black struggle against it. Ambrose Reeves wrote that 'History, I believe, will recognise that Sharpeville marked a watershed in South African affairs. Life can never be quite the same again for any racial group in the Union, because of what happened on that Monday at Sharpeville.' Yet it was only after the end of apartheid that its significance could be officially recognised. Since 1995, 21 March has been Human Rights Day in South Africa, 'to commemorate and honour those who fought for our liberation and the rights we enjoy today'. In 1996 South Africa's new constitution was signed into law at Sharpeville's George Thabe Stadium, just a few hundred metres from the site of the massacre.

None of the police officers who killed at least sixty-nine people in Sharpeville on 21 March 1960 ever faced prosecution.

5

Defending Bram Fischer (1965)

DEFENDING A FRIEND is one of the hardest things any lawyer can do. Generally, sound advice requires human distance and emotional neutrality. The need for cold objectivity can clash with the softer ties of friendship. Nonetheless when the legendary South African advocate Abram Fischer QC, known to everyone as 'Bram', who had been a colleague and friend of Sydney Kentridge over many years, faced his own moment of ultimate crisis, it was to Kentridge that he turned.[1]

Most white opponents of apartheid were either of British heritage or, like Kentridge, members of the Jewish diaspora. Very few Afrikaners actively opposed apartheid, and even fewer were from prominent Boer families. But Bram Fischer, scion of a notable Bloemfontein dynasty, was both a leading anti-apartheid activist and lawyer and an Afrikaner of impeccable pedigree. His grandfather had been prime minister of the Orange River Colony and his father judge president of the Orange Free State. His wife Molly was a niece of Jan Smuts. Fischer was also a dedicated Communist, having joined the South African Communist Party (SACP) following a visit to the Soviet Union in 1932 while studying as a Rhodes Scholar at Oxford. After this epiphany his faith in the cause of international communism would never waver, undiminished even by the emergence of the truth about Stalin's atrocities and the Soviet invasion of Hungary in 1956.

As was the case in the United States, to be a Communist in 1950s South Africa was to be regarded as, by definition, an enemy of the state. The Nationalists' hatred and fear of communism was visceral. The moderator of the Dutch Reformed Church, the brother of the future prime minister B. J. Vorster, wrote that 'Communism is *the* anti-Christian force ... It is the most evident foreshadowing of the AntiChrist.' Fischer's home on Beaumont Street in the leafy Johannesburg suburb of Oaklands was first raided in 1953, after he had helped to establish the Congress of Democrats, an anti-apartheid organisation dominated by, but not formally part of, the SACP. It was regularly searched from then on, and by the late 1950s Fischer knew that it was bugged. After the passing of the Suppression of Communism Act in 1950 the SACP, now officially proscribed, went underground, but amid the state of emergency declared in 1960 following the Sharpeville massacre, it boldly declared its continued existence on Bastille Day, 14 July. Bram Fischer QC, one of the most prominent members of the Johannesburg Bar, was its de facto leader.

Kentridge and Fischer were colleagues at Group 621 in Johannesburg; as we saw in Chapter 3, the two advocates spent the late 1950s and early 1960s engaged in the gargantuan Treason Trial. Although Fischer was well known for appearing in political cases, his main expertise lay in commercial work. Much of his income derived from mining and insurance companies engaged in litigation far removed from Fischer's political preoccupations. It was partly through introductions from Fischer that Kentridge built up his own commercial practice in the 1950s. Kentridge remembers Fischer's courtroom manner as meticulous and precise. 'He was not an orator in the old-fashioned sense. Instead he was thoughtful and deliberate, striving for the right words to convey his point.' They were also friends. For all Fischer's devotion to his political creed, he was no adamantine ideologue. Kentridge describes a man of warmth and sparkling humour who maintained ties of friendship with advocates regardless of political persuasion. He recalls Sunday afternoon parties at Fischer's house, a place of warm hospitality where people of all ethnic backgrounds mixed happily and swam in his pool. There was no apartheid at Beaumont Street.

In January 1961, shortly before the final denouement of the Treason Trial, Fischer was handed a five-year banning order by the justice minister. It did not stop him from working as an advocate but, on the face of it, would have a serious impact on his ability to continue his political work. Fischer increasingly led a double life. A professional advocate by day, he was an active cadre in the struggle against apartheid by night, taking extraordinary risks which put not only his career but his liberty, even his life, at stake.

When on 11 July 1963 a number of members of the uMkhonto we Sizwe (Spear of the Nation) high command were arrested at Liliesleaf Farm, in the Johannesburg suburb of Rivonia, it was only by chance that Fischer was not among them. As acting chairman of the SACP's central committee he had regularly attended meetings there with Nelson Mandela, Walter Sisulu, Ahmed Kathrada, Govan Mbeki, Denis Goldberg and others, all of whom were now detained. The detainees were charged under section 21 of the Sabotage Act 1962,[2] which created an offence of sabotage, carrying a potential sentence of death. At the heart of the prosecution case against them was the allegation that the ANC's armed wing had commenced a sabotage campaign and was preparing to embark upon guerrilla warfare in order to overthrow the state, as evidenced by documents found at Liliesleaf Farm. The trial would be a new departure in South African criminal law. Recent legislation meant that, for the first time, the state could (and of course did) hold the accused incommunicado in detention for months before their trial started. Potential witnesses could likewise now be detained without charge until they provided statements satisfactory to the prosecutors. The days of the Treason Trial seemed halcyon by comparison. The state held all the cards.

Despite his narrow escape, Fischer agreed to act as lead advocate for his friends and comrades arrested at Rivonia, as well as for Nelson Mandela, who had been detained a few months earlier. He had at first been reluctant to take on the brief, as well he might. After all, he had been party to the plan of sabotage that the prosecution would attempt to prove in court. At any moment Fischer was at risk of identification as a regular visitor to Liliesleaf Farm and a close political associate of the accused. On the day that some farmworkers who might well have recognised the gowned advocate as one of the conspirators were called into the witness box, Fischer was unaccountably absent from court; when incriminating documents in Fischer's own handwriting were presented by the prosecutor as evidence they were, by sheer fluke, misattributed by handwriting experts as being in another man's hand. At no stage did the mask fall; despite the extraordinary stress he was under, Fischer kept his nerve, and his advocacy remained as measured and precise as if he were arguing an abstruse case about mining rights.[3]

The Rivonia Trial lasted some eight months and by its end, Fischer and his fellow defence lawyers had ensured that the number of acts of sabotage alleged by the prosecution had been reduced from 193 to just 12, none of them causing any human injury. But unlike at the Treason Trial, there was never any realistic chance of acquittal for most of the accused. The national atmosphere was very hostile, with white paranoia about the supposed *swart gevaar* (black peril) at fever pitch and many gun shops sold out as the white population armed itself against a feared revolution. And in truth many of the allegations were admitted, and proudly so, by the accused. The Rivonia defence was more a political statement than a forensic exercise in rebuttal. The only real doubt was whether the defendants' lives could be spared. Rather than subject himself to cross-examination (to avoid any risk of incriminating his comrades rather than through fear of the questions), Nelson Mandela delivered his extraordinary five-hour dock statement, a political testament which ended with these famous words:

> During my lifetime I have dedicated my life to this struggle of the African people. I have fought against white domination, and I have fought against black domination. I have cherished the ideal of a democratic and free society in which all persons will live together in harmony and with equal opportunities. It is an ideal which I hope to live for and to see realised. But, My Lord, if it needs be, it is an ideal for which I am prepared to die.

Decades later Mandela revealed that Fischer had opposed the inclusion of the 'prepared to die' finale, fearing that it appeared positively to invite the judge, Justice Quartus de Wet, to hand down a death sentence. On 11 June 1964 the judge read out the expected guilty verdicts on all but one of the defendants.[4] The next day, after evidence in mitigation was given by the Liberal Party leader and novelist Alan Paton, de Wet delivered his sentence: life imprisonment. It is a strange thing to feel elation on hearing that you will spend the rest of your life in prison. But that is what many of these defendants, who were sure that they were to receive a capital sentence, felt on 12 June 1964. One of the accused, Denis Goldberg, was heard to shout out to his elderly mother in the public gallery, straining to hear what sentence had been imposed on her son: 'Life. Life is wonderful!'⁵

The authorities were not unaware that Fischer remained a leader of the clandestine SACP and a key figure in the resistance movement. While he may have been safe from arrest while he was leading counsel for the Rivonia accused, that immunity expired when the case ended. Bram Fischer was now fair game. Even in the short period of freedom that remained to him he had no opportunity to celebrate the outcome of the trial. The very day after its end his beloved wife Molly died in a freak car accident, with Fischer at the wheel. On 13 June they had been driving to Cape Town to celebrate their daughter Ilse's twenty-first birthday, and for Fischer to consult the Rivonia defendants, now incarcerated on Robben Island, about a possible appeal. Just after dusk Fischer swerved to avoid a cow that had strayed into their path; the car left the road and plunged into deep water. Fischer and another passenger managed to escape, but despite their efforts Molly was trapped in the car as it sank. Just one day after Mandela and his co-accused had been spared death, it was the cruellest blow of fate.

Fischer was devastated by grief and guilt. Kentridge recalls that he seemed to withdraw from his legal practice, now rarely coming to his chambers. Instead, Fischer devoted himself more than ever to his secret life in the SACP, as if the struggle for liberation was now all he had to live for. At Molly's funeral an Afrikaner family friend took Fischer's brother Paul aside. 'Tell Bram to get out,' he warned. 'They're chasing him, they're chasing him hard, and they're going to catch him.' But Fischer ignored the warnings. 'After Molly died, Bram wasn't rational any more,' recalled one friend. 'He was driven to an excessive point. He took incredible risks . . . He went over the brink.'

A few days after the funeral Fischer was able to make the journey to Robben Island to consult with his clients. It was unanimously agreed that to challenge the verdicts would be to legitimatise the trial. Even Ahmed Kathrada, against whom the case had been thin, and who had a decent chance, refused to exercise his right of appeal. It was preferable to show solidarity with his co-accused. Kathrada went on to serve twenty-six years in prison.

By the time Fischer returned to Johannesburg, many of those closest to him had been detained, including the fiancé of one of his
daughters. The moratorium on sabotage attacks which had subsisted
during the Rivonia Trial was now over: across the republic, carefully
targeted sites were being bombed. On 11 July, just four weeks after his
wife's death, Fischer was arrested and detained. During his questioning the police revealed that they knew all about his illicit activities, as
if to deliver a final warning to him to leave South Africa at once or
face the consequences. It was a warning he ignored.

After three days of detention Fischer was released. But his freedom
proved to be temporary. On 23 September he was rearrested and
charged with various offences under the Suppression of Communism
Act 1950, which were really no more than variations on a theme: being
a member of the Communist Party; participation in the activities of the
Communist Party; and furthering the aims of the Communist Party. It
was an extraordinary turn of events. Bram Fischer, one of the outstanding advocates of his generation, who had been a member of the
Johannesburg Bar Council since 1942 and served as its chairman in
1961, who had been made a Queen's Counsel in 1951, was himself now
a defendant to a serious criminal prosecution.

Fischer appeared alongside thirteen other SACP members before a
magistrate the next day. The question of bail was immediately raised
by Fischer's friend and colleague Harold Hanson QC, who appeared
on his behalf. Two days before his arrest Fischer had received a passport permitting him to fly to England to appear in a case in the Privy
Council, on appeal from the Rhodesian Court of Appeal. Fischer had
been involved in the case for years and it would bring him much
needed income after many months' work on the Rivonia Trial for a
meagre fee. His only hope of appearing in the case was if the magistrate granted him bail, allowing him to travel to London. Hanson told
the court:

> The accused Mr Fischer has been a member of the Bar for many, very
> many years. Today he holds one of the leading positions. The matter
> that concerns your Worship, is whether, if he were released on bail
> there is any danger that he will not stand his trial. I am sensible of the
> fact that there are certain persons that have given undertakings to the

authorities and have let the authorities down, but I do propose in this matter to lead evidence on the value of Mr Fischer's undertakings and to give your Worship certain undertakings from leading members of the profession . . . And, I am safe in saying that Mr Fischer's colleagues at the Bar are confident of the fact that Mr Fischer, no matter what he is charged with here, is the sort of man that will stand his trial and they equally would put any sum of money at all, no matter how large it is, to guarantee his return.

To much surprise, and despite vigorous protestation from the prosecution, the magistrate granted Fischer bail, by the mid-1960s a rare indulgence in political cases. Once a recognisance of 10,000 rand had been paid, he was released from prison and flew to London on 3 October. Fischer was adamant that he would return to face trial, which had been fixed to start in mid-November 1964. 'I have no intention of avoiding a political prosecution. I fully believe I can establish my innocence. I am an Afrikaner. My home is South Africa. I will not leave South Africa because my political beliefs conflict with those of the Government ruling the country', Fischer had said publicly to the court. Privately he was equally resolute, telling friends: 'I will go back because I said I would.' After two days of argument in London before the judges of the Privy Council, judgment was pronounced in his client's favour. The case was a technical one, of limited interest to any but the litigants themselves, but its outcome was reported as 'Fischer's triumph' in the British press.[6] Bram Fischer was already well known across the world.

His daughter Ruth now lived in London with her husband, and the newly widowed Fischer must surely have been tempted to join them for good, and escape the tribulations that plainly awaited him in South Africa. Reports emerged that many of his fellow defendants, who had been denied bail, had been tortured while in detention. It was being suggested that the justice minister was contemplating banning Communists permanently from practising at the Bar. Fischer had clandestine meetings with a number of SACP exiles, who all urged him to join them. Fischer's son-in-law likewise implored him to stay in England, at least, as he said, 'for the sake of your legal career'. 'Fuck my career!' Fischer is said to have replied. He flew back to Johannesburg on 2 November, as scheduled, in good time for the start of his trial two weeks hence. It would prove a fateful decision.

Fischer was now Accused Number One alongside numerous other white Communist activists at what was soon dubbed the Fischer Trial. He was again represented by Harold Hanson. Fischer had been confident that another prominent fellow Afrikaner Communist, Piet Beyleveld, who had been detained in September 1964, would not co-operate with the authorities, as rumoured. As president of the Congress of Democrats, Beyleveld had chaired the Congress of the People at Kliptown in 1955 at which the Freedom Charter had been agreed (see Chapter 3). Shortly before his arrest, Beyleveld had advised other SACP members on how to withstand interrogation. But human frailty intervened. Worn down by sleep deprivation, Beyleveld agreed to talk. When he appeared as a prosecution witness Fischer was stunned. Beyleveld gave candid evidence to the court about the SACP and its role in the armed resistance.

As the trial dragged on it must have become increasingly clear to Fischer that a guilty verdict was inevitable. At some point in January 1965 he made a momentous decision: to estreat his bail and go underground. Having made elaborate preparations for the precarious life of a fugitive from justice, over the weekend of 23/24 January 1965 Fischer secretly fled Johannesburg. On the Monday morning, the day the trial was due to resume, his bedroom was found empty. He had left a pile of letters on the bed. One was an open letter to his counsel. On the morning of 25 January Harold Hanson, now an advocate without a client, read it out to an astonished courtroom:

> By the time this reaches you I shall be a long way from Johannesburg and shall absent myself from the remainder of the trial. But I shall still be in the country to which I said I would return when I was granted bail. I wish you to inform the Court that my absence, though deliberate, is not intended in any way to be disrespectful . . . I realise fully that my eventual punishment may be increased by my present conduct. My decision was made only because I believe that it is the duty of every true opponent of this government to remain in this country and to oppose its monstrous policy of apartheid with every means in its power. That is what I shall do for as long as I can . . .

Fischer's open letter continued with a denunciation of the policies of the Nationalist government and an indictment of the complacency of South Africa's white population, grown rich on the back of black labour. It ended with a personal message for Hanson: 'Please accept my deepest thanks for handling my case as you have. I do hope that my conduct will not embarrass you in any way.'

It was hardly unexpected that the prosecutor was unmoved by Fischer's words. He poured scorn on 'the desperate act of a desperate man, and the action of a coward'. But in reality Fischer's decision had been an act of supreme courage. By making himself an outlaw, and so irrevocably severing every link to the comforts and status of his former life, Fischer showed a level of sacrifice which Nelson Mandela, himself no stranger to self-sacrifice, would later describe as being 'in a class by itself'.[7] Two members of the Johannesburg Bar later wrote about Fischer's decision:

> What appears from his letter was that he estreated bail and went underground within South Africa not because he underestimated the significance of such a step, but for the very significance that such a step would have in the eyes, especially, of black South Africans. In doing so, he turned his back on the privileges that his race, his ancestry, his status and his profession afforded him, and identified himself with the struggle of those who were perceived to have much less to sacrifice . . . Far from securing any personal advantage, he realised that his actions would result in increased punishment.[8]

Most of Fischer's friends, Kentridge included, had had no idea of what he was planning. Very few people, apart from his closest SACP associates, knew. Phantom sightings of 'the Scarlet Pimpernel' across South Africa were eagerly reported in the press. 'Is the "short one" still at large?' asked Nelson Mandela, speaking in code during one of his regular meetings with George Bizos, his personal lawyer, on Robben Island. One newspaper, *Dagbreek*, put up a reward of 2,000 rand for the recapture of the 'undermining communist, wherever he hides'. Rumours began to circulate that Fischer had escaped the country, even that he had committed suicide. The fugitive soon broke his silence, issuing a message from 'somewhere in South Africa', extracts of which were published by the *Observer* in London. Fischer wrote caustically:

> In 1965 South Africa presents a surface of ebullient confidence: the ebullience of a white electorate basking in phenomenal prosperity; and the confidence of a Government which, during sixteen years, has with increasing violence attempted to crush every effort by the majority of the people to win human rights until today it appears supremely stable ... Not one of the three Prime Ministers produced by the Nationalist Party since 1948 ever met or talked with a single non-white leader.[9]

When copies of the *Observer* went on sale in South Africa, Fischer's words had been excised by the censor from their pages.

Meanwhile the trial from which Fischer had absconded continued in the absence of its most famous – and now notorious – defendant. On 13 April 1965 the majority of the other accused were duly found guilty of membership of the Communist Party and given sentences ranging from one year to five years in prison. The prosecution against Fischer had been suspended pending his expected rearrest. But he now was to be subjected to a more immediate ordeal: the prospect of being disbarred from his profession. Immediately after Fischer's disappearance Justice Minister B. J. Vorster had publicly challenged the profession to take action. In fact privately he made clear to the then chairman of the Johannesburg Bar Council that unless it proceeded against the fugitive advocate the government would itself move to regulate the Bar, ending its independence and introducing criteria for membership, chief among which would be that Communists (as loosely defined by the Suppression of Communism Act) were not permitted to practise. A meeting of the Bar Council was urgently convened, where it was resolved, as the lesser of two evils, to bring disbarment proceedings against Fischer. He first learnt of this in newspaper notices announcing that 'Abram Fischer, male, Queen's Counsel, formerly residing at Beaumont Street, Oaklands, Johannesburg, but whose present whereabouts are unknown' was being proceeded against by what was technically known as the Society of Advocates of South Africa (Witwatersrand Division). One option would have been simply to ignore the Bar Council's application; but for Fischer, living incognito in a safe house, the insult it represented was too much. 'For Bram it was an unjustifiable and utterly dismaying betrayal,' wrote Fischer's biographer, although some senior lawyers I have spoken to believe that the position was much more nuanced.[10] In a letter which was passed to Kentridge, Fischer expressed his distress at the proceedings brought against him by his profession. He wrote that during the trial he realised that the only really effective protest he could make

> would have to be made in a much sharper form – in an open defiance, whatever the personal consequences might be, of a process of law which has become a travesty of all civilized tradition. A political belief is outlawed, then torture is applied to gather evidence and finally the Executive decides whether you serve a life sentence or not. I cannot believe that any genuine protest against this system which has been constructed solely to further apartheid can be regarded as immoral or as justifying the disbarment of a member of our profession . . .
>
> When an advocate does what I have done, his conduct is not deter-mined by any disrespect for the law, nor because he hopes to benefit personally by any 'offence' he may commit. On the contrary, it requires an act of will to overcome his deeply rooted respect of legality, and he takes the step only when he feels that, whatever the consequences to himself, his political conscience no longer permits him to do other-wise. He does it not because of a desire to be immoral, but because to act otherwise would, for him, be immoral.

When I read out those words to Kentridge, more than fifty-five years after they were written, he commented quietly how clearly they revealed the moral bearing of his old friend.

From his place of hiding, Fischer complied with the Bar Council's request to lodge an objection to the disbarment application and appointed his own attorneys. He also wrote to Kentridge to ask his junior colleague to represent him at the hearing. Kentridge immedi-ately agreed. It was a strange inversion of their relationship: Kentridge, who had been Fischer's junior at the Treason Trial several years before, and in many other cases, would now represent Fischer at his leader's disbarment hearing.

George Bizos recalled that Kentridge had been 'livid' at the Bar Council's decision to launch disbarment proceedings against one of its most eminent sons. But it is right to acknowledge that Fischer's actions divided opinion, even among the liberal members of the Johannesburg Bar. John Coaker, who had defended one of the Rivonia accused, was of the opinion that, regardless of his motives, Fischer had acted improperly by breaking the undertaking he had offered the court when it granted him bail. Many others agreed.

Heard on 28 October, Fischer's disbarment hearing was presided over by Quartus de Wet, judge president of the Transvaal, the very man before whom Fischer had acted as counsel for the defence at the Rivonia Trial the year before. Kentridge appeared with Arthur Chaskalson as his junior for an absent client whose current location remained unknown to them. (Chaskalson would later help Kentridge's wife Felicia to set up the Legal Resources Centre in the late 1970s and subsequently became South Africa's chief justice). Neither charged a fee. The applicant was represented by Douglas Shaw QC, chairman of the General Council of the Bar, and a member of the Natal Bar, retained because so many advocates in Johannesburg were friends of Fischer.

No full transcript of the disbarment hearing survives, but Kentridge recalls that a heavy air of sadness pervaded the courtroom. The judges hearing the application had all been at the Bar with Fischer and knew him personally. His politics had been well known but that had not prevented Fischer being a popular and respected colleague. Shaw was measured in the case he presented. He emphasised that Fischer had ensured that Peter Rissik, an attorney who had paid his bail of 10,000 rand, which was forfeited when Fischer vanished, had been fully reimbursed from Fischer's own pocket. But, argued Shaw, Fischer had broken his professional duty to respect the administration of justice, and running away from his own trial so flagrantly after he had given a solemn promise not to, could not go unmarked.

Kentridge argued essentially two points: first that the conduct relied upon did not relate to Fischer's profession as an advocate; and second that that conduct should not be stigmatised as dishonourable. In support of his second submission Kentridge referred to a long tradition in South Africa that politically motivated activity should not count against a person's professional standing. He referred in particular to two famous cases from South Africa's past. The first was an attempt in the early 1950s by the Transvaal Law Society to strike off Nelson Mandela as an attorney because of his then recent conviction for subversive activity. The application had failed because Mandela's conduct had been held to be unrelated to his work as a lawyer.[11] The second was a case at the other end of the political spectrum. At the start of the century an Afrikaner advocate, Fritz Krause, who had practised at the English Bar after fighting against the British in the Boer War, had been found guilty in England of inciting the murder of a man who had expressed anti-Boer sentiments. He had been sentenced to two years in prison, and was also disbarred by the Middle Temple, the London Inn of Court he belonged to. When Krause eventually returned to South Africa his application to join the Johannesburg Bar had been successful and he had gone on to become judge president of the Orange Free State.[12] Kentridge's point was clear: if an advocate could be judged 'fit and proper' in Johannesburg having been convicted of inciting murder in England, why should Fischer be judged dishonourable merely for having skipped bail, when his motives were plainly political? Kentridge referred to the South African principle of separating professional integrity from political conscience; apart from Krause there were many instances of Afrikaner rebels who had gone on to enjoy illustrious legal careers. Nothing, Kentridge argued, about Fischer's conduct during his own trial made him unfit to practise law. Disbarment was normally reserved for corrupt lawyers who had abused their position for personal gain or advantage – one thing that Fischer could not be accused of. 'My Lords,' Kentridge concluded, 'it is doubtful if there were any member of the Bar who had known Mr Fischer who would be prepared to stand up and say "He is a less honourable man than I am."'[13] Nobody in court disagreed.

Judgment was given on 2 November and, as expected, Abram Fischer QC was ordered to be removed from the roll of advocates. The judges did not explain what distinguished Fischer from Krause, other than the immaterial consideration of differing political outlooks, but they took it upon themselves to stray into irrelevance. 'The letters of the respondent, together with absconding from his trial, clearly lead to the inference that not only was he guilty of subversive conduct in the past but that he intends continuing such activity and probably at the time is still engaged in such activity.'[14] At the end of his judgment de Wet seemed to suggest that a time might come when Fischer could seek rehabilitation: 'It is impossible for this Court to foresee what will happen in the future. We are concerned with the laws in force at the present time and with the structure as it exists in this country at the present time.' It was as if there was a tinge of shame in the judge's mind at having facilitated the vindictiveness of the apartheid regime. Bram Fischer's long and illustrious career at the Johannesburg Bar may have been *de facto* over; now it was *de jure* over too, not because of some grubby piece of embezzlement but rather for an act of supreme self-sacrifice.

Nothing hurt Fischer more than being disbarred, George Bizos later wrote.[15] In 1997 the Truth and Reconciliation Commission condemned Fischer's disbarment and found that 'The organised professional bodies . . . were obsequious in their attitudes to government policies, hounding those of their members who chose to buck the system politically.' Before the commission the Fischer family testified that the striking-off had been carried out with indecent haste and had been regarded by Bram as the 'worst professional and personal betrayal' he had ever experienced.

Rather than fleeing abroad as rumoured, in fact Fischer did not venture far from Johannesburg after going underground. At first he travelled to Rustenburg, sixty miles north-west of Johannesburg, staying in a cottage owned by the mother-in-law of a sympathetic journalist. There he lost weight, shaved off much of his hair (dying what remained auburn), grew a goatee beard and started smoking a pipe. Many of the small coterie he stayed in contact with thought he had the air of a latter-day Lenin, or Trotsky, though the children of one SACP couple described him as a sort of Professor Calculus, the absent-minded character from the Adventures of Tintin books. Fischer's new identity – as a photographer called Douglas Black –

convinced everybody: at one point he even returned to his own chambers, where (it seems) no one saw through his disguise.

After a few weeks in Rustenburg Fischer returned to Johannesburg, holing up for six months in a house barely a mile from his former home in Beaumont Street. But fear of exposure kept him on the move. He relocated again to a larger house in another northern Johannesburg suburb, Bramley. It was a period of loneliness, anxiety and frustration, anchored only by Fischer's unswerving dedication to his political ideals. Even from his precarious hideouts he was still working hard to revive the moribund SACP. And he managed to maintain a tenuous and occasional link with normality. Fischer attended cricket matches with one of the close circle of political comrades who knew his identity and sometimes enjoyed picnics in the veldt with his friend Mary Benson, the anti-apartheid writer and campaigner.[16] One assumes that he took considerable pleasure in these audacious small acts of defiance, as if taunting the authorities to catch him if they could. They certainly show the cool nerve of the man.

Fischer had always known that his decision to abscond was bound to end in arrest and eventual imprisonment for a term far longer than the sentence he would have been handed at his first trial. He had only expected to remain underground for at most a few weeks before he was tracked down. In the event he managed almost ten months – 294 days – before his whereabouts was revealed. In September 1965 an SACP member, Issy Heymann, had been detained. Heymann did not know Fischer's location; like others he had deliberately kept himself ignorant lest he was forced to reveal his comrade's address under torture. But having been subjected to the usual sleep deprivation techniques deployed with such effectiveness by the security police, Heymann steered them to Violet Weinberg, who was part of the inner circle which did know of Fischer's whereabouts. Out of shame, Heymann attempted suicide shortly afterwards, slashing his ankles and wrists in prison, but he did manage to send out a message that Comrade Aunty – a code name for Weinberg – was in danger. The message did not reach her in time, and she was arrested on 8 November. Interrogated without break for seventy hours and tormented by threats against her children, on 11 November Weinberg finally capitulated and revealed the location of Fischer's safe house. He was arrested that very evening, just as he was making preparations to move again. His disbarment had been decided just nine days earlier, and he may have been so disheartened that he did not react swiftly enough to the news of Weinberg's arrest.

In the house police found documents evidencing quite how active Fischer had been during his months as a fugitive. They bore titles such as 'Notes on the Experience of our Portuguese Branch', 'A Note on Discipline and Training' and 'Rally and Unite Anti-Imperialist Forces – an appeal from the Central Committee of the Communist Party', along with a false moustache, beard and eyebrows, two wigs, a corset, a woman's blue hat and make-up, and fake registration plates for his Volkswagen. Many of these items were later among the 200 prosecution exhibits at Fischer's second trial.

The recapture of Fischer was a major news event. The front pages of most South African newspapers the next day carried photographs of the arrest, a still disguised Fischer being led away by the ubiquitous Captain Theunis Swanepoel, who, as we will learn, was one of the security police's most notorious torturers. He was brought straight to Pretoria Central Prison where George Bizos came to visit him in the very room where they had both consulted with Mandela and the other Rivonia defendants two years before. Bizos asked him whether the forfeiture of his profession, his status and his family for his time underground had been worth it. Fischer angrily responded 'Would you ask Mandela that?' Bizos agreed that he would not. 'Well then, don't ask me.'

Fischer appeared in Johannesburg Regional Court on the Monday after his arrest. At the trial from which Fischer had absconded in January 1965 he had been charged under the Suppression of Communism Act with offences carrying, individually, a maximum sentence of three years imprisonment. The proceedings against him had been suspended on his disappearance. He now faced those charges again, together with a much more serious charge under the Sabotage Act that carried a maximum sentence of death, and a battery of other charges of fraud and forgery, alleged to have been committed in order to maintain his false identity while he was underground. Fischer was surrounded by no fewer than 145 policemen, almost outnumbering the spectators packed into the courtroom and its surrounding corridors. Police claimed gleefully that he was 'a broken man with little of the spirit of Bram Fischer', but reporters noted the 'same alert twinkle' in his eyes.[17] All of Fischer's children were in court, including Paul, who had returned from London in poor health (he suffered from cystic fibrosis). Bail was, naturally, out of the question, and as he awaited his trial Fischer was held in solitary confinement for twenty-three hours a day at Pretoria Central Prison.

In the last days of January 1966 there was a preliminary examination of the prosecution evidence before a magistrate. It revealed the extent to which the SACP had been infiltrated by government spies and broken by police interrogation. On 2 February Fischer entered an elaborate plea. 'I plead not guilty,' he began, adding that 'Some of the evidence led is correct and at my trial I shall not seek to deny that evidence. On the other hand, important evidence has been given which is either grossly distorted or which I shall maintain is untruthful.' Because 'the truthful and the false evidence is so inextricably interwoven . . . it is not possible by means of a plea to unravel the one from the other', explained a man who was constitutionally incapable of mendacity. 'Therefore, I plead not guilty to all the charges.'

On 23 March 1966 Fischer's second criminal trial started, in the central court of the Palace of Justice in Pretoria, South Africa's most imposing courtroom, which had hosted the Rivonia Trial two and a half years before. Kentridge, who had been appointed a senior counsel (the South African equivalent of a British QC)[18] in late 1965, had again been asked by his colleague to represent him; he had again agreed, of course for no fee. Fischer's biographer painted the scene that first day. 'As the fans revolved unhurriedly overhead' the advocate-turned-accused took his place alone in the huge dock, specially enlarged two and a half years earlier to accommodate the Rivonia defendants. Fischer was seen to be 'laughing with Sydney Kentridge . . . Even here, aged and thinner, he had that engaging aura about him which attracted others and put them at their ease.'[19] Kentridge himself remembers meeting his old friend, so incongruously in the dock, that day. It was an emotional encounter. Even at this moment of crisis Fischer's first question was to enquire after his junior colleague's recently born son Matthew. 'Is the baby crawling yet?' Kentridge later recalled that 'He was on trial actually for his life because the crimes for which he was charged carried a death penalty and, I mean, he was always able to think of other people.'

This was a trial with no hope of acquittal. The pall of tragedy seemed to hang over it. Kentridge's role was to challenge the excesses of the prosecution case and the exaggerations of witnesses striving to satisfy those detaining them. To the central charges Fischer had no answer other than principled self-justification. Like the Rivonia defendants, he had no wish to disown the political decisions which had brought him into the dock. The trial got off to a rapid start. Immediately after the charges were read out and Fischer repeated his not guilty plea, the prosecutor called Bartholomew Hlapane, the state's first witness. Hlapane had joined the SACP's central committee in 1962 and had emerged unscathed from 172 days of detention after the Rivonia raid in July 1963. Maybe the SACP already suspected he was disloyal, but despite fears that the police might be following him Hlapane had been reappointed as an SACP organiser. In September 1964 he had been detained again, 'cracked', and had become a police informer.

The scale of Hlapane's betrayal now became painfully evident. His evidence was devastating. He claimed that the SACP was at the head of uMkhonto we Sizwe, the ANC's armed wing: an allegation of potentially enormous political value to the regime, which had long sought to discredit the anti-apartheid movement as a mere tool of international Communism and thus the implacable foe of the free world.[20] Fischer had been at the meeting in late 1962 or early 1963 at which Operation Mayibuye, the alleged plan for guerrilla war which had been debated at length during the Rivonia Trial, had been approved. Hlapane claimed that, far from urging restraint, Fischer had demanded 'positive action' on violence, had pointed out that 'Mealie [maize] fields were now dry' and ripe for burning, and had been instructed by the SACP to find funds for the purchase of an arsenal of weaponry and explosives.

Kentridge started his cross-examination of Hlapane with patrician nonchalance: 'You seem to have served many years in the Communist Party, Mr Hlapane?' Having put the witness at his ease, Kentridge suggested that following his most recent arrest on 20 January and his appearance at the preparatory examination (where he had given evidence to the magistrate), Hlapane seemed to have been coached in his evidence:

Q: Are you still being interrogated?
A: Not that I am interrogated, after my statement [*sic*].
Q: That is what I mean, since you gave evidence in the Court below, have you not been interrogated again?
A: No.
Q: Has no one spoken to you from the Police?
A: The police do speak to me.
Q: About what?
A: What my needs are, and so on.
Q: But I mean, about your experiences in the Communist Party?
A: I have not discussed that since I made my statement.
Q: So from the time you gave your statement in the magistrate's court by way of evidence, and your evidence today, have you not had a discussion about these facts with anybody?
A: I have not, My Lord.
Q: Not even with my learned friend, the Prosecutor?
A: Well he did come and discuss some matters, with me, about my statement.
Q: And did he go through it? I don't want you to tell me what he said, I just want to know, did you go through your statement?
A: He read my statement back to me. And that is all he said. I will be giving evidence.

Hlapane had denied discussing his statement with anybody, only to have to contradict himself just seconds later. Kentridge forced Hlapane to admit that he had never been a member of the 'high command' of uMkhonto we Sizwe, but had been on the Central Committee of the SACP that supposedly it was 'responsible to' – something he had not said at the preparatory examination. Yet Hlapane could not offer any examples of orders given by the SACP Central Committee to uMkhonto we Sizwe, other than the supposed adoption of Operation Mayibuye, which now Hlapane asserted Fischer had masterminded. But at the preparatory examination Hlapane had said nothing about the adoption of Operation Mayibuye, a discrepancy Kentridge took full advantage of.

Q: Did you tell the magistrate the Central Committee had approved of Operation Mayibuye?

A: I am not sure whether I used the word precisely 'approved'.

Q: I am not asking for a precise word – did you convey to the magistrate that it had been approved?

A: I conveyed that it had been approved.

Q: [*With emphasis*] You know, Mr Hlapane, you did not do anything of the sort!

A: I am sorry, My Lord, at this stage, but I am correct that I did it.

Q: You will see in a moment, Mr Hlapane, what you did and what you said.

Hlapane claimed that the SACP Central Committee had considered Operation Mayibuye 'very practical', but Kentridge responded that in fact Fischer had felt it was 'an impractical and ridiculous' plan, involving four planes flying from elsewhere in Africa over South Africa's neighbours – which had yet to achieve independence – and each dropping off thirty guerrilla fighters, hardly enough to wage a war of liberation. Even the Operation Mayibuye document itself had acknowledged that 'the absence of friendly borders, and long-scale impregnable natural bases from which to operate, are both disadvantages'.

Kentridge asked again why Hlapane had not told the magistrate that Operation Mayibuye had been approved by Fischer. 'I can't explain why.' Kentridge turned to Hlapane's evidence that it had been agreed that a planeload of guerrillas should be flown in to attack a target in the North-Western Cape.

Q: Look, Mr Hlapane, the point is where does an aeroplane come from to drop people in the North-Western Cape?

A: That was the sort of question that was asked.

Q: How was that replied to? I want to know what the reply was?

A: In his explanation, My Lord, Joe Slovo said it was not difficult for aeroplanes to fly across Bechuanaland [i.e. present-day Botswana] and drop people and fly back. And also . . .

Q: To the North-Western Cape?

A: And also the sea could be used? They were sure they could drop people there and sail back.

Q: And that explanation, Mr Hlapane, would not satisfy a child, let alone Mr Fischer, don't you agree with me? Does that really satisfy you? You seem pretty intelligent?

A: As far as I was concerned, I was quite satisfied.

Q: You were satisfied?

A: That is right, My Lord.

Q: Didn't you think these thirty men would die of thirst?

A: I don't think so.

Kentridge had established that the hypothetical plans outlined in the Operation Mayibuye document were laughably impractical. The document had said that 'Our target is that on arrival the external force should find at least 7,000 men in the four main areas' (Hlapane, when re-examined later by the prosecutor Henry Liebenberg, said that in 1963 only 300 uMkhonto we Sizwe personnel within South Africa had received military training). At the preparatory examination Hlapane had said that Joe Slovo was going to go abroad to 'mention' the Operation Mayibuye document to foreign supporters. When Kentridge put it to Hlapane that this meant Slovo was merely going to discuss its long-term feasibility, rather than put it into action, Hlapane's excuse – an inadequate interpreter at the preparatory examination – was not convincing.[21]

Piet Beyleveld then made a reappearance. Examined by the prosecutor he was strangely vague, saying that all he knew about uMkhonto we Sizwe was 'what I read in the press' and that he had known nothing about Liliesleaf Farm until after the Rivonia raids. The prosecution's supposed star witness was not living up to expectations. The meetings that Beyleveld attended after he became a member of the SACP's Central Committee in the latter part of 1963 had discussed 'the disorganisation of both the Central Committee and the District Committees in the various centres', and other meetings were cancelled as members stopped turning up or were detained. The SACP hardly sounded like the mastermind of an armed insurrection against the most formidable military on the continent.

As with Hlapane, Kentridge started his cross-examination of Beyleveld with kid gloves on. Beyleveld accepted that he had been in 'a prominent position' in the Congress movement and later a 'king-pin' in the SACP, and he readily agreed to Kentridge's suggestion that at the preparatory examination he had answered all questions fully and not held anything back. Continuing his cross-examination on 24 March, Kentridge extracted an admission from Beyleveld that monies he had handled on the SACP's behalf had gone towards the welfare of detainees' families, not to starting a civil war. Beyleveld agreed with Kentridge that Fischer was a sincere and kind man, that the acts of sabotage undertaken had been designed to avoid loss of life, that there was no formal connection between the SACP and Umkhonto we Sizwe, and that there had been no commitment to violence at meetings he had attended with Fischer. Perhaps Beyleveld was entertaining second thoughts about having agreed to testify against Fischer, a man he still evidently revered, but Kentridge had also done much to limit the damage his renewed testimony might cause. When re-examined Beyleveld refused to take the bait of leading questions that the prosecutor asked him about uMkhonto we Sizwe, of which Beyleveld now denied ever having been a part.

After the brief testimony of a servant at Liliesleaf Farm (Fischer of course could not now avoid being identified by absenting himself from court) came Gerard Ludi, a government spy who had infiltrated the SACP, and who produced a torrent of words in response to each of the prosecutor's questions. Ludi boasted of his importance as a champion informer: 'I attended meetings of a large number of organisations which I suspected were somehow tied up with the Communist Party, including the Congress of Democrats – in fact the entire Congress Alliance,' he bragged. At one point the exasperated prosecutor had to ask him 'Will it be difficult for you to confine yourself to those parts played by the accused in these . . .?' 'No, My Lord,' interrupted Ludi, before digressing to irrelevancies such as the fact that 'two members of my cell demanded that a protest be sent to the Communist Governments of Rumania and Russia because a South African wrestling team would be sent to Rumania soon, and because South African schoolboys would be playing chess in Russia during that time.' Ludi had next to nothing to say about Fischer, and

Kentridge refused to dignify him with a cross-examination, telling the doubtless grateful judge, who had had to feign interest in so much prolix nonsense, that 'I am instructed by my client that a number of the witness's statements are incorrect, but, My Lord, they have no effect on the legal responsibility of the accused . . . and I don't propose to ask him any questions.'

There followed a parade of witnesses – estate agents, landladies, accountants and bank managers – who testified to Fischer's time underground. None of their evidence was contentious but they all agreed with Kentridge that they had not been financially defrauded in any way by Fischer. A witness from the tax authority conceded that the accused had in fact overpaid tax by nearly 2,000 rand. The prosecution case was closed.

On the following Monday, 28 March, just after the court day had started at 10 o'clock Kentridge told the court: 'My Lord, I have no witnesses for the Defence. The Accused, who is of course well aware of his legal rights, wishes to make a statement from the dock.' Just as Mandela had done at the Rivonia Trial, from the same dock, Fischer exercised the privilege of an accused to make an unsworn statement to the court. While he thereby deprived the prosecution of their right to cross-examine him, the quid pro quo was that his statement would be accorded very limited evidential weight. But that was hardly Fischer's primary concern; this speech would be perhaps the most important of his legal or political career, and its true audience was far removed from the judge to whom he nominally addressed himself.

Extending to five uninterrupted hours, Fischer's speech was an amalgam of political testament, critique of the current state of South Africa, narrative of his own political journey, and, finally, apologia for his conduct. Notwithstanding its length, and occasional descent into an overly detailed exposition of Marxist theory, *The Times* reported 'rapt attention as in quiet, unemotional tones the slight, silver-haired man explained the standpoint from which his actions had flowed'.[22]

'I am on trial, My Lord, for my political beliefs and for the conduct which those beliefs drove me to,' Fischer began, speaking in a voice both low and deliberate.

Whatever labels may have been attached to the fifteen charges brought against me, they all arise from my having been a member of the Communist Party and from my activities as a member. I engaged upon those activities because I believed that, in the dangerous circumstances which have been created in South Africa, it was my duty to do so. My Lord, when a man is on trial for his political beliefs and actions, two courses are open to him. He can either confess to his transgressions and plead for mercy, or he can justify his beliefs and explain why he has acted as he did. Were I to ask for forgiveness today, I would betray my cause. That course, My Lord, is not open to me . . .

I accept, My Lord, the general rule that for the protection of a society laws should be obeyed. But when the laws themselves become immoral, and require the citizen to take part in an organised system of oppression – if only by his silence and apathy – then I believe that a higher duty arises. This compels me to refuse to recognise such laws.

The law, My Lord, under which I have been prosecuted, was enacted by a wholly unrepresentative body, a body in which three-quarters of the people of this country have no voice whatsoever. This and other laws were enacted not to prevent the spread of Communism, but, My Lord, for the purpose of silencing the opposition of the large majority of our citizens to a government intent upon depriving them, solely on account of their colour, of the most elementary human rights . . .

My conscience, My Lord, does not permit me to afford these laws such recognition as even a plea of guilty would involve. Hence, though I shall be convicted by this Court, I cannot plead guilty. I believe that the future may well say that I acted correctly.

How prophetic that last sentence would turn out to be.

For Fischer, personal and professional integrity were keystones of his existence and he now explained the decision to estreat his bail, the act which had led to his disbarment.

It was to keep faith with all those dispossessed by apartheid that I broke my undertaking to the Court, that I separated myself from my family, pretended I was someone else, and accepted the life of a fugitive. I owed it to the political prisoners, to the banished, to the silenced and to those under house arrest not to remain a spectator, but to act . . . surely there was an additional duty cast upon me, that at least one Afrikaner should make this protest actively and positively, even though as a result I face fifteen charges instead of four.

Fischer was also anxious to correct some of the falsehoods which Hlapane had peddled from the witness box. Far from being a founder of uMkhonto we Sizwe, he had been unaware of its existence until after its formation; he had never advocated the burning of fields; above all else Fischer insisted that Operation Mayibuye was 'an entirely unrealistic brainchild of some youthful and adventurous imagination . . . if any part of it at all could be put into operation, it could achieve nothing but disaster'. He had never condoned guerrilla war.

All the conduct with which I have been charged has been directed towards maintaining contact and understanding between the races of this country. If one day it may help to establish a bridge across which white leaders and the real leaders of the non-whites can meet to settle the destinies of all of us by negotiation, and not by force of arms, I shall be able to bear with fortitude any sentence which this court may impose on me. It will be a fortitude, My Lord, strengthened by this knowledge, at least, that for the past twenty-five years I have taken no part, not even by passive acceptance, in that hideous system of discrimination which we have erected in this country, and which has become a byword in the civilized world.

Fischer turned round to smile at his three children, who had listened from the public gallery to their father's words. Before a silent court he then sat down.

Surprisingly, a trial that had lasted less than a week was followed by a six-week adjournment, as the judge, Mr Justice Boshoff, examined the evidence and transcripts before delivering his verdict. On 4 May Fischer was back in the Palace of Justice to be found guilty on all counts. It was not a verdict about which there had been any doubt. On 9 May he returned again for sentencing. Kentridge delivered a short mitigation speech. There was very little to say beyond Fischer's own words. Kentridge paid a heartfelt tribute to his friend as a brave man whose gifts of intellect and personality were such that 'there was no status nor honour to which he could not have attained if he had not adhered to the beliefs which had resulted in his trial'. But there could be no apology for his actions: 'My client has accepted full responsibility for his actions and declared that for him to ask for forgiveness would be a betrayal of his associates.' Kentridge recalls as one of the most shocking moments of his career hearing prosecution counsel actively seeking the death sentence for his fellow advocate: 'Even the judge looked appalled.' Still, apart from the preservation of his life, Fischer could expect no other form of leniency from the court. The sentence was life imprisonment; and life meant life. As he was led down the staircase within the dock to the cells beneath, Fischer gave the ANC salute – his right fist raised with the thumb extended – and called out 'Afrika! Mayibuye!' – 'Africa, may it return!'

Fischer's first months in prison were brutal. Regarded as a traitor to his heritage, he was put in the charge of a sadistic warder who compelled him to clean toilets on his hands and knees in a sanitary block sarcastically christened the Potemkin, after the battleship famed for its role in the 1905 Russian Revolution. Kentridge tried to visit Fischer there but was denied access without explanation. To his immense sadness, Kentridge never saw his friend again. He received one memento of his colleague. Fischer gave him his briefcase, which Kentridge passed on to his son William, who used it as a prop in his plays.

Gradually conditions improved for Fischer. In 1967 the USSR awarded him the Lenin Peace Prize, an act not exactly calculated to soften the heart of the South African government; nevertheless, the following year he was moved to a more comfortable, newly built section of Pretoria Local Prison, which was reserved for political prisoners, of whom some fifteen to twenty were held there at any one time. Fischer became their unofficial leader, and kept busy tending the flower beds in the exercise yard and dispensing gratis legal advice to some of the warders.

Several campaigns for Fischer's release were launched, highlighting the fact that even Robey Leibbrandt, the pro-Nazi nationalist condemned to death for high treason in 1943 for plotting the overthrow of Jan Smuts's government, had had his sentence commuted to life imprisonment, and was then released and pardoned after only five years in jail. But the campaigns got nowhere. Fischer had, in the eyes of the Nationalist government, committed treason against his own people, and there could be no leniency. Even when Fischer's son died in 1971, aged only twenty-three, he was not permitted to attend the funeral.

In 1974 Fischer's health deteriorated: a botched prostate cancer diagnosis meant the tumour spread to his hip before he could be properly treated, by which time he had fallen over in a shower and broken his femur. When Fischer was admitted to hospital some days later he was aphasic, speaking only with great difficulty. On his return to prison two weeks later he was virtually immobile, and had to be fed and carried to and from the lavatory by other prisoners. Only after Fischer fell into a coma, in December 1974, did a renewed release campaign, backed by a number of statesmen including the former US presidential candidate Senator George McGovern, the British ambassador to the United Nations and no fewer than three future leaders of the British Labour Party (Jim Callaghan, Michael Foot and Neil Kinnock), pay off. After rallying slightly and receiving a round of radiotherapy – useless, as the cancer was so advanced – Fischer was finally released in March 1975, on condition that he live with his brother Paul on his farm outside Bloemfontein.

The authorities still seemed to fear that Fischer might become a rallying point for opponents of apartheid if allowed to return to Johannesburg, the city 'with the greatest percentage of subversives in the country' according to one government minister. Paul Fischer's house was officially designated as a prison, and even on his deathbed Fischer was kept under surveillance and not allowed non-family visitors without official permission. Another attempt by Kentridge to visit his friend and former client in his last days was predictably refused. After relapsing into a coma on 23 April 1975 – his sixty-seventh birthday – Fischer died on 8 May. His ashes were never given to his family, lest they became a shrine to apartheid's opponents.

Having been fictionalised in novels by André Brink, Mary Benson and Nadine Gordimer in the 1960s and 1970s, Fischer became a posthumous hero after the end of apartheid, seen as a prototype for a new type of Afrikaner. His life has been much analysed and debated; and while his saintlike qualities have been singled out, it is also right to recognise the contradictions and compromises in his life.[23] Here was a man whose admiration for Stalin continued undimmed until his death. For all his hatred of capitalism, he enjoyed a comfortable lifestyle paid for by briefs from major beneficiaries of apartheid and its non-unionised cheap black labour, like the Anglo-American Corporation. His decision to represent the Rivonia defendants was open to question by reference to the ethics of advocacy. In an article Stephen Ellmann makes a fascinating comparison between Fischer and Oscar Wilde, both of whom, in their differing ways, sacrificed their lives for an ideal.[24] An annual Bram Fischer Memorial Lecture was instituted in 1995. President Nelson Mandela gave the first lecture, telling his audience that Fischer 'could have become prime minister or the chief justice of South Africa if he had chosen to follow the narrow path of Afrikaner nationalism. He chose instead the long and hard road to freedom not only for himself but for all of us.' In his autobiography *Long Walk to Freedom* Mandela described Fischer as 'the bravest and staunchest friend of the freedom struggle that I have ever known'.[25]

In 1995 the Johannesburg Bar Council and the General Council of the Bar of South Africa officially apologised for the injustice that had been perpetrated when Fischer was struck from the roll of advocates. They said that they would support any application for Fischer's post-humous readmission. He was eventually readmitted in 2003. Even Fischer's home city of Bloemfontein, capital of the former Orange Free State Republic and the spiritual home of Afrikanerdom, has come to revere its 'lost' son: in 2012 its airport was renamed as Bram Fischer International Airport.

The Legal Resources Centre's director Geoff Budlender wrote in 1995:

The story of Bram Fischer dramatises and illuminates the difficult question of what the duty of conscientious lawyers is, when the government (and particularly a nonrepresentative government) represses its citizens. Many options present themselves. Does one simply go about one's business, hoping that this unpleasantness will go away? Should one work within the (immoral) system as a lawyer, trying to mitigate the evils of the system and to assist those who are its victims? Or should one distance oneself completely, and attempt actively to undermine and subvert the system?[26]

These questions are equally applicable to Sydney Kentridge, as the lawyer who represented Fischer at both his disbarment hearing and at the trial that led to his life imprisonment. Kentridge chose one path, Fischer – finally – chose another.

6

The Trials of Winnie Mandela (1970–86)

T HE CONTROVERSIES OF her later life have tended to dominate current perceptions of Winnie Mandela. But if we go back to the 1960s, when she was a young woman struggling to bring up two children alone while her husband was incarcerated in a faraway prison for the foreseeable future, we discover a very different person. At that time Winnie Mandela was not only the wife of perhaps the most famous political prisoner in the world. She also came to occupy a position as a leading opponent of the apartheid regime, acquiring iconic status within the banned ANC. This role came at a high cost: constant police surveillance and harassment, culminating in her arrest in 1969 and a concerted attempt by the state to have her imprisoned and neutralised. Sydney Kentridge now received the second 'Mandela brief' of his career.

Mandela had met the woman who would become his second wife in 1957. Winnie was twenty-one, some sixteen years younger than Nelson, and training to be a social worker. Their first encounter occurred during a break from the interminable Treason Trial proceedings, while Nelson was appearing in Johannesburg's regional court (as a lawyer rather than a defendant), representing one of Winnie's colleagues. 'I just saw this towering, imposing man, actually quite awesome,' she recalled.[1] While Nelson Mandela, then in his late thirties, was a seasoned veteran of the anti-apartheid movement, Winnie found herself caught in the centre of its maelstrom in her early twenties.

In June 1958 Nelson and Winnie were married. 'I hope it is not the Mandela of the ANC,' Winnie's stepmother had asked optimistically when she heard of the forthcoming wedding. As he was then subject to a banning order, restricting his activities and movements, the groom had to get special permission to attend his own marriage. Straight after, the Mandelas returned home to 8115 Orlando West, a red-brick matchbox bungalow in the Orlando township of Soweto, which had been Nelson's home since 1947. Hung on the wall was a poster with a photograph of Lenin addressing a revolutionary crowd in 1917.[2]

Two daughters followed, born in 1958 and 1960, to whom Winnie was effectively a single parent almost from the start. Throughout the early 1960s her husband was either on trial for his life as a defendant in the Treason Trial (see Chapter 3), illicitly travelling abroad or living a precarious underground existence. But Winnie had been under no illusions. 'When I married him, I married the struggle, the liberation of my people,' she said. Mandela was arrested in August 1962 and soon after sentenced to five years' hard labour, having been found guilty of inciting an illegal strike in 1961 and leaving South Africa in 1962 without official permission. After the capture of the rest of the leadership of uMkhonto we Sizwe, the armed wing of the ANC,[3] in the Liliesleaf raid of July 1963, Nelson was again put in the dock alongside his comrades at the Rivonia Trial. (Kentridge had been due to defend one of Mandela's co-accused, Bob Hepple, but his client was released and then absconded to England before it started.)[4] Following his conviction in June 1964, Mandela's term of imprisonment was extended to a life sentence. He would remain a prisoner until 1990.

Winnie had her own brushes with the law. She had been detained for two weeks in 1958, while five months pregnant with her first daughter, for participating in a demonstration protest against the intolerable and humiliating effect of the pass laws on black women. Upon her release she was told that her employer Baragwanath Hospital was 'terminating her services' and she had to find a new job. The loss of employment and search for its replacement would be a constant in her future life. Winnie experienced her first police raid at home when Nelson was arrested and interned in March 1960. In June 1962 her home was ransacked again. There would be many more such violent intrusions.

Winnie was subject to her first banning order in 1962, imposed after she gave a speech to a meeting of the Indian Youth Congress.

Under state pressure her then employer, Johannesburg's child welfare department, dismissed her. Her banning was justified by Colonel Coetzee of the security police with a distinctly Boer (and insulting) metaphor: 'If you have a field with a lot of pumpkins and you see a pig next to those pumpkins, you don't have to be told that that pig is going to eat those pumpkins.' Winnie remained under successive banning orders almost continuously from the early 1960s until the late 1980s – orders restricting where she could live, what she could do and who she could speak to. Throughout this time she was at the centre of much pedantic legal debate about what constituted a 'meeting' and the definition of 'visitors' and 'gatherings' – all words which appeared in the texts of orders against her – encapsulating the unique juxtaposition of legalism and oppression that epitomised apartheid South Africa.

Winnie's contact with Nelson during the first decade of his imprisonment was intermittent. Even when she was permitted to visit, Winnie was not allowed to discuss politics with her husband and could only pass on nuggets of political information 'parcelled in family talk'. Winnie's daughters were not allowed to visit their father at all until they reached the age of sixteen, which meant they would not see him for more than a decade after his initial arrest in 1962. By 1968, four years into his imprisonment at Robben Island after the conclusion of the Rivonia Trial, Nelson had received a total of only five visits – four from Winnie and one from a son by his first marriage. That same year Mandela's mother visited and died shortly afterwards: Nelson, her only son, was denied permission to attend her funeral.

In the early 1960s Winnie Mandela's own persona had been subsumed by her role as wife of Nelson. She recalled later that 'I was aware of the fact that suddenly I discovered "Oh, I have no name now" – everything I did as "Mandela's wife", I lost my individuality: "Mandela's wife said this", "Mandela's wife was arrested". It did not matter who the hell I was; it did not matter that I was a Madikizela: it did not matter that I was a human being.' But by the end of the decade, still in her early thirties, Winnie had acquired a political identity of her own. As one historian of the apartheid period wrote:

> Beyond Robben Island, there was no more conspicuous figure in the [anti-apartheid] movement than the feisty Winnie Mandela. With her 'Mother Teresa' status in the townships, you could almost hear Afrikaner MPs spluttering that all would be quiet in the land if only that *kaffir meid* ('kaffir girl') was out of the way. And they had tried.[5]

★

With most of its leadership either in exile or in prison, the ANC was at a low ebb by the late 1960s. The international media had mostly lost interest in Nelson Mandela and the other political prisoners on Robben Island. The flight of foreign capital after the Sharpeville massacre in 1960 had been quickly reversed and the largely symbolic economic sanctions against South Africa did not prevent it enjoying an industrial boom, founded on the sweat of cheap black labour. In 1967 Vorster's government introduced the Terrorism Act, which effectively allowed for indefinite detention without trial. In July of that year the ANC's president Chief Albert Luthuli died suspiciously, run over by a train: some suspected that he had been murdered. By the end of the decade the ANC would admit in an internal document that it was 'almost dead'.

In 1969 the apartheid state decided to press home its advantage by rounding up the few prominent ANC leaders and activists who still enjoyed freedom. In the early hours of 12 May Winnie was woken by the noise of her door being kicked down and the blinding light of torches shone simultaneously through every window. In front of her two young daughters, crying in bewilderment and fear, she was arrested under section 6 of the Terrorism Act and detained – along with over a hundred others – at Pretoria Central Prison. The first person to be arrested under this draconian new power, Winnie was held in solitary confinement for two weeks before being subjected to a five-day interrogation, the first of many, led by the now-promoted Major Theunis Swanepoel. Bull-necked, crew-cut and ruddy-faced, Swanepoel was a terrifying figure. Known as 'Rooi Rus' (Red Russian), a moniker inspired either by his red hair or his brutal treatment of those he classed as Communists or fellow travellers (opinions differ), he was the most notorious of the state's torturers throughout the 1960s and early 1970s. During those years scores of political prisoners were subjected to his barbaric interrogation techniques. Mac

Maharaj, an ANC activist and associate of Nelson Mandela, reported that after his arrest in 1964 Swanepoel beat his penis with a stick studded with rusty nails and hung him by his ankles from a seventh-floor window. Bob Hepple, who was subject to a protracted interrogation in 1963, after the Liliesleaf Farm raid, recalled one of Swanepoel's ploys. He would 'leave a revolver on the desk then pick it up and play Russian roulette after showing me the one bullet: "Would you like this or the rope?" he says.'[6] Babla Salojee, an activist and lawyer, did not survive to leave an account of Swanepoel's treatment of him. After sixty-five days in detention he was thrown from the same seventh-floor window from which Maharaj had been suspended. The subsequent inquest concluded that he had committed suicide.

Winnie's prison diaries would be published in 2013 under the title *491 Days*, a reference to the total period of her eventual incarceration. They depict in stark language, devoid of self-pity, the appalling experience she sustained; the indignities and humiliations inflicted on her in a futile attempt to break her will. Bodily functions had to be performed in a bucket which was emptied once a day and delivered back unwashed. The mat and blankets which made up her rudimentary bedding were bespattered with the dried blood – and who knew what else? – of former inmates. Winnie was detained in the execution cell; a closed door led directly to the gallows chamber. Execrable food, cold and unchanging, was served up on dirty plates. But worst of all was the isolation, unmitigated by human interaction – other than the screams of prisoners being beaten in adjacent cells or the bellows and insults of prisoner guards – and unleavened even by the sense of day turning into night, and back again.

> In the dim grim walls with the electric light burning day and night, the difference between day and night or daybreak and dawn is hard to tell when you can't sleep and all you do is to doze off now and again whenever the mind decides to stop over functioning for a while.
>
> The cell measures 15' x 5' or is it? I've walked miles and miles in this cell, round and round, backwards and forwards in a desperate attempt to kill the empty long lonely minutes, hours and months which drag by at a snail's pace gnawing at the inner cores of my soul, corroding it, battering it about . . .[7]

Winnie would eventually be charged in October 1969 for offences under the Suppression of Communism Act 1950. The prospect of a trial after months of blank emptiness was a relief, bringing with it the hope of some form of resolution, and an interruption to the dreary days of incarceration – 'full of nothing', as Winnie described them. Many of the details of the charges faced by Winnie, and the twenty-one others who would eventually be tried alongside her, seemed trivial, even laughable: 'polluting' youth; trying to 'revive' the ANC by giving its official salute; singing ANC songs; discussing and possessing ANC literature; 'arranging a funeral under the auspices of the ANC'; and 'encouraging people to listen to radio broadcasts of the ANC in Tanzania'. But while they were never accused of actual acts of violence, the Twenty-Two – as the accused became known – also faced more serious charges: 'propagating the communist doctrine'; 'discussing sending people outside the country'; 'inspecting trains to find sabotage targets'; and 'devising means of obtaining explosives'. The gravamen of the charges was clear: the Twenty-Two were accused of a conspiracy, vaguely delineated and devoid of specificity, to overthrow the state. As the indictment read: 'The State alleges that the accused acted in concert and with a common purpose to re-establish and build up the ANC, knowing that its ultimate aim was the violent overthrow of the State.'

Winnie's lawyer, Joel Carlson, had learned of her arrest and detention under the Terrorism Act within hours.[8] Carlson was a tireless Johannesburg attorney who had acted in many of the higher-profile political cases of the previous few years. His services went beyond the purely legal: he arranged for a caretaker to deter looting and vandalism of the Mandelas' empty house, and for clothes to be delivered to Winnie. But as to her treatment in prison, Carlson was virtually powerless to offer her protection. Winnie's 'self-confidence brought out every vestige of hostility and hatred in the white wardresses', Carlson later wrote in his memoir No Neutral Ground (1977). For the first 200 days of their detention the five women of the Twenty-Two were not permitted a bath or shower, nor even provided sanitary products during menstruation. They were only able to wash properly after George Bizos, whom Carlson had retained as a member of their legal team, obtained a court order.

During her interrogations Winnie was repeatedly offered her freedom, and that of her husband, if she agreed publicly to urge black
South Africans to abandon the armed struggle. (Mandela himself had
received directly similar proposals from a state anxious to disencumber
itself of its most famous political prisoner, requiring him to retire from
political life as the price of his release: he rejected them all.) Winnie
was already in poor health, with a heart condition that led to frequent
palpitations and blackouts. How many in her position would have
succumbed to the terms held out by her interrogators? It says much
about her fortitude that she consistently refused them, even as
Swanepoel and his fellow interrogators ratcheted up their verbal abuse.
'You are going to be broken completely, you are shattered, you are a
finished woman . . . Now what is it going to be with you? Broken
bones or the statement we want?' Swanepoel screamed at her. 'You
know, people think Nelson is a great man, they think he is in prison
because he wanted to sacrifice for his people. If I had a wife like you,
I would do exactly what Nelson has done and go and seek protection
in prison. He ran away from you . . .' Prison guards took up the theme:
'You're still alive? We don't know if you will be alive tomorrow . . .
For God's sake leave us some inheritance when you pop it.'

It had quickly become clear which detainees had succumbed to
the intolerable pressure and agreed to turn against their comrades and
act as state witnesses at the forthcoming trial. Visits from their families
and special privileges marked them out. Carlson certainly did not
judge them.

> I had learned not to make any moral judgement about the reaction of
> people in prison. I had known over a hundred detainees and not one
> of them had managed to hold out completely. All of them had eventu-
> ally made statements to the security police. Even without physical
> torture, their assault on the mind eventually breaks all resistance.[9]

Delirious after days of sleep deprivation, Winnie finally confessed to
her role in the ANC, but she went no further. She did not implicate
any others.

The trial of the Twenty-Two, technically known as *The State v
Ndou*,[10] did not begin until December 1969, almost nine months after

their arrest, in the familiar surroundings of the Old Synagogue in Pretoria. Winnie, Accused Number Four, attended dressed resplendently in the ANC colours of green, black and yellow. Those dreadful nine months had not broken her defiance. When asked to plead, rather than simply utter the standard response of 'Not Guilty', she replied, 'I find it difficult to enter any plea because I regard myself as already having been found guilty.' But the judge on the bench – Mr Justice Bekker – was a lawyer of integrity and no state lackey.[11] Almost ten years previously he had been part of the three-judge tribunal that had acquitted Nelson Mandela and his co-accused at the Treason Trial, which had played out in the same court in which he was now sitting. 'I think you are wrong in that assumption. I will enter a plea of not guilty on your behalf,' he responded in a mild voice.

The witnesses called by the state to testify against the accused were a sad parade of the broken and the terrified. Most had been held in detention for months, subjected to the security police's usual tactics to secure co-operation. One witness, a twenty-four-year-old Englishman called Philip Golding, reluctantly told the court, in answer to defence advocate David Soggot's persistent cross-examination, that he had signed a statement only after he had been required to remain standing, without sleep, for over seventy-two hours. His hesitancy was understandable: the witness's interrogator and tormentor, Rooi Rus Swanepoel, was sitting close by the witness box, eyeballing him. Knowing that the decision whether or not to allow him to return home to England rested with the police, Golding could hardly bring himself to admit the treatment meted out to him. 'I believe I was assaulted in some way,' he finally conceded in a quiet, almost apologetic, voice. 'Yes I was punched a bit,' he stuttered, before adding that the interrogation had been 'physically, but not emotionally, painful'. Years later Carlson remembered in particular Swanepoel's eyes: 'I saw the essence of the man in his eyes: cold, oily and frightening. I had seen the evil of the man's soul and it made me shudder.' Even Winnie's younger sister, Nonyaniso Madikizela, was called as a witness by the prosecutor, the ubiquitous and dreary Henry Liebenberg (see Chapter 7). It was as if the state wanted to demonstrate the reach of its dominion: it could even turn families upon each other. Under cross-examination, her voice a whisper, she told of the threats she had received should she refuse to give evidence against her sister. 'They said "You are not going to leave this office until you make a statement."' When Liebenberg rose to object to such questions by defence counsel he was silenced by the judge. 'It may be irrelevant, but if these things happened I want to know about them.'

There were also displays of extraordinary courage by some of the prosecution witnesses. Shanti Naidoo simply refused to take the oath. She told the judge that her conscience prevented her from giving evidence against her friends. As she must have known, this stance would lead to her immediate imprisonment for contempt of court. Bekker gave her as light a sentence as he could: two months in prison. It was an act of mercy: Naidoo was now a prisoner in the regular prison system, the length of her sentence prescribed and her rights clearly demarcated, rather than a plaything of the security police. The case was adjourned for several weeks and Carlson informed the prosecutors that the defence would seek a subpoena from the judge requiring Nelson Mandela to be called as a defence witness. The thought of Mandela, already an internationally acclaimed figure, in the witness box was too much for the security police to bear. Carlson now experienced the rage of the state against him. Shots were fired and a petrol bomb was thrown at his Johannesburg home.

At the resumption of the trial on 16 February 1970, something unexpected happened. Into court, without prior warning, marched the attorney general of the Transvaal, Kenneth Moodie, now apparently leading the prosecution team. He told an astonished courtroom that the state was withdrawing all charges against the accused. The judge duly entered formal verdicts of not guilty. (George Bizos later explained that the prosecution was concerned that Bekker was giving defence counsel too much latitude to elicit from prosecution witnesses the grim circumstances of their detention, but other theories as to why the prosecution dropped the charges have also been put forward.)[12]

But this was far from the end of the ordeal for Winnie Mandela and her co-accused. Even as the Twenty-Two were struggling to comprehend the elation of their acquittal, the courtroom doors were being locked and armed security police were surrounding them. As they exited the dock they were all rearrested under the Terrorism Act and carted back to prison in blacked-out vans waiting outside.

The nightmare of solitary confinement without any defined end date recommenced.

The fact of Winnie's rearrest had another consequence. Once she had been formally charged with a criminal offence back in October 1969, she finally became legally entitled to see her attorney. That right ceased with her acquittal and rearrest. She was now, along with her co-accused, thrown back into the maw of the security police. A person detained under section 6 of the Terrorism Act for interrogation was held incommunicado: entirely isolated from contact of any kind with friends, family and lawyers. The trial before Bekker had demonstrated with horrifying clarity what interrogation actually meant in practice. The state witnesses, like the defendants, had been subjected to torture in order to obtain statements incriminating the Twenty-Two who were on trial. They were now thrown back into the same chasm they had occupied the year before.

It was at this moment that Sydney Kentridge found himself thrust centre-stage into the proceedings. The counsel from the aborted trial before Bekker, George Bizos and David Soggot, urgently sought a consultation with him. The subject of their discussions was novel: could an injunction be obtained against the minister of police to protect all the detainees from further torture and beatings? Kentridge agreed to clear his diary. While he saw the application as difficult, it was worth trying. Every minute counted: once new statements had been beaten out of the demoralised detainees by Swanepoel and his gang, the damage would have been done, and any injunction, even if it could be obtained, would by then be futile.

The defence needed to move very fast, but in the analogue age of 1970 the task of formalising written evidence to present before the court took time. Existing handwritten statements made by the Twenty-Two for Carlson some months earlier, recounting their experiences while in detention, had to be deciphered and typed up. What was vital was to put forward to the court evidence that there existed a reasonable apprehension that the Twenty-Two would again be subjected to assaults by the security police. For three days the defence lawyers worked around the clock, and in great secrecy, to get their paperwork ready. Carlson knew that his offices and telephone were bugged. There was a constant fear of police raids. If he needed to discuss matters with the legal team they would use the lift in the building in which his firm was located. Kentridge recalls discussions with Carlson as they walked around his garden, safe from electronic listening devices. A petition by fifteen applicants, all family members of the Twenty-Two, was filed on the Friday of the same week in which they had all been acquitted. It had to be family members who brought the application: the Twenty-Two were now lost to the world, uncontactable even by their lawyers in the prisons to which they had been returned. At eight o'clock on Friday morning, after two hours' sleep the previous night, Carlson served their petition, and the voluminous supporting evidence, on a bemused official at security headquarters in Pretoria.

As Kentridge arrived in court later that morning, accompanied by George Bizos and David Soggot, he was confronted by eight security policemen, who 'had come to stare at and intimidate those people who had dared to challenge them'.[13] The hearing commenced at 11 a.m. before a judge of a very different stamp to Bekker. Mr Justice J. K. Theron, 'a ruddy-faced man in his fifties with a shock of white hair',[14] was a state placeman with a reputation as a hanging judge.[15] Kentridge knew he would have an uphill struggle before such a man, but what followed far exceeded his greatest fears. It was to be a disgraceful exercise in studied judicial obtuseness.

The best advocacy simplifies rather than complicates. And the application Kentridge presented was simplicity itself. Here was copious evidence, obtained from the Twenty-Two themselves, that after their original detention under section 6 of the Terrorism Act in May 1969 they had been subjected to various forms of torture to extract forced confessions. Once the statements had been provided, the assaults ceased: they had served their purpose and so the Twenty-Two could be charged with the crimes they had apparently admitted. Now that they had been rearrested under the same Act, they were placed back in the same position in which they had been during the spring and summer of the year before. The court needed to urgently intervene to grant an injunction 'restraining the servants of the respondents from assaulting these detained persons in making them stand for prolonged periods or performing any act calculated to induce fear or prolonged discomfort or any act calculated to degrade them'. The language may have been legalistic but the purpose was clear. The minister should be ordered to take steps to ensure that the detainees were unmolested by Swanepoel and his interrogation team, the so-called 'sabotage squad'.

With such incendiary material an advocate might be tempted to overplay his hand. But Kentridge was emollient. He accepted that the minister had not had an opportunity to respond to the evidence served on his lawyers just hours beforehand. Yet this was a case of supreme urgency. The application could not be allowed to proceed according to the court's usual snail-like timescales, whereby weeks would pass before it came on to be heard. By then the harm feared, the prevention of which was the very purpose of the application, could well already have occurred. Who knew what was, even at that moment, going on in the interrogation rooms of Pretoria Central Prison? And what possible prejudice would the minister suffer by being subject to such an order on an interim basis pending a full hearing, even if – as might be expected – he were to strenuously deny the evidence which had been served? All the application sought to do was to ensure that no legal wrong was committed – something that a law-abiding police force surely could not reasonably object to.

Kentridge referred to the statement of one of the Twenty-Two, the trade unionist Rita Ndzanga:

> Now, it is not my intention to read to Your Lordship every one of these statements, but one can read them almost at random. Your Lordship will see that they are in the words of the persons themselves – I think a fairly typical statement is that on page 72 by Rita Ndzanga, in which she explains how she was taken to Compol [the security police headquarters in Pretoria] and there is a detailed account of her interrogation. And if Your Lordship looks at page 74, there are allegations of assault and kicking, and then at the bottom of page 74 she says – 'Major Swanepoel told me if I do not want to make a statement, I will stand on my feet until I decide to speak.' Then on page 75 – 'I was standing on my feet all the time, the man who slapped me was in this team. The interrogation continued, I was stiff and could not walk properly.' And then if Your Lordship goes on to page 77, she says how

she was hit and began to scream, and then in the second paragraph –
'The Security police produced three bricks and told me to take off my
shoes and stand on the bricks. I refused to stand on the bricks' and she
indicates what happened. She was pulled onto the bricks, she fell
down and hit a gas pipe, her hair was pulled and eventually, of course,
she made a statement.

Kentridge also referred to some of the other statements. The
evidence before the court told of beatings to knees, feet and genitals
with *sjamboks* (a heavy leather whip much favoured by the South
African police); of prolonged sleep deprivation ('I could not distinguish
day from night' said one of the Twenty-Two); of degradations such as
the forcing of one detainee to kill with his bare hands cockroaches that
infested the interrogation room, or another detainee denied access to a
lavatory eventually having to urinate into his trousers; of terrifying
threats ('I know how painful it is to break a woman, and I will do it
with you'); of hours of abuse ('kaffir, your life is worth nothing'). 'My
Lord, this material is really so revolting that it would be unpleasant to
read it out time and time again. But every one of these statements given
in the words of those persons themselves makes similar allegations.'
The hastily instructed counsel for the minister of police, D. J.
Curlewis SC, had been sitting in the row down from Kentridge. A
senior Pretoria advocate, he had boarded the *Winchester Castle* together
with Kentridge at Durban in 1946 to make the three-week journey
to Southampton and from there to, respectively, Cambridge and
Oxford to study law. But his time at Cambridge had not instilled in
Curlewis a liberal outlook: Kentridge remembers him as an ardent
racist with 'an aggressive right-wing intellect'. Curlewis now rose to
deliver an unfocused – though, as it would prove, effective – response.
It was a veritable wall of cod indignation – still a much used technique of advocacy that works all too often. Curlewis protested that
any injunction granted by the court would be wrongly perceived by
the world at large as a finding of culpability against the security police
– as if the court should be influenced by such considerations! He
objected to the absence of sworn affidavits from the Twenty-Two
themselves – but of course Carlson was unable to actually take instructions from his clients now that they were back in detention under the

Terrorism Act. The allegations of violence all dated back to the year before, well prior to the trial which had been heard by Bekker; so even if true, they were all historic and of no possible relevance to the present situation. What urgency, Curlewis asked, could really be shown? He complained of

> the blithe way in which it is set out in [Mr Carlson's affidavit, where it was said]: 'As a result of their rearrest in terms of the Terrorism Act they are again at the mercy of their interrogators . . .' A highly emotionally charged statement which seems to be completely out of place. But there is nothing to suggest that they are going to be reinterrogated.

However unsympathetic he may have been to the predicament of the Twenty-Two, Curlewis was doing his job as an advocate to present his client's case. Yet, knowing what in fact had happened to the Twenty-Two, and the brutalities to which they had been subjected, it is easy to feel real anger at the cavalier submissions he made, as if all that were at stake were competing interests in some dry contractual dispute. Straight-facedly, he complained how 'unfair' it would be for the police to be subject to the injunction sought, founded on 'a mass of hearsay, third-hand evidence, referring to a period of about nine months ago'. Given what everyone knew about the *modus operandi* of the security police, did Curlewis really believe what he was saying? Did, indeed, the judge believe it?

In his reply Kentridge did not allow indignation to cloud clarity of submission:

> My Lord, with regard to the date of the assaults, my Learned Friend is right. But with great respect, he has missed the significance of it. These people were detained under the Terrorism Act in May 1969. My Learned Friend is absolutely right in saying that the assaults which they allege took place shortly after their detention and that thereafter, right until they came to trial in December 1969, the assaults were not repeated. But the reason is this, what they all say is this, that when they were detained they were then assaulted in order to induce them to make a statement. By reason of the assault they all made statements, and then of course, the assaults ceased.

Now, that is exactly the apprehension here. They have now been detained again under section 6, which provides specifically for detention for interrogation. In other words, they are now going to be interrogated again.

There was no answer to this straightforward logic. But Theron feigned incomprehension. Why had no application for injunction been made during the trial before Bekker? Kentridge wearily explained that by that stage they had stood in no further danger. The Twenty-Two had access to their attorney; they were coming to court every day; they were not being interrogated. But since their rearrest everything had changed.

If there is any point in bringing an application it must surely be brought now as a matter of urgency. If they are assaulted and they make a statement, well then, that will be the end of it. What we want to stop is the defendants being assaulted in order to make another statement . . . I do submit that if one is going to say that these people cannot get even interim relief [i.e. a temporary injunction at this very early stage] unless they produce proper affidavits and adhere to the rules of Court, then the respondents are saying they have no rights in a Court of law . . .

Curlewis leapt up in a lather of confected rage: 'This is ridiculous. I must object to these comments made about the respondents. We don't take that attitude. You know that, My Lord. It is ridiculous for my Learned Friend to make that sort of comment.'
Kentridge was not to be deflected:

That is what it amounts to, My Lord . . . if this relief is not granted it would mean, in effect, that persons in this situation were helpless; they are at the mercy of their interrogators because if this application, on this evidence, does not qualify for interim relief, it is impossible to conceive of any circumstances in which interim relief could be granted.

The hearing ended and the judge said he would deliver his decision the next Monday. But no one had any hopes that Theron would do the right thing. When he came to read out his judgment he ruled that no urgency had been shown and that the application for an injunction should be heard in the 'normal' way, at some point in May or June, and so many months hence. Legal process and harsh reality had yet again parted company. 'An applicant desiring an injunction, or any temporary relief in this form, is required to make out a case and not leave it to speculation as to whether the allegations are or are not true,' the judge simpered, as if the accounts of Swanepoel's cruelties might be simple inventions. It is impossible to interpret his judgment as given in good faith. Here was an Afrikaner judge blatantly placing loyalty to the apartheid state above fealty to his judicial oath. The court had compelling evidence laid before it of the practices of Swanepoel and his associates, and still the judge effectively washed his hands of the Twenty-Two, condemning them to legal oblivion. His ruling was greeted with howls of anguish by legal commentators.[16]

Yet it may be that the mere fact of the application being made had the desired effect of restraining Swanepoel and his goons. Kentridge recalls Joel Carlson as not perhaps the most legally adept of attorneys, but one who more than made up for that by his remarkable assiduousness. Carlson's commitment to his clients was total and he had, in those frenetic days spent preparing the evidence to be presented to Theron, found time to brief the press about the application that Kentridge was to present that Friday. The result was that the hearing before Theron was reported internationally, the *New York Times* devoting four columns to the case. If the South African court had decided to withhold its protection from the Twenty-Two, at least the knowledge that the rest of the world was watching provided some measure of comfort in its place.

Still, the months that followed were a time of renewed misery for Winnie Mandela, who was, like her co-accused, cast back into the limbo of solitary confinement. She contemplated suicide by hoarding her medication and overdosing. She chose instead deliberately to aggravate her heart condition by under-eating, in an attempt to pressure the authorities to hurry up and bring the second trial on sooner. Throughout May, June and July 1970 Winnie was in and out of the prison hospital. She was by no means a docile patient: she frequently

On Muizenberg Beach, Cape Town, 1933.
Back row: May and Morris Kentridge and Nellie, the family nanny.
Front row: Arnold Kentridge and the eleven-year-old Sydney.

The young sergeant. Kentridge in
South African Air Force uniform, *c.*1943.

Sydney (in cricket whites) and
Felicia with their first child,
Catherine, 1954.

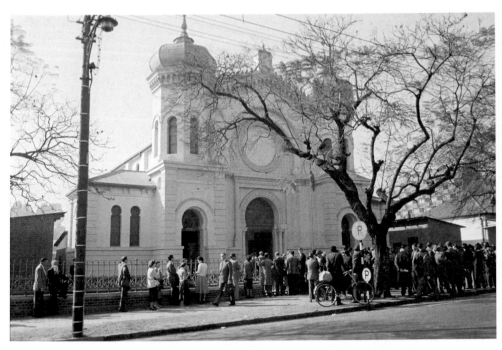

Crowds gather outside the Old Synagogue, Pretoria, in 1958.
It would be the location of many of Kentridge's most important cases.

Kentridge's copy of the indictment in the Treason
Trial, bearing the date 22 November 1958.
Accused Number Six is Nelson Mandela.

William Papas's drawing of the courtroom
in the Old Synagogue, 1958, for the *Observer*.
Kentridge, legal textbooks in front of him, is
depicted on the right.

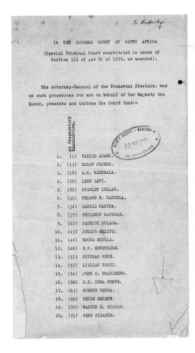

IN THE SUPREME COURT OF SOUTH AFRICA

(Special Criminal Court constituted in terms of
Section 112 of Act 56 of 1955, as amended).

The Attorney-General of the Transvaal Province, who
as such prosecutes for and on behalf of Her Majesty the
Queen, presents and informs the Court that:-

		At Preparatory Examination.
1.	(1)	FARIED ADAMS.
2.	(13)	HELEN JOSEPH.
3.	(18)	A.M. KATHRADA.
4.	(20)	LEON LEVY.
5.	(22)	STANLEY LOLLAN.
6.	(32)	NELSON R. MANDELA.
7.	(34)	LESLIE MASINA.
8.	(37)	PHILEMON MATHOLE.
9.	(42)	PATRICK MOLAOA.
10.	(43)	JOSEPH MOLIFE.
11.	(44)	MOOSA MOOLLA.
12.	(46)	E.P. MORETSELE.
13.	(51)	PHINEAS NENE.
14.	(52)	LILLIAN NGOYI.
15.	(54)	JOHN N. NKADIMENG.
16.	(56)	P.P. DUMA NOKWE.
17.	(63)	ROBERT RESHA.
18.	(66)	PETER SELEPE.
19.	(70)	WALTER M. SISULU.
20.	(71)	GERT SIBANDE.

Kentridge makes a point
in conversation with Chief
Albert Luthuli outside the
Old Synagogue, 1960.

An illicit photograph taken from the
public gallery of the Old Synagogue,
during the Treason Trial, early 1961.
Kentridge and Bram Fischer are
distinctly visible.

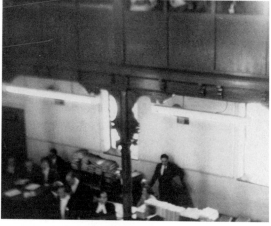

Laughter in the face of
oppression. Helen Joseph,
Nelson Mandela and
other accused during the
Treason Trial.

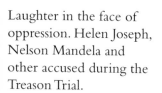

Ian Berry captures history on 21 March 1960.
Protestors running for their lives as the
Sharpeville massacre unfolds.

Nelson Mandela burns his passbook in
protest against the Sharpeville massacre,
26 March 1960. A state of emergency
was declared four days later.

'A dividing line in history.' The funeral of
the victims of the Sharpeville massacre.

The leader and his junior. Sydney and Felicia Kentridge with Bram Fischer (left), late 1950s.

The 'Scarlet Pimpernel' finally caught. A disguised Bram Fischer is arrested on 11 November 1965 and led into custody by 'Rooi Rus' Swanepoel, most notorious of all the security police.

A heavy weight of responsibility. Kentridge, now a senior counsel, and his junior George Bizos, during Bram Fischer's trial, 1966.

'When I married him, I married the struggle, the liberation of my people.' Winnie Mandela outside the Palace of Justice, Pretoria, December 1963, during the Rivonia Trial.

Kentridge (right), in relentless mood, walking to the Old Synagogue during the trial of Winnie Mandela and her co-accused, August 1970.

After 491 days of incarceration, Winnie Mandela enjoys the taste of freedom, 20 September 1970. The *Rand Daily Mail* recorded 'scenes of appreciation towards Mr Kentridge'.

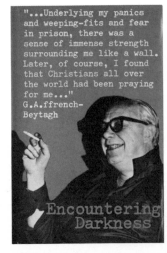

"...Underlying my panics and weeping-fits and fear in prison, there was a sense of immense strength surrounding me like a wall. Later, of course, I found that Christians all over the world had been praying for me..." G.A.ffrench-Beytagh

Encountering Darkness

'A truly saintly man despite his penchant for gin, whisky and cigarettes.' Gonville ffrench-Beytagh publishes his autobiography from the safety of England, 1973.

Kentridge organises his papers at the start of the Biko Inquest, November 1977. George Bizos, ever the helpful junior, looks on.

Steve Biko's brother, wife, sister and mother listen intently to the evidence during the inquest.

'Are these leg irons a necessary part of your equipment?' Captain Daantje Siebert (left) and Major Harold Snyman prepare to be cross-examined by Kentridge during the Biko Inquest.

Steve Biko. According to the journalist Donald Woods, he was 'the greatest man I ever had the privilege to know ... He walked tall in all things, without deference or apology.'

Aged eighty-eight, Sir Sydney Kentridge about to deliver the Steve Biko Memorial Lecture at the University of Cape Town, 2011.

Sydney and Felicia, 2006.

shouted at her guards and at a prison psychiatrist, a Dr Morgan. When Morgan asked her if she ever 'heard God's voice sometimes telling you to lead your people', Winnie replied: 'I deeply resent the indirect insult on my national pride and my husband's. Would you ask Vorster's [the prime minister's] wife the same question?' When asked the preposterous question whether she felt depressed, Winnie responded angrily: 'Of course I am . . . how else can I be when I am subjected to the brutal conditions we have been subjected to for a whole year?' Not until June – more than a year after she had been detained – was Winnie's sister allowed to visit her in jail. On 14 June, her twelfth wedding anniversary, she recalled, 'I lay on my back gasping for breath with a temperature of 103.'

While the Twenty-Two remained incarcerated, Carlson was subjected to further intimidation and worse. Bullets were fired at his offices, apparently from a government building across the road. A parcel bomb concealed in a hollowed-out volume of the works of Mao Tse-tung (presumably the security services' idea of a joke) was sent to him. Fortunately it failed to explode. It was put about by government sources that Carlson was himself the author of these attacks, motivated by a desire to generate publicity. And then, on the morning of 18 June 1970, the news he was waiting for came: his clients had been charged again and there was to be a hearing later that day. When he hurried over to the Old Synagogue, Carlson saw only eighteen of the Twenty-Two in its dock. Once again the prosecution took the defence by surprise. Prosecutor Dennis Rothwell explained that Winnie was in hospital and three other detainees, finally broken by the mental torment of solitary confinement, had now become state witnesses. Even more mysteriously, Rothwell said that a new defendant was on his way to join the remaining eighteen in the dock. It was the first time since February that Carlson had actually seen his clients. They confirmed that, whatever the privations they had experienced, they had at least not been tortured. To that extent, Kentridge's application to Theron in February had been successful.

That new defendant turned out to be an uMkhonto we Sizwe bomb maker, Benjamin Ramotse, who was entirely unconnected to Winnie Mandela and her co-accused. Almost a decade earlier, in December 1961, Ramotse had planted a bomb which had exploded prematurely, killing a fellow bomb maker, Petrus Molefe, and seriously injuring Ramotse himself. Ramotse had promptly fled South Africa, but in May 1968 he had been seized in Botswana by Rhodesian police, who then illegally rendered him to Salisbury, the Rhodesian capital (now Harare, capital of Zimbabwe). There Ramotse was tortured before being handed over to Swanepoel, who brought him back to Johannesburg. He had now endured over 700 days of solitary confinement. As so often, the apartheid state was doing all it could to link peaceful political activists and trade unionists with violent freedom fighters, and to manufacture guilt by association. Winnie Mandela herself later insisted that the Twenty-Two had 'nothing to do with' Ramotse. 'Ramotse did not for a moment deny the part he played until his capture and arrest,' wrote Carlson, 'but it was clearly ridiculous to hold the other accused guilty with him. Many of the 22 had never heard of him and none of them knew what he had been doing for the last eight or nine years.'[17]

A few weeks later a new fifty-eight-page indictment, in which Ramotse had replaced Samson Ndou as Accused Number One, was handed to Carlson. The accused now faced charges 'of participating in terroristic activities' under the Terrorism Act. The maximum sentence under the Suppression of Communism Act was ten years in prison, whereas the Terrorism Act imposed a minimum five years' imprisonment and a maximum of death. Yet, apart from the substitution of 'Terrorism' for 'Communism', the allegations against the remaining members of the original Twenty-Two were essentially the same. However, twelve new allegations, aired in court by the prosecution during the earlier trial but not included in the original indictment, were now tacked on.

Wading through the new indictment, the defence team, again led by Kentridge, could see the cynical game being played by the state. It was simply bringing forward the same prosecution it had abandoned before Bekker, now dressed up as a series of new offences, in the hope of getting an easier ride before a more compliant judge. The lawyers posed themselves an intriguing question: could they stop this prosecution once and for all before it ever got to a full trial? South African law recognised an ancient common law principle developed by the English courts and known by its Norman French designation as *autrefois acquit*. In essence it held that where a person had been acquitted of one offence, they could not be charged again where the alleged facts founding the second prosecution were materially the same as those which had founded the first, even if the new prosecution was formally presented as constituting a different offence. The underlying principles were that a person should not be harassed twice in respect of the same underlying facts; nor should they be placed in double jeopardy. An acquittal should be final in relation to the underlying facts alleged.

Kentridge and George Bizos were now joined by a new advocate: Michael Kuper, only twenty-three years old and a recent recruit to Kentridge's Johannesburg chambers.[18] He recalls this as his first significant case, requiring a huge expenditure of effort.[19] The two indictments had to be subjected to meticulous analysis to demonstrate that this was indeed just an example of the state rerunning its first, abandoned, prosecution under a different guise. Elaborate charts were drawn up to show how the second indictment tracked the first. Kuper remembers Kentridge as an exacting taskmaster, demanding absolute precision of analysis. But as the process continued so Kentridge's mood lightened. In his memoirs George Bizos described a meeting in Kentridge's room in his chambers one Saturday morning:

> Sydney paced up and down, wringing his hands, and trying hard to contain his excitement. The proposition was unanswerable, he declared . . . I questioned Sydney's optimism . . . But I had never heard Sydney so confident. It didn't matter who heard the case, the argument was unanswerable.[20]

★

When the second trial was reconvened in Pretoria in late August 1970 there was yet another judge presiding. Mr Justice Gerrit Viljoen was an Afrikaner who had recently achieved notoriety by sentencing four white men convicted of raping a black woman to a nominal fine.[21] Carlson entered court with anxiety gnawing at the pit of his stomach; if Kentridge had similar feelings, he did not show them. He greeted prosecutor Liebenberg, who had been retained by the state to defend the new indictment. For Kentridge, however much the opposing advocate was identified with the interests of the government, courtroom civility had to be maintained.

The second trial attracted even more international attention than the first. Representatives from foreign embassies and human rights groups were in abundance. Winnie had recovered and was back in court, joining her co-accused in the dock. Her prison experiences had somehow not diminished her beauty, which radiated through the courtroom. The journalist from the *Washington Post*, just one of many from across the world, was so enamoured that he composed a laud-atory sonnet, which started doing the rounds. A copy found its way to Kentridge; but he was not a man for levity in the tense minutes before the start of a court day, and cast it aside. Kuper remembers the air of total concentration that enveloped Kentridge. It was as though all external influences had been banished from his mind. The case had become everything. Standing to make his submissions, the advocate would hold his left arm tense behind his back, hand clenched, as if channelling the stress of litigation through it.

Kentridge had also now been instructed on behalf of Benjamin Ramotse, the new Accused Number One. Unlike the Twenty-Two (now the reduced Nineteen), Ramotse had not previously been pros-ecuted and anyway admitted the offences with which he was charged. The only hope of achieving an acquittal was founded on an argument that his arrest – or, as the defence would contend, his kidnapping – and rendition to South Africa had been illegal as a matter of inter-national law because, as Kentridge put it, 'one state may not exercise police powers on the territory of another state'; and therefore the South African court should not exercise jurisdiction over Ramotse. Swanepoel gave evidence concerning the circumstances of the arrest. He angrily denied Kentridge's suggestion that Ramotse had been tortured by him, but few in court believed it.

Kentridge led the judge through a wide-ranging body of case law, encompassing English, American and international authority. The most immediately relevant was the prosecution in Jerusalem a few years earlier of the Nazi war criminal Adolf Eichmann. Eichmann had challenged the jurisdiction of the Israeli court on the basis that he had been illegally arrested and brought from Argentina to Israel by Israeli state operatives.[22] It was an uncomfortable but close analogy. Crucially, however, the Israeli court only accepted jurisdiction over Eichmann because Argentina had agreed retrospectively to waive the breach of international law which Eichmann's abduction had involved. No such approval of the violation of its territory had been forthcoming from the Botswanan government. Kentridge wrapped up his submissions on this subject:

> I would ask Your Lordship to consider this as a matter of important general principle; I would ask Your Lordship to consider whether it is right that if there has been a breach of International Law, our Courts – which observe international comity – should appear to condone it by exercising jurisdiction over a person who has been brought before it in breach of International Law.

It sounded persuasive, but in truth the law of South Africa said something different: its judges had consistently held that, for the purposes of jurisdiction, once a person was upon South African soil the circumstances in which they had arrived there were irrelevant. Kentridge knew that Benjamin Ramotse's hopes of evading conviction were slender.[23]

Kentridge now turned to the very different position of the other nineteen defendants, who had been prosecuted the year before and acquitted by Bekker. Here he was on much stronger ground. 'Kentridge spent the next three days carefully and methodically spelling out to the judge, word for word, all the hundreds of allegations made against each of the nineteen defendants,' recalled Carlson, sitting behind his advocate in the Old Synagogue.

> The proceedings dragged on, hour after hour, only lightened occasionally by some of Kentridge's ironic comments: 'It is inconceivable, My Lord, that by merely rearranging the sequences of allegations as they applied to the defendants numbered 2 to 9 in the first indictment, and having them now apply from 9 to 2 in the second indictment, the prosecutor hoped to deceive the court and the defence, for such a deception would be too patently obvious and could not even have entered the prosecutor's mind.'[24]

It was, of course, only too conceivable that such tactics could be employed, and Liebenberg shifted uncomfortably in his seat as

Kentridge's sarcasm hit home. This was advocacy that needed to be slowly, methodically played out: the very process of comparing the two lengthy indictments paragraph by paragraph, line by line, created its own rhetorical heft. 'I wasn't going to rush anything; the judge had to realise that he had no escape from the logic of the defendants' case,' recalled Kentridge. Layer upon layer of submissions built up as Kentridge painstakingly constructed a vast variorum of the accusations:

> Now, as Your Lordship recalls, in the first indictment the classes of activity carried on by the accused are also set out, and there it is said right in the forefront, that what the accused did was to establish 'groups and committees within the ANC', exactly as is said in this second indictment, excepting that here the prosecutor chooses to use the phrase 'committees or branches' instead of 'groups and committees'. Then sub-para (2) of the first indictment – it is said that the accused 'did administer and/or take the oath of the said organisation;' whereas in the present indictment the term is 'administering the ANC oath to the said members'.
>
> In sub-para (3) of the first indictment the activity was that they 'did recruit members or encourage one another to recruit members for the said organisation;' here it is 'recruiting and encouraging the recruitment of members of the said African National Congress.'
>
> My Lord, these alterations in the precise language have no significance. If they were intentional, they would be completely hopeless as devices for avoiding the plea of *autrefois acquit*, but I don't *for a moment* believe that these changes were adopted with that end in view.

The words 'for a moment' were laden with sardonic emphasis: he meant, of course, the exact opposite. And so it went on; Kentridge laid bare the cynicism of the state's attempt to prosecute anew, under the carapace of a different statute, the very same case as the one it had abandoned seven months earlier.

> My Lord, it is said that a reviewer of books who was dealing with a novel by an author who tended to repeat himself, wrote that it was simply a case of the old characters and the old incidents under new

names. My Lord, these are the old characters and the old incidents under the same name.

As Michael Kuper later recalled, ruminating on the different experience of having Kentridge as an opponent rather than a leader:

> Sydney would take – say – five points and he would deal with the first point and you would listen to him and you would say, hell, that's a good point. Can the other side survive that point? And then Sydney would say, 'but that's just the first point', then would come the second. But of course that's just the second, and so forth. So by the end you are actually, certainly when you were against him, you were screaming internally, stop it, stop it, and he would just go on remorselessly.[25]

Even the judge seemed to be experiencing this reaction; as the inexorable dismantling of the prosecution case entered its third day, as if a man gasping for air, he invited Kentridge to dispense with further comparison. Everyone knew what that meant. It was as if he were saying to Kentridge: yes, I understand your point and it is obviously right: you need not proceed any further.

Liebenberg stood up to try to defend his new indictment. But it was a feeble effort. He could stutter out a few minor differences between the indictments. Winnie Mandela caught the advocate with exactitude in a letter she wrote to her husband from prison: 'I watched [a man] in billowing academic gowns, an achievement I would have given my whole life for, stooping so low in court that I thought he needs a ladder to look at the back of a worm, so narrow minded that if he fell on a pin with his face the pin would pierce both eyes.'[26]

After several days of legal argument Viljoen adjourned. He would give judgment on 14 September. That day the lawyers came back to the Old Synagogue, the accused were brought back into the dock, and the public gallery on the first floor, looking down on the proceedings below, was packed with their supporters. Viljoen entered court and took his seat. He explained that he would not read out his full judgment but would save time by only stating his conclusion on each of the two arguments presented by Kentridge three weeks earlier. Quietly and without emotion, he first ruled on Ramotse's application: 'I have, therefore, concluded that his seizure was lawful and his trial should proceed.' This was hardly unexpected; Ramotse shrugged his shoulders from the dock. Viljoen turned to the *autrefois acquit* plea. Again, he only read out the last sentence of his judgment: 'I have, therefore, come to the conclusion that the plea taken on their behalf is a proper one and they are acquitted. All nineteen for whom the plea succeeds may go.' His written judgment, published soon afterwards, was damning: the prosecution of the Nineteen had been 'oppressive, vexatious and an abuse of the process of the court'.

The outcome of this second trial was even more astonishing than that of the first. As Viljoen left court, Carlson looked at George Bizos and saw that 'his mouth was open, his face was white, and he registered stunned amazement at our success'. Bizos recalled Kentridge, usually so composed in court, shouting at the security police 'Let them Go! Let them Go!', as if he feared that any delay might lead to further arrests and detentions. Swanepoel bowled up to Kentridge and thrust out his hand, as if to say 'it was a fair fight well won and well lost'. Kentridge reluctantly took it. The fight had, of course, been no such thing. Throughout his career Kentridge found himself cross-examining Swanepoel – described by R. W. Johnson after his death in 1998 as 'South Africa's most notorious torturer' – on a number of occasions, challenging his veracity and the abuse he subjected detainees to. (Any doubt as to the insincerity of the security policeman's show of magnanimity in defeat on this occasion would have been finally quashed a few years later, when Kentridge's son William was prosecuted for attending a demonstration in Johannesburg. The state's principal witness was Rooi Rus himself, who entered the witness box to swear to William's leadership of the demonstration. It was only the fact that a press photographer happened to have captured the occasion that saved William from conviction. The magistrate was reluctantly forced to acquit in the face of incontrovertible evidence that Swanepoel had perjured himself. There was no proffering of the hand that time.)

Michael Kuper remembers pandemonium in the courtroom as a great sea of supporters, shouting excitedly, descended the stairs from the public gallery to mob the Nineteen. The *Rand Daily Mail* stolidly recorded 'scenes of appreciation towards Mr Kentridge'. But there was a poignant moment amid the excitement. Ramotse's wife, confused by the judge's words, approached Joel Carlson. 'Is my husband free to go?' she asked quietly. Carlson, who was so devoted to the welfare of his clients, turned away, unable to provide the answer she hoped for. She did not need to repeat the question: as the Nineteen left the dock, to be engulfed in the jubilation of the crowds, Ramotse was dragged off to an iron cage behind the courtroom.

On the street outside the Old Synagogue there were 'cries and tears of joy and high-pitched laughter, shouts of recognition as friends and relatives found their loved ones and congratulated them'.[27] One of the accused lifted a small child high above his head and shouted 'my baby, my baby'. After nearly a year and a half in prison the Nineteen were experiencing the delight of freedom and reunion. Yet even this moment of elation could not go unmolested by the security police. Unable to rearrest them under the Terrorism Act, a grim-faced police captain toting a Sten gun warned the crowd that they were an 'illegal gathering' and ordered them to disperse. A Black Maria pulled out into the road. As Kuper and Kentridge left court they saw Benjamin Ramotse clutching the bars at the window of the van as it drove past his wife and son mournfully standing on the pavement, hoping for a last glimpse of him as he returned to prison. That image has remained imprinted on Kuper's memory ever since. 'He shook the bars with such ferocity that the whole vehicle seemed to tremble. And he shouted out "Amandla, my son, Amandla!"'[28]

Kentridge's victory again made news around the world. *The Times* of London's leader pulled no punches:

The acquittal of 19 Africans in the political trial in Pretoria yesterday was understandably greeted with rejoicing outside the Supreme Court. It is greatly to be hoped that the men and women freed yesterday will not be arrested again, as they were earlier this year after acquittal on charges which the court found had 'substantial identity' with the later charges under the Terrorism Act. The Act provides a brutal instrument of repression that has been attacked even within South Africa, and is detested by international lawyers . . . An even greater danger lies in the point made by Mrs Winnie Mandela, perhaps the best known of the accused, who said that even as she went free, she did not know when she might be detained again . . . the judge in ruling for acquittal invoked considerations of fairness and justice. It is difficult to believe that even this second acquittal can remove the history of unfairness and injustice implicit in the conditions under which the accused were arrested and held. The arrests were made in a series of raids which began nearly two years ago, and the prisoners have been held since, mostly in solitary confinement. Several of them have made sworn statements of torture used against them, and by right of South African law they were held without access to their families or lawyers . . . The Africans who were acquitted yesterday are only a handful of those who have suffered under the system of arrest without safeguards and prolonged, arduous detention. The South African Government should take this opportunity of reviewing the whole apparatus of cat and mouse imprisonment and interrogation.[29]

Similarly, the New York Times warned that 'In Prime Minister Vorster's country, however, not even a second acquittal ensures that the Africans will long be free. The courts have spoken, but the Government still could put the nineteen under house arrest by administrative action and thus deprive them of the chance to earn a living.'[30] Sure enough, Winnie Mandela's taste of freedom was brief. 'The security police now exacted their punishment for our victories in the courts,' noted Carlson. Two weeks after leaving the dock in the Old Synagogue, all nineteen were served with five-year banning orders preventing each from leaving home between 6 p.m. and 6 a.m. on weekdays and 2 p.m. to 6 a.m. on weekends and holidays, receiving any visitors, engaging in 'social intercourse' or meeting with more than one person at a time. The apartheid state thumbed its nose at the world.

They were not alone in feeling the full force of the state's revenge. Joel Carlson's passionate devotion to his clients' cause had won him powerful enemies. The campaign of intimidation and harassment intensified. His employees and friends were also targeted. Yet what affected Carlson most of all was the nagging sense that for him to go on working within the South African legal system was somehow to lend it a veneer of integrity. That moral dilemma tormented many liberal lawyers, Kentridge included. For Carlson, the painful answer was clear: he should leave the country for good and find a new home. Although he had been deprived of his South African passport by the government, both his and his wife's parents were British-born, so they were entitled to British citizenship. A timely offer of a job at a New York university arrived and Carlson moved, amid great secrecy, to obtain a British passport. He flew to London, renouncing his South African citizenship as he did so, soon followed by his wife and children. Carlson spent the next twenty years as an assistant district attorney in the borough of Queens. Like so many exiles, he did not see South Africa again until after the fall of apartheid. When he died in New York in 2001, obituaries told of a man who had sacrificed much for the cause of freedom.

This is not to say that the acquittal of the Nineteen was a thing writ in water.[31] Had Kentridge's argument failed, a full trial would have followed, with guilty verdicts and – for those who escaped the death penalty – very long prison sentences the likely outcome. Beyond its disastrous consequences for the accused and their families, that would have been a further demoralising blow for the ANC and the liberation movement. As it was, the case entered the folklore of the struggle against the apartheid state. Avoiding protracted incarceration, Winnie remained – to the fury of the authorities – a beacon of hope and a rallying point for the resistance throughout the 1970s and 1980s.

Still, her 491 days in prison, most of them spent in solitary confinement, had taken a terrible toll. Carlson said that she 'wavered between sanity and insanity'. Helen Suzman observed that the experience turned Winnie 'from a warm-hearted person into a mad creature'.[32] Who could blame her for emerging from prison a changed person? The years after her release offered no respite. She was subjected to successive banning orders curtailing her freedom so harshly that her life continued as a form of perpetual house imprisonment, overlaid with the knowledge that she was under constant surveillance, the authorities waiting to pounce at the slightest infraction.

Winnie managed to obtain a relaxation of her banning order to allow a visit to Robben Island in November 1970 – the first time she had seen Nelson in almost two years. They were permitted just thirty minutes together. After returning from her strenuous day trip (she was not even allowed to stay in Cape Town overnight), Winnie suffered a minor heart attack. At home in Orlando, she was plagued by vexatious prosecutions and violent attacks. In 1971 she was jailed for twelve months, suspended for three years, for breaching the terms of her banning order by talking to her brother-in-law, who had called at her house to collect a shopping list. Over the next few years intruders ransacked the house, a gunman was found in her yard, a petrol bomb was thrown through a window, and her car windows were smashed. In May 1974 three men broke in, poisoned her Alsatian guard dog and tried to strangle her as she lay in bed. Nelson wrote to the minister of justice asking for his wife to be issued with a passport and a firearms permit 'for the purpose of self-defence'. Both requests were predictably refused.

Even as the prosecutions and periods of incarceration mounted up, Winnie Mandela's ascent to the status of 'mother of the nation' continued. Her suffering, and her refusal to be bowed by it, sanctified her. Kentridge, who acted for her on some of her later prosecutions, recalled that after one hearing a chauffeur-driven car was waiting for her as she left court: 'There was a crowd of children who ran after the car as it drove away. They all wanted to touch the car carrying Mrs Mandela. It was as if it was sacred.'

After the Soweto uprising in 1976, when black students in the townships took to the streets in revolt against the imposition of Afrikaans in schools as a mandatory language of education, Winnie was detained without trial for four months. On her release, under the terms of a new banning order, she was banished from her home in Orlando to a black township outside a small, dusty town in the Orange Free State called Brandfort, 200 miles away. Winnie had never heard of the godforsaken place, knew no one there, and could not speak the local language. Situated in the very heart of Afrikanerdom, it was where former Prime Minister Hendrik Verwoerd had spent part of his childhood. The malicious symbolism was obvious. It would be her Siberia for seven years.

The emptiness of unbearable loneliness now took its place alongside the intrusion of constant police surveillance. Winnie continued to be harried by prosecutions for trivial infringements of her banning order. Once, while she was casually talking to a neighbour, a man approached and offered to sell her a chicken. Forbidden to meet more than one person at a time, Winnie was charged with illegally attending a 'gathering'. But she had hardened. She wrote of herself then: 'I have ceased a long time ago to exist as an individual . . . My private self doesn't exist.'[33] A small band of supporters loyally made the long journey to Brandfort to deliver the necessities, and sometimes the small luxuries, that could make life more tolerable. The former Treason Trialist and veteran activist Helen Joseph (by now in her seventies) and Barbara Waite, wife of the cricketer Johnny Waite, made the trip together in September 1977. The moment Winnie, delighted with the balm of human company, embraced her visitors, she breached the terms of her banning order. A snooping police office promptly emerged from nearby bushes and required the two white women to follow him to the police station to make statements. Helen Joseph had decades of experience sparring with the authorities; but Barbara Waite, a nurse and a devout Christian, had never previously had any brush with the law. Both women refused to make statements against their friend. Barbara Waite, whose faith made dissembling impossible, knew that to do so would be to incriminate Winnie in a breach of her banning order. She and Helen Joseph were subpoenaed to appear at court. They again refused to speak against Winnie and the court sentenced Mrs Waite to a year in prison. She explained: 'I didn't look for this situation. I was suddenly faced with it. Everyone comes to a crisis when they are living in an evil society and I believe apartheid is evil.' Kentridge was retained by Barbara Waite to argue her appeal against sentence and in spring 1978 succeeded in having it reduced to two months.[34] That reduction meant a lot to Mrs Waite. The case also marked Kentridge. He recalls his disgust at the treatment meted out to Barbara Waite, a private woman dedicated to her caring work and her faith, enmeshed in the bitter madness of apartheid and the unbearable choices it forced upon decent people. It would in part inspire his own departure from South Africa.

By 1985 Winnie's exile in Brandfort had lasted for seven years. It was by then clear that the state's endeavour to isolate and silence her had proved as futile as its incarceration of her husband on Robben Island.

During those years her international standing had reached new heights, as had her resilience. She became increasingly willing to flout the restrictions placed upon her and defy the authorities to react. She would make a point of entering whites-only shops in Brandfort. If challenged she would shout abuse at the shopkeepers – they were 'white dogs' or 'pigs' – while prim Afrikaner housewives scattered in panic.[35] The celebrated South African writer J. M. Coetzee noted at the time that 'persecution, far from breaking Mrs. Mandela, as it has undoubtedly been intended to do, has turned her into a formidable and far from temperate antagonist (from one tussle with her a police-man emerged with a broken neck)'.[36] In August 1985, while she was undergoing medical treatment in Johannesburg, her house (she always described it as a prison cell) in Brandfort was burned out in an arson attack. This was Winnie's cue to return to her home in Orlando, in overt breach of her banning order. After repairs had been completed to the Brandfort house the security police required her to go back to it. She refused and the stage was set for another stand-off. Under massive international pressure, and aware of her domestic standing, the state partially buckled. In December it replaced the banning order confining her to Brandfort with one which permitted her to live wherever she wished – with one exception. Winnie was forbidden to live in, or enter, the magisterial district of Johannesburg and Roodepoort, where Orlando was located. The perverse – and, of course, intended – effect was that she was now at liberty to reside anywhere except in her own home.

The new banning order had been issued under section 19 of the Internal Security Act 1982 by the minister of law and order, Louis le Grange. This section, which replicated similar legislation in place since almost the dawn of the apartheid era, allowed the minister to serve a notice on any person who 'engages in activities which endanger or are calculated to endanger the security of the State or the maintenance of law and order', preventing that person 'from being within or absenting himself from . . . any place or area specified in the notice . . . or communicating with any person or category of persons specified in the notice or receiving any visitor or performing any act so specified'. This breathtakingly wide power was a key element of the apparatus of the police state which South Africa had become under the Nationalist government, permitting the executive to crush the personal and working life of anyone actively opposing the system, without the need to show that a crime had been committed. There was one token qualification to the minister's otherwise untrammelled ability, at will, to turn a home into a prison: section 25 of the Act required him to set out 'the reasons for such notice' and gave its subject the right to make representations (to the minister himself) as to the terms of the order. But the notice served on Winnie merely quoted the wording of section 19, stating that the minister 'being satisfied' that Mrs Mandela was a danger to the state, she was forbidden to be within the district of Johannesburg.

Winnie's response to the new order was twofold. First, she ignored it, remaining in Orlando – indeed flaunting her presence there – and continuing her policy of daring the state to move against her. When she was eventually arrested, 'kicking and screaming', by twenty policemen armed with shotguns and tear gas launchers, international opprobrium followed. On her release, Antigone-like, she simply returned. Second, she brought urgent legal proceedings challenging the order's legality. It was now that Kentridge undertook his final case for Winnie. The attack was straightforward: in order to make meaningful representations about the terms of a banning order, a person had to know the reasons underlying the decision to issue it; but the minister had given no reasons, just his conclusions. The notice was therefore invalid and the order (or, as lawyers would say, the purported order) a nullity.

Gilbert Marcus, now an eminent senior counsel, acted as Kentridge's junior. He recalls Winnie's astonishing charisma as well as her chutzpah. She was insistent on going to the courtroom wearing an ANC T-shirt, itself a criminal offence. Marcus eventually prevailed upon her to cover the offending garment with a coat. He also has vivid memories of Kentridge in the courtroom. Although the use of photocopies in court was by then standard practice, Kentridge still preferred to have the actual tomes of law reports before him as he presented his argument.

Each volume would have a little piece of paper inserted at the page to which he wished to refer. Sydney would then make his submissions and seamlessly reach for one of the many books arrayed in front of him and read the selected passage. All of this was done without hesitation and with extraordinary fluency. There were some excruciatingly stupid questions from the bench which Sydney answered with his customary patience and precision.[37]

Kentridge quoted a famous legal dictum:

A man cannot meet charges of which he has no knowledge. A man who has to give evidence that he is of a respectable and deserving character is merely beating the air if the tribunal before which he goes declines to give him any indication of the points against him and which have to be met.[38]

Judgment was handed down on 13 January 1986, dismissing Winnie's application. Leave to appeal was granted and Kentridge and Marcus got to work preparing for the main event before the Appellate Division; then, fortuitously, a decision of the appeal court in another case was handed down, deciding that the minister's reasons had to be given in an analogous situation.[39] Le Grange was forced to concede Winnie's appeal and the banning order was lifted. He did not attempt to issue a new one justified by proper reasons. Winnie was now a free woman. Cheering crowds surrounded the little house in Orlando she had first occupied in 1958 as Nelson's wife. Not only could she live where she wanted, she could now do and say – almost – as she pleased. Just weeks later she made the speech that would taint the rest of her life, extolling the gruesome practice, known as necklacing, of setting light to a car tyre hung round a person's neck: 'With our boxes of matches and our necklaces we shall liberate this country.' A new, equally fraught, chapter in her life was starting.

7

'The Dean': Gonville ffrench-Beytagh (1971–2)

FROM ITS INCEPTION the apartheid state had claimed a God-given right to exist. Daniel Malan, a former minister in the Dutch Reformed Church (DRC) who had swept the National Party to victory in 1948, once said that 'Afrikanerdom is not the work of men but the creation of God.'[1] The speeches and writings of National Party politicians constantly extolled their vision of South Africa as a bastion of Christian civilisation against the forces of godless international communism. But South Africa's Christian churches were always divided in their response to apartheid. While the DRC, founded in 1652 by Dutch settlers and thereafter central to Afrikaner identity, generally fell in line (there were honourable exceptions, most notably Beyers Naudé), many clergymen in the Anglican church, a relative latecomer to South Africa and a confession predominantly of English-speaking whites and the non-white population, were opposed to the tenets of apartheid. The differences were not merely doctrinal; rather, they followed the cultural fault lines that had existed in white South Africa since its creation as a British dominion, divisions only deepened by the establishment of the apartheid regime.

In 1967 B. J. Vorster, the prime minister of South Africa for twelve miserable years whose permanent air of gloomy menace is emblematic of the period of his rule, launched a bitter attack on those 'who wish to disrupt the order in South Africa under the cloak of religion'. Clerics seeking to emulate the role of Dr Martin Luther King, who brought all the moral authority of his ministry to the Civil Rights movement in the United States, were told to 'cut it out, cut it out immediately, for the cloak you carry will not protect you if you try to do this in South Africa'.[2] These were not empty words. In the 1960s a number of Anglican clerics were deported, detained and prosecuted for their opposition to apartheid, starting, as we have seen, with the expulsion of Ambrose Reeves, bishop of Johannesburg. The conflict between church and state reached its apogee with the prosecution of the Very Reverend Gonville Aubie ffrench-Beytagh (pronounced 'beater'), dean of Johannesburg and one of the most senior clergymen in South Africa. For several months in 1971 and 1972 Sydney Kentridge's professional life would be dominated by the defence of a man whose very name, as Kentridge later noted, was an affront to the ideologues of the Nationalist government.

Despite carrying a British passport and a name that seemed to have been dreamt up by P. G. Wodehouse, Gonville ffrench-Beytagh was only nominally English, and he had not always led a cloistered life. He was in fact one of the most eccentric, well-travelled and worldly clients that Kentridge ever represented. 'An interesting man', the dean was, paradoxically, 'not a political priest'; and despite his vigorous engagement with the world outside the church door, his principal 'field of expertise and interest was the ritual of the Church', Kentridge recalled.[3] Wearing chunky black-framed spectacles above an impish grin, ffrench-Beytagh was no sanctimonious prude. His 1973 memoir *Encountering Darkness* displays a sensitive intelligence and much self-deprecation; yet he was a man of passionate convictions, described by contemporaries as *un homme d'action*.[4] After his death in 1991 an obituarist wrote fondly of 'the kindly priest who brought me home from the agnostic jungle . . . here was a truly saintly man despite his penchant for gin, whisky and cigarettes'.[5]

A citizen of the world, ffrench-Beytagh had been born in 1912 in Shanghai to unconventional Anglo-Irish parents. By his late teens he was in New Zealand, leading an *avant la lettre* Kerouacian existence, drifting aimlessly, working irregularly on farms, sleeping rough, getting into fights and writing poetry. In the early 1930s he wound up in South Africa, where, penniless and lonely, and craving spiritual consolation, he took a job with Toc H, a philanthropic Christian movement. A religious epiphany followed, leading to a determination to be ordained. His decision caused much surprise – a girlfriend 'rocked and rocked with laughter' on hearing the news – but ffrench-Beytagh had felt 'touched by the hand of God'.[6] After his ordination he became an assistant curate in a tough mining parish outside Johannesburg. A good head for alcohol was a distinct asset: ffrench-Beytagh spent much of his time drinking with miners. He ascended to becoming priest in charge of another parish. His house was open to all; he once hosted a drunken army deserter who committed suicide by shooting himself in the head in the rectory study.

In the early 1950s ffrench-Beytagh was appointed dean of St Mary and All Saints Cathedral in Salisbury, Rhodesia, where he established educational bursaries, a black orphanage and a branch of the Samaritans. He also befriended a young English journalist, Alison Norman, who apparently had substantial financial resources and enthusiastically provided funding for the dean's charitable ventures. Norman was well connected and encouraged members of her London circle, all of them respectable establishment figures, to donate as well. None of her contacts could be described as revolutionary firebrands intent on the violent overthrow of apartheid. On the contrary, their names read like a roll-call of the British great and good. Yet ffrench-Beytagh's seemingly innocuous association with Alison Norman would later be his undoing.

In April 1965 he returned to South Africa as dean of St Mary's Cathedral in Johannesburg. The newly created republic was very different from the country he had left more than ten years previously. 'Practically every vocal liberal, or person who dared to speak out for freedom, had been imprisoned, exiled, banished, detained, or forced to flee the country,' he wrote; 'it did not take me long to get into political hot water'. While in Rhodesia ffrench-Beytagh had once said that South Africa was ruled 'by the whip and the gun', and as he arrived at Johannesburg's Jan Smuts Airport reporters were quizzing him about the remark. He quickly threw himself into activities which, if not overtly political, were at odds with the prevailing orthodoxy. ffrench-Beytagh's energy and drive turned the cathedral into a place of racially inclusive activity. He was not afraid to use his position to tell white worshippers uncomfortable home truths about how the country's black population was being treated. Although careful not to associate himself with banned entities such as the ANC, he urged parishioners to join multiracial organisations. And rather than just preach to his white congregation about the daily experience of black life, he brought the communities together under the same roof. The cathedral's black and white congregations, which had hitherto held separate services, now worshipped alongside each other. Whatever his theological interests in abstruse liturgical matters, ffrench-Beytagh believed in making things happen. Blacks and whites were now invited to the same lectures, dances and barbecues in the deanery garden.

The integration of black and white congregations was not welcomed by everyone. Some conservative whites stopped coming to cathedral services or pulled their children out of multiracial Sunday school. But there was to be no apartheid in St Mary's. He erected signs proclaiming that all races were welcome in the house of God. He encouraged black choirs excluded from the city's large auditoria to hold concerts in the cathedral. He ensured that charitable funds were distributed more equably. He spent Saturday nights wandering around Hillbrow – Johannesburg's Soho and 'a Pagan part of the city' – wearing a cassock and dog collar, seeking to spread the word of God to whites and blacks equally.

Another cause the dean took up was that of political detainees and their families, who were often left destitute when the main breadwinner was incarcerated. In March 1966 the International Defence and Aid Fund (IDAF), a charity established in the 1950s by Canon John Collins of St Paul's in London to give financial help to detainees and their dependants (and which had funded the defence of the accused in the Treason Trial), was banned. Its bank account was impounded and it was made an offence to receive any money from the fund. Although ffrench-Beytagh had never been directly involved in the IDAF before, its proscription made him 'extremely angry'. Finding himself 'at something of a vocational loose end', he resolved to try to continue its work. The dean was initially, as he put it, 'rather uncertain whether or not I would be contravening a law which forbids the use of foreign money for "political purposes"', but having obtained comforting legal advice, he pressed ahead, taking the view that while the IDAF itself may have been banned, the activity of helping political prisoners and their dependants remained both legal and pressing. With that mixture of ingenuousness and enthusiasm, which were his defining features, ffrench-Beytagh asked a fellow priest who had worked for the IDAF to go to security police headquarters at John Vorster Square, Johannesburg, to tell them about the new venture and ask to retrieve the IDAF's old files. The police actually handed them over. So the Dean's Discretionary Fund was born.

News of the fund quickly spread on the grapevine. Swamped by applications for assistance, ffrench-Beytagh was soon, according to one account, the 'largest single dispenser of private welfare in the Transvaal'.[7] The dean again turned to the ever-generous Alison Norman, who had now returned to Britain. In May 1966 she had written to him: 'As you know I am quite indecently well off and I feel it is time I got rid of some lolly, especially as my pay has been increased and I might have to pay supertax.' 'What fun it is to have wealthy friends!' ffrench-Beytagh replied. By 1971 the dean's fund had received a total of more than 50,000 rand from her.

The beneficiaries of ffrench-Beytagh's fund were not only political prisoners. Anti-apartheid books were underwritten, and the fund paid for the construction of a higher wall around the back garden of the home of Helen Joseph, the former Treason Trial defendant, who was concerned about being overlooked by a policeman living next door.[8] But most of the money went to support the spouses of black political detainees. The fund sent Christmas parcels to prisoners and paid the fares of women to visit their husbands on Robben Island – a four-day round trip just for a half-hour meeting through glass, under heavy supervision. An ANC member's widow received funds to pay for an artificial leg. Many loans were, unsurprisingly, never repaid. 'I suppose we were rather amateur in our investigations,' ffrench-Beytagh later admitted: shortly before his arrest it emerged that a Mrs Dhlamini was not a penniless ex-detainee unable to find work – as she claimed – but rather one of Soweto's most notorious shebeen queens (illegal liquor vendors). More hazardous was ffrench-Beytagh's willingness to administer legal aid for the accused in the terrorism prosecution of Winnie Mandela and twenty-one other co-accused (see Chapter 6). But for the most part his operation tried to avoid controversy by not giving money directly to recipients, instead paying rent or school fees on their behalf.

Inevitably, the dean's activities attracted the attention of the security police. 'Having silenced the Liberals who once ran the Defence and

Aid committees, the police were not about to let it operate under another guise,' wrote one commentator: 'And there was the bonus of being able to discredit another busy-body Anglican slanderer of Afrikanerdom.'[9] The state's retribution would be only a matter of time.

Soon after arriving in Johannesburg ffrench-Beytagh got to know an apparently liberal Afrikaner called Ken Jordaan, a server at the cathedral and an active member of its congregation. After some months Jordaan came to see the dean privately. He seemed to be a man in turmoil. During a long heart-to-heart in ffrench-Beytagh's office, Jordaan angrily demanded to know why the Anglican church wasn't taking violent action against apartheid. He eulogised Dimitri Tsafendas, the Greek Mozambican who had assassinated Prime Minister Hendrik Verwoerd in September 1966, as 'one of the great men of South Africa'. He claimed he had experience as a scuba diver and described to ffrench-Beytagh a hare-brained plan to attach limpet mines to South African warships.

Although the dean was, as he later put it, 'very considerably scared' by Jordaan's ravings, he did not report them to the police. Jordaan seemed mentally unstable, and the dean did not believe he had the wherewithal to put his mad-cap scheme into effect. He tried gently to steer Jordaan towards more peaceful opposition to apartheid. Jordaan was not to be mollified and carried on angrily demanding that the Anglican church should take up arms against the state. Perplexed, ffrench-Beytagh then proposed that Jordaan should join the National Party and try to reform it from within. To his relief, Jordaan appeared to follow his advice, soon becoming a branch secretary of his local party.

Jordaan then confided to the dean that he planned to infiltrate the security police. ffrench-Beytagh urged him to abandon the idea. 'His talk got more and more provocative and my association with him became something of a nightmare,' he later recalled. Keen to get Jordaan out of his office, the dean suggested instead that he use his new political connections to gather information about the National Party's corporate funders (with a view to encouraging boycotts of their goods and services) and immigration statistics (ffrench-Beytagh openly opposed emigration from Europe to South Africa because he did not want skilled white immigrants to take jobs from blacks). In fact Jordaan had no need to infiltrate the security police: he was already a member and had been tasked with trying to lure the dean to make incriminating statements. ffrench-Beytagh's capacity for good was matched by his naivety: despite the warning signs he still took Jordaan for an unstable parishioner with a Walter Mitty complex, not an agent provocateur bent on his downfall.

When a group of clergy – ffrench-Beytagh among them – wrote to the prime minister objecting to his belligerent criticisms of the Anglican church, Vorster replied with yet another attack on church-men 'who demean your pulpits into becoming political platforms to attack the government'. In November 1970 a speech by ffrench-Beytagh was recorded by the BBC and extracts, which inevitably severed some of his remarks from their full context, were later broad-cast. The dean was heard to say that the Anglican church should not 'wash its hands of any contact with violence'. The speech was prob-ably the final straw for the South African authorities, who had already placed ffrench-Beytagh under surveillance.

A number of incidents started to cause the dean to worry for his personal safety. He was woken early one morning to find his Citroën car on fire in the deanery's garage. Although the police dismissed the fire as having been caused by an electrical fault, ffrench-Beytagh knew that Joel Carlson had suffered similar attacks (see Chapter 6), and strongly suspected sabotage. He moved out of his house and into a supposedly more secure downtown flat. But the harassment continued, which ffrench-Beytagh interpreted as a campaign to 'frighten him out of the country'. He was certain his phone was being bugged and rightly suspected that police informers were attending cathedral services and social gatherings he hosted. But he stayed put.

In January 1971, as ffrench-Beytagh returned to his home, he noticed three or four 'noticeably large men' get into the lift with him. They followed him to his front door and announced they were police officers with a warrant to search the flat. The officers quickly homed in on a particular cupboard, in which they found a pile of anti-government leaflets hidden in a shoebox. With titles such as 'We Are at War' and 'We Bring You a Message – the ANC Calls You to Action', many were published by the banned SACP and ANC. One even described how to make a Molotov cocktail. The dean, who protested his ignorance of the leaflets, was taken to the security police's headquarters and thence to a police station in Pretoria. At first he assumed he was only to be questioned overnight, but any hopes that a terrible mistake had been made, or that the police were not in deadly earnest, were quickly dispelled.

Given the dean's prominence, by the evening the whole of Johannesburg had heard of his arrest: many churches held masses in his honour that very night, and rang their bells at noon the following day in protest against his detention. Before his questioning began he was visited by Cecil Smith, Johannesburg's British Consul, to whom he tearfully protested his innocence. In front of two police colonels, Smith pointedly told ffrench-Beytagh that his detention had 'made world headlines' as if to warn off the interrogators from any thoughts of brutality. With alarm, ffrench-Beytagh recalled the fate of Abdullah Haron, a Cape Town imam who had recently died in prison after weeks of beatings, his death officially explained as caused by his fall-ing down a flight of stone steps. But the dean's status as a white, British-born cleric saved him from physical torture. Instead, over the course of nine days of interrogation, his captors used more subtle methods of instilling fear. An electric light burned in his cell all night. Warders banged doors in the small hours to interrupt his sleep. Kentridge recalled later in a British Library interview that the dean's interrogators

> did not permit him to wash and they did not permit him any change of clothes, and when they gave him his meals they didn't give him any utensils, no knife or fork or spoon; he had to eat with his fingers . . . and he told me that he felt so filthy and so degraded that he would have told them anything just to get a wash and a change of clothes; and after about six days the British Consul was allowed in, and this consul told me afterwards that the Dean actually stank.

Ffrench-Betyagh was also subjected to vicious verbal assaults during which three interrogators would 'rise from their chairs and walk around screaming, shouting, and swearing at me'. Classic interrogation techniques were deployed: good cop alternated with bad cop, apparent solicitude was followed by abuse, and mind games were played. Pieces of paper, supposedly carrying proof that the dean had preached sedition, were suddenly plucked from pockets. One interrogator goaded the dean about interracial sex, quoting the Old Testament verse 'A man may not mix his seed with that of an animal' as biblical authority for apartheid. They raved at him: 'You don't preach Christianity, you preach shit!' It was as if decades of Afrikaner resentment against 'casual British snobbery, greed and unconcern' (as ffrench-Beytagh described it) was being vented on this particular embodiment of quasi-Englishness.

On the final day of his interrogation, ffrench-Beytagh was taken to a magistrates court, where for the first time since his arrest he saw his lawyers: Raymond Tucker, one of the few attorneys now willing to take on political cases and a man of unremitting devotion to his clients, and junior advocate Ernie Wentzel, a colleague of Kentridge's at Group 621 (Kentridge had previously represented Wentzel in a libel action against an Afrikaner newspaper who had accused him of being a Communist sympathiser). Only at the end of the hearing did ffrench-Beytagh turn round and see a huge crowd of well-wishers in the public gallery. At this first hearing the only charge ffrench-Beytagh faced was under the Suppression of Communism Act and related to his alleged possession of the subversive leaflets found at his flat, extracts of which were portentously read out by the prosecutor, Henry Liebenberg, for the benefit of the press. No mention was made of Alison Norman's funds or the dean's supposedly inflammatory speeches. ffrench-Beytagh was released on bail, though the price of freedom was the impounding of his passport and payment of a 5,000-rand bond. The next morning he said mass in the cathedral as if nothing had happened.

At his final court appearance before his trial, on 30 June 1971, Liebenberg announced that ffrench-Beytagh was now being additionally charged under section 2(1)(a) of the Terrorism Act 1967. With some understatement, the dean recalled his 'very considerable shock' at this new development. Section 2(1) contained an expansive definition of terrorism: any person proven to have committed any acts 'with intent to endanger the maintenance of law and order' in South Africa was guilty of an offence for which the maximum sentence was the death penalty. There followed a particularly pernicious section which provided that if the prosecution could show that an act committed by the accused was likely to 'cause or promote general dislocation, disturbance or disorder' or 'embarrass the administration of the affairs of the state', the court *had* to presume that it was committed 'with intent to endanger the maintenance of law and order in the Republic' – namely, the capital offence of terrorism – unless the accused could prove 'beyond reasonable doubt' that 'he did not intend' that result. Outside the legal systems of fascist or communist dictatorships, this provision, effectively requiring an accused to prove their innocence in capital cases, ranks among the most draconian criminal legislation of the twentieth century.

The dean now faced a forty-page indictment comprising ten counts of allegedly 'terroristic activities'. Alongside possession of 'Communist' pamphlets, ffrench-Beytagh was charged with having received, 'through the agency of' Alison Norman, 51,000 rand (then about £30,000) of ANC and IDAF funds. By passing it on, he had sought to 'further the aims of the ANC by relieving its members of anxiety about the welfare of their families'. He was also charged with advocating and inciting violence in various speeches he had given, and encouraging Ken Jordaan to commit sabotage and infiltrate the security police (the prosecution did not reveal at this stage that Jordaan had in fact been a security policeman all along). The prosecution claimed that ffrench-Beytagh had advised Jordaan that he 'could receive instructions in England in the use of explosives'. 'I had to punch myself to see if I was awake or having a nightmare,' wrote ffrench-Beytagh. 'It seemed so utterly unreal that a perfectly ordinary sort of person like myself should find himself facing what could be a capital charge.'

Ernie Wentzel, himself a former political detainee who had proudly acquired his old cell door to use as a garden gate after the police station in which he had been held was demolished, was a well-regarded junior advocate. But ffrench-Beytagh realised he needed a heavier hitter for the trial itself. He and his attorney discussed whom to engage and soon, as the dean recalled in his memoirs, 'decided to ask Sydney Kentridge to take on the burden of the defence'. The dean later recalled that Kentridge was 'in some ways loath' to take the case on because 'he had defended people in many of the great political trials in South Africa and found he got so personally involved that such cases were a tremendous strain upon him'. Kentridge was, ffrench-Beytagh added, 'a brilliant lawyer [who] can make a perfectly adequate income from practice in chambers so I felt very privileged and fortunate when he agreed to take on my defence'.

Kentridge had good reason to be feeling the strain. In the last three years not only had he been heavily involved in the defence of Winnie Mandela and her co-accused (see Chapter 6) but he had also appeared in the marathon Prisons Trial, which had dominated the South African news in the late 1960s. Over the course of eighty-eight court days between November 1968 and July 1969 he had defended the journalists Laurence Gandar and Benjamin Pogrund, respectively the editor and African affairs correspondent of South Africa's leading daily newspaper, the liberal-leaning *Rand Daily Mail*. During the mid sixties the *Mail* had run a series of controversial exposés of the appalling conditions in South Africa's prisons. Descriptions of torture by electric shock and savage beatings caused international outrage and severely embarrassed the South African government. It was simply a matter of time before it exacted its retribution on Gandar and Pogrund. The first ominous signs came with denunciations of their reports in the Afrikaner press. The *Transvaler*, closely linked to the government, accused the *Mail* of orchestrating 'an abominable smear campaign' and warned that 'further action can result soon'.

That further action came in the form of a criminal charge under section 44(1)(f) of the Prisons Act 1959, a provision which made it an offence, punishable by up to two years imprisonment, to publish any 'false information' about prisons or prisoners, 'knowing the same to be false or without taking reasonable steps to verify such information', the burden being placed on the accused of proving that they had taken such reasonable steps. The purpose of this section – the tenor of which has been replicated across the world both before and since – was plain: to terrorise journalists into silence. And it had generally succeeded. Pogrund, who had already willingly gone to prison for refusing to identify a source, was however not a man to be discouraged. He had researched his stories meticulously and spoken to dozens of ex-prisoners and prison guards. Yet once approached by the authorities, all his informants, terrified by the consequences of non-compliance with the security police's demands, hastily recanted. Seared into Pogrund's memory is the horror of experiencing, day after day, witness after witness giving false evidence at the behest of the state, extolling the supposedly idyllic conditions in South Africa's prisons.

Now aged eighty-eight and his recollection of events that happened over fifty years ago undimmed, Pogrund recalls ruefully:

> The trial taught me a huge lesson. I had always believed that the truth would eventually prevail. In that courtroom I saw that in South Africa that was not the case. It turned my ethical world upside down. As the prosecution's witnesses were destroyed by Sydney's brilliant cross-examination the judge just seemed to swallow their evidence. It was a case of organised perjury.[10]

One journalist attending the case noted sardonically:

> To the defence it appeared that some of the evidence was patently incredible. There were, for instance, the warders who said that in long careers with the prisons service they had never seen or even heard of an assault on a prisoner and that when African prisoners were noisy, far from shouting and swearing at them, it was customary for the warder to say 'Hush'. [11]

The same journalist noted Kentridge's increasing deployment of the word 'ludicrous' – 'a word he used with perhaps forgivable frequency'.

Even when Kentridge called into the witness box the then editor of *The Times*, William Rees-Mogg, to explain the function of a free press on behalf of the accused, the judge remained unimpressed. That judge was Mr Justice Petrus Cillié, a personal friend of Prime Minister Vorster and shortly to be made judge president of the Transvaal.[12] He had maintained a mediocre practice at the Bar and his elevation to the bench was widely thought to have been earned through his political allegiance to the Nationalist government. Kentridge, when later asked what had been his greatest achievement as an advocate, replied archly that it was making Cillié disbelieve a police officer – once.

Kentridge's already low opinion of Cillié did not improve during the trial. His contempt for the judge's handling of the case, manifested through a veneer of impeccable courtroom courtesy, provided for Benjamin Pogrund the only moments of pleasure in an otherwise gloomy experience. In his memoir *War of Words* (2010), Pogrund recalled his senior counsel:

> Kentridge, with his aquiline nose and his deep voice, looked and sounded like a movie depiction of a British barrister; he was already highly regarded and this trial was to confirm him as the country's foremost lawyer. A few weeks before the start of the trial I shaved my beard, as some thought it made me look like an anarchist, and Kentridge thought I was in enough trouble already.

For Cyril Dunn, a reporter from the London *Observer*, attending the trial was like stepping into an alien world. He explained that 'what happened in Court III was essentially a conflict between Fundamentalism and Modernism, related in kind to that more notorious encounter in 1925 between those two concepts at Dayton, Tennessee', a reference to the so-called Scopes Monkey Trial, which pitted creationists against Darwinists in the courtroom. Dunn saw the South African trial as one that went to the very core of the Nationalist mindset, revealing its obsession with authority and subordination to it. It explained the prosecutor's apparently sincere submission that 'It is the duty of a newspaper not to make public attacks on Government departments and their officials . . . it must not cause stirs or rumpuses', and his display of outrage at Laurence Gandar's answer to a question put to him: 'I do not think journalists were brought into the world to be discreet and obsequious.'

When Cillié eventually came to deliver his judgment it was no surprise that Gandar and the still clean-shaven Pogrund were convicted. After the verdicts were announced Kentridge rose to his feet. The packed courtroom expected a lengthy plea in mitigation. Instead Kentridge uttered one sentence: 'Both the accused gave evidence in the case and do not wish to say anything further.' The judge seemed to shrink into himself as if shamed by Kentridge's moral authority. Gandar was fined 200 rand and Pogrund given a suspended sentence. This was the state's paltry reward for its concerted persecution of two journalists whose only offence had been the pursuit of truth. Both accused left court free men to jubilant applause. The outcome was generally viewed as a victory.

Now, two years later, Kentridge threw himself into what was bound to be yet another protracted battle against the state. He insisted that his first meeting with ffrench-Beytagh and Tucker should take place at a secret location – a flat belonging to a friend – because of fears of surveillance. 'It was the first time I had met Kentridge and I found him a forbidding figure,' said the dean.

> He looks rather like the pictures I have seen of Disraeli – handsome, but seemingly cold and intellectual. He is certainly intellectual, but he is anything but cold and I came to be extremely fond of him. He, like Raymond Tucker, is Jewish, while Ernie Wentzel is a lapsed Anglican, but these differences in religions seemed, if anything, to cement our friendship.

Most clients hope for warm sympathy from their counsel. But generally they are better off being subjected to relentless and clinical probing, however discomforting that may be. It is only through the early identification of the weaknesses in a client's case that a lawyer can hope to devise strategies to neutralise them. ffrench-Beytagh endured a 'long succession of almost interminable interviews' with Tucker and Wentzel, followed by lengthy meetings at Kentridge's home. Never a smoker himself, Kentridge's daughter Catherine recalls plumes of smoke emerging from his study as he sat late into the night with his nicotine-addicted legal team and client, working through the case. In his later account of the case ffrench-Beytagh provided a description of Kentridge's *modus operandi* in the run-up to a trial. Kentridge was 'quite ruthless in identifying the gaps that I had left and things that I had forgotten and demand[ed] the reasons why I had done this or that', recalled ffrench-Beytagh. 'I was extremely grateful to him for this since it forced me to get the facts really clear in my own mind, but it was pretty hard going at the time.' When ffrench-Beytagh told Kentridge that he thought something he had done was okay, Kentridge 'stood up and almost screamed at me "What do you mean, 'OK'?" . . . He would have no truck with anything that wasn't quite exact and accurate. He wanted precise detailed facts and he wanted them clearly presented in a coherent and unemotional way.' Advocacy before a jury can afford – sometimes – to smoothe over difficulties with bland generalities; but this case would be tried by a judge sitting alone (juries had been abolished in South Africa two years previously),[13] who would be immune to flourishes and flighty rhetoric. Absolute precision would be required. Kentridge knew that sentimental lawyering was bad lawyering.

The trial of Gonville ffrench-Beytagh began on 2 August 1971 at the Old Synagogue in Pretoria. No other case in Kentridge's career shows the paranoia of the apartheid state so starkly. There was throughout a yawning gulf between the mild-mannered, slightly eccentric accused – who could be seen daily outside court in a black clerical suit with improbably baggy trousers drawing vigorously on a cigarette – and the dark plots in which he was accused of having participated. Like others who had gone on trial there, the irony of apartheid-style justice being delivered in a former synagogue was not lost on the dean, who considered it to be

> a curious building, more like a mosque than a synagogue from the outside, with its two onion-shaped turrets . . . During the trial I often thought of the Jews of Pretoria, who for so many years had offered their prayers here, and it seemed somehow blasphemous that so much injustice had been committed in a place where the God of justice has been worshipped.

On the bench was Mr Justice Cillié. It was not a good sign.

Henry Liebenberg had faced Kentridge at both the Bram Fischer and Winnie Mandela trials. As a prosecutor he was a state employee rather than an independent member of the Bar. His politics aligned with those of his paymasters. Yet throughout his career Kentridge remained adamant that, whatever his views on his opponents' political affiliations, he would maintain absolute cordiality towards them. (When Liebenberg later joined the Johannesburg Bar he would not hesitate to ask for Kentridge's advice on knotty points of law.) As many clients do, ffrench-Beytagh found it 'difficult to get used to the way Liebenberg and my own counsel were apparently on the friendliest of terms as soon as a formal court session was over'. But the dean was still able to take a mocking pleasure in Liebenberg's 'tiny little voice' and 'incredible capacity for asking the same question over and over again – apparently under the impression that he was pursuing a ruthless cross-examination'. Who could blame him? 'Kentridge's cross-examinations are a great deal more quotable than Liebenberg's sledge-hammer techniques,' the accused noted with satisfaction.

On the first day of the trial the public gallery was filled with clerics from across South Africa and beyond, many Western diplomats (including the Canadian ambassador) and the British Labour MP Joan Lestor, all of them duly photographed, as they arrived at court, by security police. Throughout the trial at least one of the interrogators who had connived in the dean's degradation sat in court opposite him. It was a standard form of intimidation. Still, he was able to articulate his plea of 'not guilty' with confidence after the charges were read to him. 'The dean looked calm generally but displayed slight signs of nervousness immediately before the trial opened and during discussions with his counsel,' noted the *Rand Daily Mail*. His anxiety was understandable and prescient. Later that first day the first prosecution witness turned out to be the Judas-like Ken Jordaan. Even after the dean's release on bail, and in a brazen attempt to incriminate him further, Jordaan had had the effrontery to continue to meet ffrench-Beytagh, offering to have him smuggled out of South Africa. It was a proposal that the dean, by now entertaining suspicions about Jordaan, wisely declined. Yet it was only when Jordaan appeared in the witness box at the Old Synagogue that ffrench-Beytagh realised the full extent of his parishioner's double-dealing.

Smuggled in and out of court each day (press photographs show him hiding his face behind a copy of the *Rand Daily Mail*), Jordaan had done his duty according to his own perverted lights. He told the court that, having befriended the dean he had become alarmed by his radical views. He had first approached the police in early

1969 and been recruited as a security police constable with instructions to report on the dean's words and deeds. In answer to Liebenberg's questions, Jordaan proceeded to wrench everything ffrench-Beytagh had ever said in his presence from its true context. His claims were varied, in some cases almost comical. In May 1969 ffrench-Beytagh had apparently described the notorious (now) Colonel Swanepoel (his promotions came at pace), who had overseen the ill-treatment of Winnie Mandela and the rest of the Twenty-Two after their arrest, as an 'out-and-out sadist who should be shot' (see Chapter 6). ffrench-Beytagh had described himself as a 'distribution point' for ANC funds. He had supposedly 'advocated the wildest schemes for sabotage', including assisting Robben Island prisoners to escape from their confinement by submarine (a plan only abandoned when the dean was alleged to have expressed fears that the remaining prisoners would be executed). He had encouraged Jordaan to adopt the role of a 'disgruntled Afrikaner' and infiltrate the National Party and the security police. Jordaan even testified that ffrench-Beytagh was part of a secret group bent on 'destroying Portugal' by aiding Frelimo freedom fighters in Mozambique, then still a Portuguese colony. After that the next steps would be the destruction of Rhodesia and then South Africa in some vast revolutionary domino effect engulfing the southern part of Africa. 'By the time [Jordaan] had finished it sounded as though I was mad, rather than bad, but certainly a very dangerous character to have around. Several of my congregation looked at me very askance after that first day's evidence,' recorded ffrench-Beytagh. Still, a daily interdenominational service in his honour would continue to be held at the cathedral throughout his trial. He was to need all the congregation's prayers.

When Kentridge rose to cross-examine Jordaan his task was to expose him as a fantasist with an inbuilt motivation to exaggerate and invent conversations with ffrench-Beytagh in order to please his police handlers. It is of course hardly unknown for a spy to embellish the quality of the intelligence they feed up the line. But there was a real problem lying in Kentridge's way: Jordaan had filed near contemporaneous typed reports relaying all the inflammatory statements and admissions supposedly made by the dean. Kentridge could not evade the fact that his case had to be that Jordaan had furnished his security police superiors with a whole range of distortions over a prolonged period. But not pure lies: Jordaan's reports contained accounts of many conversations he had had with the dean. To suggest that they were all entirely made up would stretch credulity. The approach Kentridge took, with deadly effectiveness, was to accept that there was a kernel of innocent truth in many of the reports, but to show that Jordaan had wilfully perverted the innocuous into the criminally compromising.

Jordaan objected to Kentridge's use of the term *agent provocateur.* Yet he also had to admit that he had persistently induced ffrench-Beytagh to break the law, inducements which the dean had consistently refused:

Q: I think it is clear from your reports that for a period of 18 months you were urging the dean to commit unlawful acts.

A: I wanted action.

Q: There was no response from the Dean to your suggestion of sabotage of South African warships? The Dean did not assist you in your plans for sabotage?

A: He did not.

Q: You offered to help him escape; he rejected it?

JORDAAN: [*No reply.*]

Q: You showed him a gun; he did nothing. [*Jordaan had once produced a pistol with the words 'perhaps you need this, father'; ffrench-Betytagh recalled that he had recoiled in terror at the sight of it.*]

A: Yes.

Q: You offered to photograph documents and he rejected that.

A: Yes . . .

Q: The Dean never gave you any money at all?

A: No . . .

Q: Can you identify one instance of money spent by the Dean on ANC activities?

A: No.

Q: Over the long period of time that you enjoyed the Dean's confidence can you tell us of one unlawful act committed by the Dean?

A: No . . .

Q: Perhaps [you also felt] a sense of disappointment because you had nothing spectacular to report? [*Note the quiet insinuation of this question; far more effective than if it had been put as an assertion.*]

A: I merely submitted the information, whether it was spectacular or not . . .

Q: You used to initiate conversations about revolution and violence?

A: It would be more correct to say that I made myself available . . .

Q: I am suggesting you first raised the question of sabotage.

A: The accused raised the question of sabotage.

Q: I am putting it to you that you spoke of it first.

A: I did speak of sabotage . . .

Q: In January [1971] the Dean was detained by the security police. After he came out of detention you offered to get him across the border, didn't you?

A: I offered to give him a lift to Ficksburg [a town on the border with Lesotho].

Q: To get him over the border?

A: To further convey to the accused that even at this stage I was his agent and acting on his behalf.

Q: No, not for that reason at all. In order to attempt to get him into further trouble.

A: No.

Q: But if he had said yes, thank you very much, what would you have done?

A: I would have said to him that he must reconsider this action.

At that ludicrous answer 'a large group of spectators laughed, and Mr Justice Cillié ordered them to be silent', reported the *Rand Daily Mail*. Those same spectators had to bite their collective tongue when Jordaan insisted that the dean had urged him to obtain a job as a prison guard on Robben Island in order to relay information to and from political detainees. Kentridge could barely conceal his contempt: 'I can only suggest to you that this is nonsensical.'

And as to the dean's supposed plan to commandeer a submarine to orchestrate a mass escape from Robben Island – 'Does not that even now strike you as completely ridiculous, that the Dean should be involved in such a plan?' – Jordaan's response struck a note of

fastidious understatement. 'It did not seem capable of implementation.' Jordaan had also reported that the dean envisaged taking part in
the interracial revolution which he predicted was inevitable. Again it
did not seem an immediately credible proposition:

Q: Tell me, what part did the Dean envisage taking in this interracial
violence? Did he tell you that?

JORDAAN: [*No reply.*]

Q: You have to think a bit here, Mr Jordaan. You may . . .

A: Do you mean what part he personally would have in it?

Q: Yes, that is right. Think.

A: I do not know what part he personally would have taken in it.
Whether he would be involved in it in an active capacity or in a
directive capacity.

Q: But surely you asked him?

A: I gave him to understand that I understood he directed these affairs,
that he was concerned with the planning and strategy involved.

Q: Listen to my question again, Mr Jordaan. Surely you asked him
what part he foresaw himself playing?

A: I cannot recall asking him that question.

Q: But if he said what you say he said surely it was a natural question
for you as a police agent to ask him?

A: I didn't ask him the question, if it be a natural question, because
at that time, even at this moment, I am something of an amateur
in this sort of business.

Q: [*Sarcastic*] Oh, I see. A very talented one, Mr Jordaan.

A: Thank you, sir.

Jordaan was inexorably, unconsciously, revealing himself as a con-
ceited buffoon. And would ffrench-Beytagh be a sort of 'general' in
this insurrection, Kentridge asked, maintaining a straight face. Jordaan
suggested he envisaged the dean being a 'senior commander'. 'Did you
seriously believe this?' It seemed that Jordaan was still living out a
self-regarding fantasy in which he had helped bring down a key
ANC mastermind, albeit one wearing a dog collar. Kentridge's cross-
examination continued in delineating the fantastical world that Jordaan
inhabited. He spoke of a 'ffrench-Beytagh organisation' plotting the

downfall of the South African state ('a figment of a fevered imagination', suggested Kentridge). Jordaan even seemed to think that other
agents of the state were checking on him: 'I was convinced that I was
being watched so I had to be careful.' It was as if the Nationalist mindset
was being laid bare in all its paranoia and wounded pride. But Kentridge
also revealed the individual psychology of a man who craved recognition. Jordaan had proudly reported that, based on a few inconsequential
conversations with the dean, he had 'been accepted as an accredited
agent of the ANC'. Kentridge responded with contemptuous formality: 'I think it is my duty to suggest to you that this was a wholly
extravagant and fictitious conclusion to have drawn.'

Q: And you felt this work of yours was important?
A: Yes.
Q: Won't you agree with me that it is perhaps a human failing to
  exaggerate the importance of one's work?
A: We all try to make ourselves out a little bit bigger than we are, I
  suppose that is human.
Q: [*Withering*] That is a fair enough answer.

Not only fair but revealing. It is a common phenomenon that
agents will tend to gild the truth if it is dull and workaday, in order to
enhance their own significance and importance to their handler.
Kentridge asked Jordaan why, over a year and a half of regular meetings between mid-1969 and late 1970, he had deliberately not tried to
establish the truth about ffrench-Beytagh's exact role in the plots he
ascribed to him, or to which clandestine organisation in London he
apparently reported. For an agent in the service of the security police,
Jordaan seemed to be remarkably incurious:

A: I did not wish to alarm the accused by asking him questions
  which might lead him to believe that I was seeking information
  that I shouldn't be asking, merely that I was carrying out my
  instructions . . .
Q: Over the whole 18-month period . . . You asked no questions to
  elucidate the Dean's organisation?
A: No, I did not want to probe too deeply.

Q: Perhaps if you had asked one or two straightforward questions instead of drawing inferences in your reports this whole bubble of yours would have burst and you would have been out of a job as a police spy?

A: No.

. . .

Q: I suggest that your reports are a farrago of faulty recollection and distortion.

A: No.

Q: It is as though, when the Dean said something to you, there was an evil spirit looking over your shoulder and compelling you to distort what he said.

A: [*Ever the literalist*] I do not know about evil spirits.

A fantasy can only hold good if reality is not allowed to intrude. At one stage Jordaan had reported that the dean had said that he should go to England to be trained in 'electronic sabotage' by ffrench-Beytagh's mysterious associates. If this was true, then here was an opportunity to get to the heart of the dean's supposed secret organisation, bent as it was on the destruction of South Africa. Surely Jordaan had seized this opportunity?

Q: Well now, this for you was surely a great breakthrough, Mr Jordaan?

A: It looked encouraging, yes.

Q: Yes, he was prepared to put you in touch with the right people in England?

A: Yes . . .

Q: This was promising, wasn't it? . . . Because now you might find out who these people were?

A: Yes.

Q: Right. Now what did you do about it?

A: I waited for him to continue.

Q: [*Insistent*] What did you do about it?

A: How do you mean, what did I do about it?

Q: Well, what did you do? Did you say to him, right, I am ready to go, who are the people, give me their addresses?

A: No.

Q: Did you take any steps to meet these people?

A: I passed the report through to my superiors, who would then decide what should be done after that.

Q: You got no instructions to do anything more about it?

A: No.

Q: Perhaps your superiors took this no more seriously than I do, Mr Jordaan?

During his re-examination by Liebenberg Jordaan simpered that he had received anonymous death threats for his participation as a state witness. Kentridge got up again:

Q: Have you asked for police protection because of these threats?

A: No.

Q: How did you come from Johannesburg to Pretoria today?

A: By train.

Q: Did you travel alone?

A: Yes.

Q: [*Contemptuous*] Well so much for the threats.

Jordaan had spent two days in the witness box. 'By the time Kentridge had finished with [him], it seemed to me that his evidence had been blown to smithereens,' ffrench-Beytagh noted approvingly.

On the trial's fifth day another undercover policeman, the bearded Sergeant Michael Kennedy, arrived, photographed by the waiting press with the seemingly mandatory air of menace behind dark glasses which such people wore. Kennedy testified that he had turned up uninvited to an earnest Council of Churches conference on the 'Generation Gap' in early 1969. His bizarre get-up – a blue safari suit and a comb in his sock – had signalled to all present that he was a plain-clothes security policeman. Yet Kennedy insisted that during the conference ffrench-Beytagh had stood up and advocated a violent and bloody revolution – indeed proclaimed it a 'good thing', at which about a hundred people present had apparently erupted into 'cheering, laughter and applause'. Kentridge pointed out to Kennedy that those present included a number of senior churchmen. His cross-examination was sardonic.

Kennedy's evidence was that the dean had openly advertised his approval of bloodshed. 'And that is what drew the cheers and applause from these ecclesiastical and other persons present. It was this reference to bloodshed being a good thing that drew the applause?' 'That is correct.' 'Did you hear any protest from anyone present?' 'Not that I know of.' Kentridge slowly read out the names of some of the august ecclesiastical personages present at the conference: bishops, pastors, reverends – even Desmond Tutu had attended.

Q: You are not surprised that none of these people objected to what the Dean said?
A: I would have expected it, however it did not occur.

Kentridge let the answer stand. Kennedy left the witness box a figure who had destroyed himself through absurdity.

It became apparent that the state had been shadowing the good dean's every move, seeking out evidence, however exiguous, to mount a case against him. ffrench-Beytagh had addressed various public gatherings: seemingly ever-present was a state agent with instructions to distort and misrepresent his utterances. He had given a talk entitled 'Violence, and All That' to a meeting of the Black Sash. (Despite the group's conspiratorial name, it was made up in large part of respectable and deeply committed ladies from the white community who paraded in silence wearing black sashes to protest against apartheid. The dean's attorney Raymond Tucker spent his Saturdays giving gratis legal advice under its auspices.) Warrant Officer Helberg had eavesdropped outside utilising recording equipment which, as seemed almost de rigueur with state operatives, did not work properly. A Mrs Van Heerden, who had actually attended the meeting, also testified against the dean, imperfectly recalling his supposed advocacy of violence to the pacific audience. How this woman came to be a state witness was never discovered; but having read the report of her evidence in the newspapers, her horrified employer contacted the dean's lawyers to inform them that, far from being an adherent of the liberal tenets of the Black Sash, Mrs Van Heerden was a fanatic who disseminated her own demented tracts, in which she averred that the mixing of blood would spell the end of Western civilisation and denounced fluoridation of water as a Communist plot (a well-worn right-wing conspiracy theory, parodied a few years earlier in Stanley Kubrick's *Dr Strangelove* through the mouth of General Jack D. Ripper).

The court heard from a Stephen Norman (no relation to Alison, naturally), a twenty-five-year-old undercover policeman who had been instructed to befriend the dean, all the while trying to lure him into statements that could furnish the grounds for a prosecution. Norman told the court he had attended one of the dean's Friday night 'open house' gatherings, where ffrench-Beytagh had declared himself a proud card-carrying Communist until the 1940s, talked of a plan to use magnets to sabotage computers, and extolled 'an instrument the size of a pin's head that could blow up parliament'. None of the prosecution witnesses that followed dispelled the growing sense that ffrench-Beytagh was the hapless victim of a Clouseauesque set-up. Black witnesses who had been the beneficiaries of the dean's fund reluctantly gave evidence for the prosecution, terrorised by the security police into attending court. But all they revealed was a man of generosity seeking to alleviate the misery of life under apartheid. A former nurse, a pitiful figure who been convicted of ANC membership, served two and a half years in prison, and then had her name struck off the nursing register, conceded to Kentridge that the 34 rand she had obtained from the fund had covered a train fare, food and clothing for her children – money she had needed 'desperately'. Kentridge asked if she could identify the dean in the courtroom. She looked around blankly: she had never met him. There followed a tragic retinue of other beneficiaries of the dean's fund. It had provided the sister of one detainee with 20 rand for a new pair of spectacles. Money had been paid out to a Mrs Mashaba, to allow her to make an annual visit to her husband incarcerated on Robben Island for fifteen years. Schoolbooks had been given to another. The prosecution's point was that each of these witnesses had formerly received funds from the IDAF until it had been banned and had then subsequently received grants from ffrench-Beytagh's fund. The state was seeking to prove 'terroristic activities' by such evidence of guilt by association.

On 18 August the trial entered the realm of the surreal. 'The tension of the proceedings was relieved, if not for the Dean, by a subplot with the texture of a Peter Sellers farce,' recalled one eyewitness. In an attempt to prove a connection between Alison Norman and the IDAF, and hence the ultimate source of the money the dean distributed, a Major Nicholaas Zwart of the security police had been tasked with entrapping her while she was visiting South Africa. On a sleeper train from Johannesburg to Pietermaritzburg (en route to stay with her cousin, a nun, in the small town of Tsolo in the Transkei), Norman had got talking to an ostensibly friendly young woman who gave her name as June. In a country where nothing was quite as it appeared, June was, needless to say, a security police agent. An apparent friend of June's, a Mr Morley (Zwart's alias), who described himself (inventively) as a dealer in herbs and other products, then entered their train compartment. Morley, with improbable generosity, offered to drive Norman from Pietermaritzburg to her cousin's nunnery, saving her the trouble of a long, uncomfortable bus ride. Norman would later testify that she had accepted his offer and that she and Zwart had driven to Tsolo and had a 'pretty desultory' conversation en route. Zwart's account was different: he had told Norman he was a dedicated member of the Liberal Party (the party co-founded by Alan Paton to which Kentridge had belonged until it was dissolved in 1968) and lured her into a serious political discussion during which, Zwart claimed, Norman had spoken of the blacks' 'righteous fight for freedom' and apartheid's 'fascist oppression'. Upon arrival in Tsolo, according to Zwart, Alison Norman had refused lunch, drunk at least three pints of lager and two double brandies, and then tried to 'procure' Zwart as an agent for the IDAF, reassuring him that there were 'several prominent churchmen in Johannesburg who could protect him if he got into trouble'. Unlike the bumbling Jordaan, Zwart was a senior member of the security police, well trained in giving plausible evidence. If believed by the court then the dean was in serious trouble.

This was, like so much evidence at this trial, a question of Norman's word against Zwart's. Kentridge started with some flattery.

Q: Now Major, would you say you held yourself out as a dedicated member of the Liberal Party?
A: That is so.
Q: I take it that was untrue?

A: [*Proudly*] That is very, very untrue.

Q: You say that you expressed anti-Government views?

A: That is so.

Q: Were those expressions of opinion sincere?

A: No.

Q: Well, you said that you were Mr Morley, a general dealer; that was, of course, untrue?

A: That is so.

Q: And quite apart from membership of the Liberal Party, you told her and gave her the idea that you were a liberal?

A: That is so.

Q: Was that untrue?

A: That was also untrue . . .

Q: Did you indicate that you were of Afrikaans descent?

A: No.

Q: So all these things were untrue, but as you said, she was satisfied with what you said?

A: She appeared so.

Q: And you spoke with apparent sincerity and honesty?

A: That is so.

Q: Of course, you were acting a part?

A: I was acting a part.

Q: But you were doing so with some success?

A: I trust so.

Q: So you were able to disguise your untruths with a veneer of sincerity and honesty?

A: [*Beginning to realise the hole he was digging for himself*] On that particular occasion, yes.

Q: Well, the ability to do that must have been useful to you as an agent?

A: Yes.

Q: And would you agree that it is an ability which might be useful to a witness?

A: [*Seeing even more clearly his difficulty*] Well, I know exactly what the Defence is getting at, but I would have to agree that it probably would be.

Q: Yes. I mean of course, a witness who is not telling the truth.

Effective cross-examination cannot be conducted from a rigid script. It must gently insinuate and peel away the layers of a witness's evidence. The great cross-examiner listens carefully and probes quietly: they do not grandstand or hector. They take the evidence slowly; like the patient fisherman, if you wait, something will sooner or later bite. Kentridge was interested in the liquid lunch at Tsolo where Alison Norman's tongue had apparently been so loosened that she had told a complete stranger that she was a member of an illegal organisation, a criminal offence carrying a minimum sentence of five years in prison.

Q: Major, you say she was under the influence of liquor?

A: I said that she was . . . I would not go so far as to say she was heavily under the influence, but I would say that she was to an extent under the influence of liquor.

Q: You say she had had at least three beers and two double brandies?

A: Three beers and two double brandies, pre-metrication tots.

Q: At least?

A: At least.

Q: So perhaps more?

A: I do not think more. I say at least, but I do not think they were more.

Q: Why then do you say 'at least'?

A: Well, they were not more . . . they were not less, definitely not less.

Q: Well, you have got a great memory. Did she have three beers and two double brandies or not?

A: She had three beers and at least two double brandies.

Q: So you mean she might have had a third double brandy?

A: It is not impossible, that is why I said, at least.

Q: And no food?

A: And no food.

Q: Why didn't she have any food?

A: I have an idea that the beer took away her appetite. It was . . .

Q: Really? Is that your idea? What about you, did you have any food?

A: I had food later that afternoon in Umtata [a nearby town].

Q: But at lunchtime?

A: No.

Q: Did you drink?

A: Yes.

Q: What did you drink?

A: I matched her.

Q: So what did you drink?

A: I drank three pints of lager and I had, I had actually four double
   brandies. That is why I am a little doubtful whether she joined
   me in the last one. That is why I say she had at least three.

There is a lot of forensic work going on in these short, seemingly
banal, questions. The picture of these two strangers – one a devoutly
Christian young woman on her way to a convent – drinking brandy
after brandy in a hot bush town while discussing subversion with a
man she had first met that day becomes increasingly absurd. Zwart,
without realising it, contradicts himself fundamentally. And then, to
cap it all, he reveals – with manly pride – the heroic scale of his own
alcoholic consumption, thus undermining the credibility of everything he has said so far: could he really recall through the fog of his
(pre-metrication) tots anything at all?

Q: Now of course, it will be for His Lordship in due course to say
   who is telling the truth, Major Zwart, but I must tell you that
   according to Miss Norman, what you have said about these things
   in the witness box is a total and unmitigated lie.

A: I would not expect her to have the courage not to deny it.

Q: You would not expect her to have the courage not to deny it?

A: That is what I said.

Q: [*Tartly*] What do you know about her courage or otherwise?

A: I know nothing, but I do not think Miss Norman is in a very
   enviable position at the moment.

Q: You don't?

A: No.

Q: [*Sarcastically*] And you, of course, are in a splendid position?

A: I am in court, telling the truth.

Q: Very well. Do you always tell the truth?

A: In court.

Alison Norman's cousin, Sister Phoebe of St Cuthbert's Mission, followed Major Zwart into the witness box: she testified that she had last seen her cousin in 1961 or 1962 and had kissed her warmly when she arrived at the mission. 'No, I am sure she was not smelling of brandy,' she replied to Kentridge's question, leading to the unforgettable *Rand Daily Mail* headline: 'Nun: Alison Norman did not smell of brandy.'

The trial was then adjourned for two and a half weeks, until 7 September, so that testimony could be obtained from, apart from the dean, the main defence witness: Alison Norman herself. Unusually, evidence for a South African trial was taken not in a courtroom but 'on commission' in the Temple chambers of an English barrister. Norman had already been visited in England by the dean's attorney Raymond Tucker and given him a long affidavit. She had told Tucker that she would gladly come to South Africa to testify in person, provided she received a 'satisfactory guarantee' that she would not be arrested and prosecuted as ffrench-Beytagh's co-conspirator (having been expressly identified as such in the indictment). With no such guarantee forthcoming, all the lawyers flew to London.

The Middle Temple in London was a far cry from the formality of the Old Synagogue. Transcripts show that playing an away match 4,000 miles from Pretoria, without the comforting presence of Mr Justice Cillié, Liebenberg's cross-examination of Alison Norman there was distinctly lacklustre. Luckily, Norman had kept meticulous financial records and was quite open about the money she had donated to ffrench-Beytagh – for humanitarian, not political reasons, she insisted – both from her own inheritance and from British friends. She explained that she had felt 'oppressed by the extent of my capital wealth' and compelled to give much of it away. Liebenberg's attempts to get Norman to reveal herself as a Communist revolutionary were a disastrous failure. With her horn-rimmed spectacles, she looked more like a school librarian. Norman had a first-class Oxford history degree and was a regular donor to Christian Aid. A member of the Society of St Francis, she devoted at least half an hour each day to prayer. It was difficult to imagine a figure less likely to be intent on fomenting a revolution, but Liebenberg did his best to portray her as precisely that. She dismissed

Jordaan's description of her as an 'accredited member' of the ANC as 'such a twist of the imagination that it leaves me staggered'. She denied ever trying to recruit Zwart as an 'agent' of the IDAF. Liebenberg ended up asking silly questions, greeted with barely disguised contempt from Norman. When he asked whether there were 'any Marxist groups at the LSE', Norman replied that it had 5,000 students and no doubt 'one would find among them subscribers to many philosophies'. At one point Liebenberg even asked Norman why none of her money had been spent on 'pro-Government activities' in South Africa, a question that Norman refused to dignify with an answer. Norman gave short shrift to his plodding repetitions: 'I do get tired of saying the same thing so many times'. Impossibly blinkered by the paranoias of Nationalism, Liebenberg had completely misunderstood the nuances of social class and politics in 1960s Britain, where many upper-middle-class people could – and did – openly oppose apartheid, without thereby necessarily holding Marxist views.

On 7 September the trial resumed in Pretoria and the defence started calling its own witnesses. Bill Burnett, now bishop of Grahamstown, denied that ffrench-Beytagh had said 'violence is a good thing' at the 'Generation Gap' conference, as the prosecution had alleged. Delia Gardner, a mother of three, recalled that far from inciting violence at the Black Sash meeting she had attended, ffrench-Beytagh had said that he feared it. 'Did [ffrench-Beytagh] say that if there was a revolution, you ladies should take up your rolling-pins on the side of the blacks?' asked Kentridge (who would now doubtless cringe at his question). 'No' was Gardner's unsurprising reply. A professor of computer science at the University of the Witwatersrand mocked the prosecution evidence that ffrench-Beytagh had talked of sabotaging computers with pins or magnets: 'Blows from a hammer would be more effective,' opined the professor, who had naturally never heard of explosive devices 'the size of a pin's head'.

On 14 September ffrench-Beytagh finally entered the witness box. 'No smiles as cleric enters witness box' ran a headline in the *Star*, adding that 'The dean looked unusually drawn, tired and pale.' ffrench-Beytagh had previously been seen chatting with Kentridge and his junior Ernie Wentzel 'while puffing on a filtered cigarette during breaks in the hearing . . . But today his face was tight and unsmiling.' As soon as he entered the witness box the dean appeared to relax. Examined in chief by Kentridge, he confidently stated 'I believe the doctrine of apartheid is abhorrent to Christianity', that he had never belonged to any political party, and that 'I hate black nationalism as much as white nationalism.' Asked why he had set up his fund, ffrench-Beytagh explained that as 'I am one of those fortunate people who is not married, I have no family responsibilities, and it seemed to me that it was the kind of job that a priest perhaps ought to do, really.'

Kentridge asked about Alison Norman and her English donors – among them a former headmaster of Eton. 'Could all these people be called "left-wing"?' 'Not in the English sense,' replied ffrench-Beytagh. 'Some of them would be called Conservatives.' As for a conspiracy to bring down apartheid by force, 'How can I play a part in a conspiracy of which I know nothing?' asked ffrench-Beytagh rhetorically. Suggestions that he had given financial aid to Frelimo in Mozambique were the 'sheer unadulterated essence of conglomerated nonsense', the dean said floridly. He explained his abhorrence of Communism. He was 'astonished' that his nocturnal ministry around Johannesburg's hospitals and fire stations had been described by the prosecution as 'reconnaissance for sabotage'.

That same day, the *Star* put the case on its front page for the first time, with ffrench-Beytagh's insistence that the 'Communist' leaflets found in his flat had been planted, and that he had been 'horrified and very frightened' at their discovery. Was there any truth in the allegation that he had slammed his fist on a table at a Black Sash meeting? 'None whatsoever,' ffrench-Beytagh replied. Claims that he had ordered middle-aged do-gooders at the meeting to prepare for a revolution were 'absolute nonsense'; the evidence that he had told the 'Generation Gap' conference that bloodshed would be a good thing was 'pure fabrication'. ffrench-Beytagh described Ken Jordaan as a 'man of moods' and 'rather unstable'. Far from him suggesting a plan to attach limpet mines to South African warships at anchor, this was something that Jordaan himself had proposed: 'I was horrified and said he must not do anything of the kind,' added ffrench-Beytagh, who readily admitted that he was 'a fool' not to have realised by then that Jordaan was a police agent.

Liebenberg's first question in his cross-examination – the pedestrian 'Can you hear me, Dean?' – left ffrench-Beytagh 'completely floored'. But like Alison Norman, the guileless churchman soon disarmed him. When Liebenberg asked about his description of Colonel Swanepoel as 'a sadist who should be shot', ffrench-Beytagh replied cheerfully that 'he recommended much the same treatment for several Anglican bishops'. Instead of sticking to hard facts, Liebenberg made the error of cross-examining ffrench-Beytagh about matters of theology, where the dean was not to be outwitted. He made much of an article in which ffrench-Beytagh had written 'there can be no doubt that Christians, in their consciences and in the sight of God, may reach a decision that involves them, under certain conditions, in a struggle against an obsolete, essentially impossible and unjust economic, social or political order'. This was hardly a call to the barricades, and in cross-examination ffrench-Beytagh insisted that he did not think a revolution was either imminent or justified.

ffrench-Beytagh's fund had once given 500 rand towards the cost of a car for Winnie Mandela, enabling her to travel between her workplace in Germiston and home in Soweto in time to comply with her curfew. Liebenberg, seeing some advantage in this link to a leading ANC figure, could hardly leave the point alone. Kentridge chose the opportunity to gently ridicule the plodding prosecutor. 'I do think on a precise count that this is at least the third time on which my learned friend has been back to those questions about this motor car and the 500 rand.' Even the judge was tiring of these repetitions. 'Yes I think you have asked the question a few times, Mr Liebenberg.' ffrench-Beytagh's cross-examination staggered into its ninth day. Liebenberg finally lost his temper when Kentridge objected yet again to another fatuous question. 'My learned friend feels I do it too often – I stand astonished at my own moderation,' retorted Kentridge with lordly disdain, invoking Clive of India's famous rebuke to Parliament. Eventually, on 15 October 1971, the trial had run its course. Cillié reserved judgment, to be delivered two weeks later.

★

Kentridge's defence of Gonville ffrench-Beytagh had been a technical tour de force. It had also been a wearisome experience: day after day of travelling from Johannesburg to Pretoria, cross-examining witness after witness without forewarning (the prosecution had no obligation either to inform the defence of what witnesses it was going to call, nor to provide it with a proof of their proposed evidence). But through that cross-examination Kentridge had revealed them as a ragbag of craven informers and bumbling flat-foots. For one young man watching from the public gallery, the proceedings, and Kentridge's advocacy, was a life-changing experience. The eighteen-year-old Edwin Cameron had just left school and was undergoing compulsory military service in Pretoria, leaving him with time on his hands. In his memoir he described the trial as 'the start of a very slow, fitful and protracted coming to consciousness'.[14] Almost forty years later Cameron, one of the most celebrated South African jurists of the last half-century, would become a member of the South African Constitutional Court, having spent eight years in the Court of Appeal. He has provided a vivid account of Kentridge's courtroom methods:

> Kentridge's cross-examination was meticulously detailed, but mesmerising. Trudge, trudge, trudge. Question by question. Seated in the stuffy upper gallery, reserved for women during orthodox religious observances, I learned my first lessons about good lawyering. There are few flourishes and grandiose gestures. Much more grinding slog. And intense concentration on detail . . . If convicted [the dean] faced a minimum of five years in jail. Kentridge's commitment to avoiding that result, and his mastery of the minutiae of whether Ms Norman had or had not drunk brandy with Major Zwart, was propelled by an underlying, smouldering, incensed rage at the injustice of the system that was trying to imprison the clergyman.
>
> Kentridge achieved renown as a lawyer not only because of his intellect and his mastery of the technical rules of procedure and hearsay. He made an impact because of his fervour in employing those skills against a system he abhorred. My eighteen-year-old self, gazing down through the upstairs railings, began to understand that effective lawyering lies in a combination of heart and mind and very hard work.

★

Cillié's judgment was to be given on All Saints' Day, 1 November 1971: a fortunate omen, thought ffrench-Beytagh. Kentridge and the other lawyers were cautiously hopeful. According to the dean, most white South Africans, who had initially thought 'there was probably no smoke without a good deal of fire', were now sympathetic and agreed that the prosecution's case had 'pretty well fallen to bits'. If acquitted, he did not plan to stick around in South Africa. He had been advised to leave for England at once and had a suitcase packed. Everyone assembled in the Old Synagogue to learn the outcome. The judgment took all day to read out: in a judge-alone criminal justice system the verdict is not delivered through the unreasoned utterance of the words 'guilty' or 'not guilty'. By lunchtime ffrench-Beytagh had still not been convicted of anything. As the minutes passed the sense of tension built while the judge laboriously traced through the evidence: only in the afternoon did he receive his first conviction. The judgment's 'quality seemed to deteriorate very much towards the end and Cillié's reading became tired and hurried, as if he was ashamed of what he was doing', the dean noted. By the end of the day, although the judge had rejected much of the evidence against him, ffrench-Beytagh had been convicted on three counts – inciting Ken Jordaan to commit sabotage and take part in the contemplated uprising, encouraging the Black Sash to 'support and prepare for a violent revolution', and receiving money from the IDAF, which he distributed in furtherance of a plan to give aid and succour to the ANC's plan for the violent overthrow of the state. Although Cillié found that it had been proved by the state that the leaflets had not been planted in ffrench-Beytagh's flat, nonetheless he was acquitted on that count, on the grounds that there was no evidence that the dean intended to distribute them. Simple possession did not amount to an 'act' under the terror legislation. On such slender distinctions could questions of guilt turn.

Immediately after Cillié had finished delivering his judgment a shell-shocked ffrench-Beytagh had a consultation with Kentridge in one of the Old Synagogue's private rooms. 'Suddenly Kentridge made a dash for the door,' the dean later recalled. He opened it to find a policeman standing directly outside, apparently eavesdropping. A 'furious' Kentridge complained to Cillié, the police claiming they had merely been standing guard to make sure ffrench-Beytagh did not try to escape. In fact there had not been much for the police to overhear. Client and advocate had already agreed that a guilty verdict would not prompt a long speech of mitigation. As far as ffrench-Beytagh was concerned he was not going to start grovelling for mercy now. Kentridge agreed.

When Cillié reconvened the court for sentencing he asked Liebenberg if he had the power to give ffrench-Beytagh a suspended sentence. 'Liebenberg was rather floored by this and did not seem to know what the answer was,' recorded ffrench-Beytagh. Remarkably, it was Kentridge who had – as a matter of professional duty – to tell the judge that under the Terrorism Act no suspension was permissible, and that the statutory minimum sentence was five years' imprisonment. Kentridge then made a brief submission. In its simple dignity it deserves quotation in full.

> I think it is clear from what he said in the witness box in this court that the accused is a man who takes full responsibility for everything which he has done, or which has been done in his name.
>
> My Lord, I also feel entitled to submit to Your Lordship that what the accused has done, he did out of a sense of his duty to God and to man. Your Lordship has made certain findings from which it is clear that the principal activity, if not the sole, real, overt and continuous activity for which the accused has been convicted, has been the distribution of money to persons who, by common consent, were persons in need: women without husbands to support them and children without fathers. Your Lordship has found that this money came from a tainted source and that the accused, in handling this money, did so because of, in part at least, an adherence to an unlawful conspiracy. I submit that whatever the source of the money, however tainted it may be, whoever may be the husbands or fathers of the people who were assisted, and whatever the motive with which such acts of charity were done, the fact that these acts can and indeed must lead to a prison sentence, must cause a sense of shock and stupefaction far beyond the confines of this Court. But Your Lordship's hands are tied. The Act provides for a minimum sentence of five years' imprisonment and there is little more that I can say, other than to

suggest to Your Lordship that if ever there was a case for the minimum sentence, it is this case.

Cillié duly handed the dean the minimum sentence of five years' imprisonment. Perhaps Kentridge had shamed him a second time. Still, five years in a South African prison was a frightening prospect, especially for a man in late middle age and ill health. Edwin Cameron recalled that women in the public gallery gasped and sobbed. Kentridge made an application for leave to appeal observing, as the dean recorded, 'in a very polite way, that other judges might interpret the facts differently'. Any appeal could only succeed by persuading the appeal court that Cillié had fundamentally misconstrued the evidence or misapplied the law – a daunting task. That Cillié granted that permission immediately perhaps suggests that behind his avuncular demeanour was a troubled conscience. Bail was extended to await the outcome of the appeal. ffrench-Beytagh was not to be jailed, for now at least.

A guilty verdict did not quell ffrench-Beytagh's supporters. As he left court he found 'a marvellous crowd' of both black and white supporters (captured by a Pathé newsreel) singing 'Onward, Christian Soldiers'. There were congratulations – for a fight well fought – as well as tears and sympathy. Ever the *homme d'action*, ffrench-Beytagh went straight back to his cathedral in time for evening mass. He spent the five months before his appeal was heard continuing his ministry as best he could. People would come up to him in the street with the words 'God bless you, Father'. On one occasion a bus driver, seeing the dean on the pavement, stopped his bus and dashed across the road to shake his hand before continuing his journey. Despite these shows of support, Cillié's judgment was met with gloom and apprehension among apartheid's opponents. Professor John Dugard warned that 'the morality of violence and civil disobedience . . . are subjects which will in future be practically impossible to discuss, despite the fact that they are widely debated in most Western countries'. Cillié had held that giving charity to the families of ANC members could be a terroristic activity and many people withdrew from participation in the provision of assistance to dissidents and their dependants, for fear that they too would face prosecution.

★

The volume of work required to mount the appeal was prodigious. Although the dean had been found guilty on only three of the ten counts, the judge had made numerous adverse findings on other matters which had to be dislodged if there was to be any chance of successfully overturning the convictions. The appeal had to traverse the totality of the evidence given at the trial, which filled a transcript covering over 2,500 pages. Kentridge still retains his copy of the 'Heads of Argument for the Appellant', three typed volumes running to 260 pages. This document, dated 21 January 1972, contains an extended submission – copiously cross-referenced to the evidence – as to why Cillié's judgment was flawed. It is a monument of labour and thought: it must run to over 100,000 words, all produced in about two months.

The appeal court sat in an imposing early twentieth-century building in Bloemfontein, South Africa's judicial capital. Kentridge and his junior Ernie Wentzel travelled down the night before the appeal was due to start, on 21 February 1972, in the principal, stinkwood-lined courtroom. Thirty years later Edwin Cameron would spend eight years as a judge of what had by then become known as the Supreme Court of Appeal (until 1996 it was known as the Appellate Division). Of the unchanging formality of judicial hearings there he recalled:

> even now, the protocols instilled over decades are followed. First, the judges assigned to hear an appeal assemble in the gallery outside the courtroom . . . At exactly 9.45, the court orderly enters the courtroom and summons all to rise. Then with a swish he tugs the drawstring that opens a maroon velvet curtain screening the judges' gallery from the public. The judges file in, in strict order of seniority, and take their places on the Bench . . . The judges bow gravely to the lawyers and members of the public, and take their seats. The advocates, the attorneys and the public sit. The presiding judge's registrar gets up and calls the case for hearing. After a moment of shuffling paper and pens and checking books, the presiding judge signals that counsel for the appellant may rise to address the court.[15]

The hearing ran for an extraordinary ten court days, the high ceiling of the courtroom providing some mitigation to the blazing heat of the South African summer. The magnitude of the burden on counsel to construct a coherent and ordered, and above all persuasive, oral argument over that length of time is difficult to convey. Kentridge needed instant recall of the transcript and the thousands of pages of exhibits which had been adduced at trial. Every point had to be referenced to the evidence, whether oral or written. Kentridge presented his case to a panel of three: South Africa's chief justice, Newton Ogilvie Thompson, and two judges of appeal, Mr Justice Botha and Mr Justice Trollip. Ogilvie Thompson was an Anglican from an English-speaking Cape Town family, but he was hardly a liberal. A few years earlier he had given judgment in the notorious case of *Rossouw v Sachs* – in which he decided that those detained for interrogation, even though they were not charged with any crime, could be lawfully denied access to books, pens and paper on the basis that Parliament had not intended that such people should be allowed 'to relieve the tedium of their detention with reading matter or writing materials'. Nonetheless the judges listened politely, aware that this was the first case before the Appellate Division which would consider the breadth of the Terrorism Act. When the arguing was over, the court reserved its judgment.

In the weeks that followed, ffrench-Beytagh was given no inkling of when judgment would be given. He was warned to expect at most twenty-four hours' notice, 'an awfully short time in which to get ready either to go to prison or to leave the country'. It was only after Easter that he finally learned his fate. At 3.45 p.m. on 13 April 1972 the court registrar telephoned his attorney: judgment would be handed down in Bloemfontein at eleven o'clock the next morning. Ogilvie Thompson's 42,000-word judgment was not an entire exoneration of ffrench-Beytagh, but all three judges unanimously agreed that he should be acquitted on all charges. The dean had not travelled to the appeal court to hear the verdict in person. He learned the news by telephone in Raymond Tucker's Johannesburg office before returning to his cathedral, where a black congregation 'literally danced up the aisles'.

There was much to celebrate. Appeal courts are loath to overturn the findings of judges who have had the advantage of seeing and hearing the witnesses at close quarters. But Kentridge had persuaded the appeal judges that Cillié's assessment of their evidence was fundamentally wrong. Ogilvie Thompson 'tore to shreds both Jordaan's evidence and Cillié's assessment of it', wrote the dean with satisfaction. The chief justice was scathing about Cillié's reliance on Ken Jordaan, a 'wholly unsatisfactory witness' and a 'trap . . . constantly pressing the appellant for action'; far from inciting Jordaan, ffrench-Beytagh had in fact 'discouraged and restrained' him. Jordaan had told many lies, which 'clearly demonstrate, not only his unreliability as a witness, but also his readiness to untruthfully involve the appellant with the ANC'. As for the Black Sash meeting, Ogilvie Thompson found that if ffrench-Beytagh had tried to incite it to violence, 'he could hardly have chosen a more infertile soil for sowing such seeds than an audience of women, including mothers and grandmothers, who were all members of an organisation avowedly opposed to violence and strictly committed to working within the law'. The 'cardinal feature' of the state's case, that ffrench-Beytagh had received money from the IDAF via Alison Norman, was not proved. Further, the prosecution had failed to prove that ffrench-Beytagh 'knowingly possessed' incendiary pamphlets; indeed, the possibility that they had been planted in his flat could 'hardly be said to be an unreasonable one'. As for Major Zwart, Ogilvie Thompson noted the 'inherent improbability' of his account of his encounter with Alison Norman. Was it credible that an upper-class Oxford graduate, with a first in history no less, would go binge-drinking with an unknown man at lunchtime in a dusty bar in Tsolo and then try to recruit him as an agent of the IDAF? It was sweet indeed for Kentridge to read the court's view that 'as regards the good impression Zwart made upon [the judge], it is to be borne in mind that, as was submitted by counsel for appellant, Major Zwart is *ex hypothesi* an accomplished actor'. Alison Norman's testimony, both about her finances and her encounter with Zwart, 'remained unshaken in all material aspects'.

Most importantly, the appeal judges construed the Terrorism Act in a way that clipped its capacious wings. They decided that while helping political offenders and their families 'might conceivably not meet with universal approval', it was 'manifestly not a contravention of the [Terrorism] Act'. Cillié had held that the mere act of providing financial assistance to people on trial or in prison for opposing

apartheid, and supporting their families, could involve the boosting of
the morale of members of the ANC and so could constitute a crime.
Ogilvie Thompson disagreed:

> Knowledge that his family is receiving some assistance while he is
> serving a prison sentence (or while he is . . . engaged in terroristic
> activities) is no doubt some solace to the individual concerned; but
> that can hardly be regarded as an intended boosting of morale in such
> a degree as to qualify as promotion of the activities of the African
> National Congress.

The judgment, written in the obfuscatory legal language of an
earlier age by South Africa's most senior judge, was nonetheless a
testament to judicial rectitude and honesty. It would have been very
easy for the appeal judges to uphold Cillié's judgment: that would
have required a good deal less mental labour and would have gratified
a state itching to see the troublesome dean in prison and the chill of
Cillié's judgment made permanent winter. But Ogilvie Thompson,
conservative as he was, demonstrated an uncompromising adherence
to the principles of justice, however inconvenient they might be to
the prevailing orthodoxy. That was surely an act of integrity. The
judgment, founded as it was on the legal argument presented to the
court, is also one of Kentridge's greatest achievements. By the time
Edwin Cameron read the judgment of the appeal court, he was a
first-year law undergraduate. He recalls the 'sensational news reports
of the dean's acquittal' and later explained the significance of Ogilvie
Thompson's judgment.

> The impact of these rulings was momentous. They sliced through the
> potentially unlimited scope of the Terrorism Act . . . his ruling blasted
> a torpedo through the hull of some of the statute's most menacing
> provisions. In doing so, it opened a life-sustaining space [where]
> opponents of apartheid could continue to breathe and work inside the
> country.[16]

★

After his initial conviction 'a wave of fear and caution had run
through the Republic', recalled ffrench-Beytagh. The appeal judgment

'changed all that . . . Protesting, arguing, defending and aiding *are* still legal. South Africa is not yet totally a police state', he insisted, albeit writing from the safety of London. For Kentridge – aware that the Nationalist government was quite capable of introducing new legislation to achieve its desired ends – the judgment was, more modestly, 'a happy ending for the dean and for his worried counsel'. It was also, it might be added, a triumph for Kentridge personally. It is difficult to overstate the burden of work and anxiety under which he had laboured during the previous months, a burden made all the more onerous with the eyes of the world upon him.

ffrench-Beytagh was well aware that access to justice still depended on skin colour and the ability to pay for good representation. He knew that had he not been 'a European male', and a British citizen who attracted much media attention, the outcome might have been different. Apart from the eight days in detention following his arrest, he had throughout remained a free man. 'I am deeply aware of how privileged I have been, and how far I am from being the "martyr" which I have sometimes been called. But there are many real martyrs suffering under South African "justice" and these must not be forgotten', ffrench-Beytagh later wrote.

> I find it a terrifying thought that if the generosity of people all over the world had not enabled me to go to appeal, Cillié's judgment would have gone unchallenged and I would have been in prison for five years. But it is still more terrifying to wonder what will happen to South African justice when the present members of the appeal court retire.

By the time ffrench-Beytagh wrote those words he had long since left South Africa. Just hours after the delivery of the appeal judgment, on the evening of 14 April 1972, he boarded a flight from Johannesburg to London. Like many exiles, he felt guilt about his departure, and some felt that, like Ambrose Reeves, he had deserted his congregation. But Kentridge and others had been adamant in urging him to leave immediately after the appeal judgment, in case he was rearrested and prosecuted again, as had happened to the Twenty-Two. 'I wanted to get out as quickly as I possibly could,' ffrench-Beytagh told a BBC interviewer after arriving in London. 'Discretion is the best part of valour.' While his appeal decision meant that liberal people 'could heave a huge sigh of relief', he added he would probably never return to South Africa. He never did.[17]

ffrench-Beytagh's successful appeal certainly did not stop the apartheid state's intolerance of turbulent priests. Its victimisation of churches continued. Yet ffrench-Beytagh had done much to reinvigorate South Africa's Anglican church, within which it was possible to challenge the moral legitimacy of apartheid and which increasingly started appointing black leaders. In March 1975 Desmond Tutu – another of Kentridge's clients – became Johannesburg's first black dean.

After a short spell as a curate at St Matthew's, Westminster, in 1974 ffrench-Beytagh became rector of the charmingly named St Vedast-alias-Foster in the City of London, a secluded Wren church with no resident congregation, giving him much time to write and contemplate. After retiring in 1986 he lived with friends, including Alison Norman, at an informal religious community in Tower Hamlets, where he died in 1991. Kentridge would occasionally visit him.

In 2004, long after ffrench-Beytagh's death and the fall of apartheid, Denis Herbstein's book *White Lies: Canon Collins and the Secret War against Apartheid* revealed that in 1965 ffrench-Beytagh had visited Canon Collins in London and hatched a plan to channel IDAF funds to South Africa via Norman, who owing to her wealth and class could plausibly claim that all the money donated was her own, or that of her friends. In 1997 Norman told Herbstein that she had agonised about perjuring herself by saying that none of the money came from the IDAF and had even sought the advice of Trevor Huddleston, then bishop of Stepney, who told her to 'go ahead'. 'I was lying through my head about the source of the money,' she admitted. The dean's work was thus not a substitute for that of the IDAF, but an audacious continuation of it, with IDAF money ingeniously laundered through Norman's bank account. His memoir, published in 1973, skirted around the truth to protect those at risk of detention and prosecution in South Africa. As the title of Herbstein's book suggests, effective opposition to apartheid was impossible without dissembling and subterfuge.

So did all the money that ffrench-Beytagh distributed indeed come from the banned IDAF, just as the prosecution had alleged? The question seems academic now that the IDAF is seen as a laudable organisation that helped bring apartheid to an end. But in 1971 being associated with the banned IDAF was dangerous – and for Gonville ffrench-Beytagh, a man even braver than appeared at the time, it was almost a matter of life and death.

8

The Biko Inquest (1977)

JUST AS WITH the assassination of President Kennedy or the murder of John Lennon, people remember the moment they learnt of the death, in police custody, of Bantu Stephen (Steve) Biko. His friend and ally Nyameko Barney Pityana was himself in detention when he was told the news. He recalled that on the night of Biko's death he had a dream in which he and his friend had been engaged in animated discussion. 'That was Steve as I prefer to remember him: a man full of life, jocular and yet one who had the ability to express even the deepest thoughts in a light-hearted manner.' His friend had then turned serious: he had entrusted to Pityana the well-being and future of his children. 'Like all dreams it went away as swiftly as it came. I was left to unravel the puzzle.'[1] Helen Zille, then a journalist at the *Rand Daily Mail*, also recorded her reaction to the grim news.

> There are a few events in the course of any journalistic career that are of seismic significance. You never forget where you were, and what you were doing when the news broke. You know that something has happened that will change the course of history, although you don't know exactly how. One such event occurred on 12 September 1977.[2]

Sydney Kentridge never met Steve Biko. But he was aware of Biko's political standing and when the fact, if not the circumstances, of his death emerged in the newspapers in mid-September 1977 Kentridge knew that an event had occurred which would have vast repercussions.[3] Within two months he would be appearing on behalf of Steve Biko's family at an inquest which would be one of the seminal legal and political events of the 1970s.

★

The early 1970s was a period of gloom for the anti-apartheid movement. The ANC's president Albert Luthuli had died in 1967, and Robert Sobukwe, founder of the Pan Africanist Congress, was living under house arrest in failing health (he would die in February 1978). Oliver Tambo was in exile in London. Nelson Mandela and Walter Sisulu started their second decade in prison. Most expected that Mandela would die there. Into this leadership vacuum stepped Steve Biko. Born in 1946, Biko was a generation younger than Tambo, Sisulu or Mandela. As a medical student, in 1967 Biko had been instrumental in setting up the South African Students Organisation (SASO), a blacks-only body that split from the multiracial National Union of South African Students (NUSAS). Although NUSAS was firmly anti-apartheid and some of its white leaders had even been jailed for their political activism, Biko became convinced that black students had to liberate themselves, not be liberated by so-called 'white saviours'. 'Black man, you are on your own.'

By the end of the 1960s Biko and his adherents had a name for their new movement – Black Consciousness – and in 1972 Biko helped to set up the movement's main vehicle, the Black People's Convention (BPC). Although Biko was an enigmatically shy man who never formally held a senior position in the BPC, he soon emerged as one of its most charismatic leaders. The Black Consciousness movement was founded on the espousal of a psychological shift in the minds of the country's black population, which Biko articulated in a stream of articles and speeches with themes such as 'blacks can no longer afford to be led and dominated by non-blacks' and the need to 'liberate the mind of the black man'.[4]

> We are aware that the white man is sitting at our table. We know he has no right to be there; we want to remove him from our table, strip the table of all trappings put on it by him, decorate it in true African style, settle down and then ask him to join us on our terms if he wishes . . .

So Biko had written in a 1972 book, *Student Perspectives on South Africa.*[5] Black Consciousness was a peaceful movement, as much a philosophical outlook as a political proposition, owing much to the writings of the French West Indian psychiatrist and philosopher Frantz Fanon, whose 1961 book *The Wretched of the Earth* had had a profound impact on liberation movements around the world. SASO and the BPC organised 'compassion days', set up community and education projects and were much preoccupied with 'conscientisation' of the black population – capacity building, in modern organisational parlance. Yet Black Consciousness's peaceable objectives did not inhibit the South African state from taking murderous action against it. In February 1974 the former SASO leader Abram Tiro was assassinated in Botswana by means of a parcel bomb sent by South African secret police.

In early 1976 Biko gained wide public recognition when he appeared as a defence witness at the so-called SASO/BPC Trial, held at the Palace of Justice in Pretoria. Nine defendants were in the dock, charged under the Terrorism Act as a result of rallies they had organised in September 1974 to celebrate the recent victory in Mozambique of Frelimo in their long war of liberation against the Portuguese. In the witness box Biko was disarmingly charming, making what George Bizos has described as 'one of the great courtroom statements ever delivered'[6] – later memorably recreated in Richard Attenborough's film *Cry Freedom*. Biko told the court:

> the black man is subject to two forces in this country. He is first of all oppressed by an external world through institutionalised machinery, through laws that restrict him from doing certain things, through heavy work conditions, through poor pay, through very difficult living conditions, through poor education. These are all external to him. Secondly, and this we regard as more important, the black man in himself has developed a certain state of alienation, he rejects himself, precisely because he attaches the meaning white to all that is good, in other words he associates good and he equates good with white.

In the unlikely setting of a Victorian courtroom, presided over by an unsympathetic Afrikaans judge, Biko then expounded his philosophy of black liberation.

By the mid-1970s Biko's home in King William's Town in the Eastern Cape, where he lived with his wife and two young sons, had become a Mecca to which journalists and foreign dignitaries flocked. Like virtually every other black activist, Biko was subject to a banning order, which restricted his ability to meet with more than one person at a time. Nonetheless he travelled clandestinely across the country pursuing his political activities. And, despite his political philosophy, Biko maintained friendships with a number of prominent whites. The most important was Donald Woods, editor of the *Daily Dispatch* in the Eastern Cape city of East London, a politically independent paper which had become more hostile to apartheid under his editorship. In 1971 Prime Minister Vorster had angrily confronted Woods and told him, 'the stuff you are writing is stirring the blacks to revolution'. Nonetheless many white liberals, like Woods, were suspicious of Biko and perturbed by the Black Consciousness movement of which he was the de facto leader, with its rejection of multiracialism and of co-operation with white opponents of apartheid.

'I had an idea of what Biko stood for, and I didn't like it,' Woods later admitted. But he did eventually agree to a meeting at the urging of Biko's lover Mamphela Ramphele ('You've got the whole thing wrong, man. We're not racist. We're just insisting on being ourselves,' she told him.) Although he had been a newspaper editor for almost ten years, Woods had never before met a banned person. It would be the beginning of a friendship that was only cut short by Biko's death. Although Biko's banning order meant he could not be quoted directly, Woods's paper became much more sympathetic to Black Consciousness. Woods would later state that Biko was 'the greatest man I ever had the privilege to know . . . He walked tall in all things, without deference or apology'. It was a confidence which led the minister of justice, police and prisons, Jimmy Kruger, to label Biko 'the most dangerous man in the country'. Biko's growing prominence as a political leader meant that by 1977 he had become a key target for the state security apparatus. In the period before his final arrest in August 1977, Biko was detained three times – twice briefly, and once for 101 days. On each occasion he had emerged largely unscathed. The various petty charges levelled against him – infringements of his banning order, minor traffic violations, 'defeating the ends of justice' by persuading witnesses to change statements, and so on – had all been seen off in court. In an interview in the spring of 1977 he had reflected on his experience of interrogation in words both suicidally brave and tragically prescient.

> You are either alive and proud or you are dead and when you are dead, you can't care anyway. And your method of death can itself be a politicizing thing . . . So if you can overcome the personal fear of death, which is a highly irrational thing you know, then you're on the way. And in interrogation the same sort of thing applies. I was talking to the policeman and I told him, 'If you want us to make any progress, the best thing is for us to talk.' And this is absolutely true also. For I just couldn't see what they could do to me which would make me all of a sudden soften to them. If they talk to me, well I'm bound to be affected by them as human beings. But the moment they adopt rough stuff, they are imprinting in my mind that they are police. And I only understand one form of dealing with police and that's to be as unhelpful as possible.[7]

★

In earlier chapters we have encountered the Terrorism Act 1967, under which many of Kentridge's clients were both detained and charged. Kentridge would later pinpoint the terms of section 6 of that Act as the principal reason why the police officers responsible for killing so many black detainees evaded justice. In a radio lecture in 1978 he explained:

> Under section 6, any senior officer, if he has reason to believe any person has committed an offence under the Act, or has some information relating to an offence under the Act, may detain him until he has answered questions to his satisfaction or – and this is a rather chilly phrase – otherwise until the police are satisfied that no useful purpose will be served by his further detention.[8]

The effect was that a person could be arrested and detained, incommunicado, for as long as the police thought fit, and no court was permitted to review that detention. By 1977 the situation had become more draconian still: the Internal Security Act had been amended a year earlier to allow for the detention of witnesses, as well as suspects. In practice, detention was used not just as a pretext for torture but also increasingly for state-orchestrated assassination. At inquest after inquest police officers would straight-facedly explain that detainees had slipped on bars of soap, fallen downstairs, hanged themselves or engaged in acts of self-defenestration from high windows.[9]

Since 1963, forty-five detainees had died suspiciously in security police custody, twenty of them in the eighteen months leading up to August 1977. None had been prominent anti-apartheid activists or black leaders. This was to change when at 10.20 p.m. on 18 August 1977 a car carrying Steve Biko was stopped at a security police road-block near Grahamstown, in the Eastern Cape, well outside the area to which he was restricted by his banning order.

The facts of what then happened, so far as they are verifiable, are as follows. On 19 August Biko was taken to Walmer police station in Port Elizabeth, some sixty miles away, for interrogation under section 6 of the Terrorism Act. There he was held in solitary confinement on the orders of Colonel Pieter Goosen, head of the security police in Port Elizabeth. For nearly three weeks Biko remained there in isolation. He was not permitted any exercise, books, paper – or clothes. For these first nineteen days Biko was not physically assaulted, but the psychological torture must have been appalling. In a lecture Kentridge would later speak of the experience of being held in isolation with biting sarcasm:

> First of all, the accused himself may have undergone many months of solitary detention. What of that? Well let me quote from a recent biography of a wartime internee in South Africa who had been held for several weeks alone in a small cell. 'When you are locked in a tiny cell, I can readily understand how you can go insane.' The author of that pregnant statement is Mr B. J. Vorster, who later became our prime minister. But his experience has perhaps not been thought necessary to apply to those who are detained to date.[10]

On 2 September Biko was visited by a magistrate, who later supplied an affidavit to the inquest reporting that Biko had asked for soap, a wash cloth and a comb, and for permission to buy food. 'I live on bread only here. Is it compulsory that I have to be naked? I have been naked since I came here,' Biko told him – probably the last words he spoke to be accurately recorded. The magistrate refused the requests.

On the morning of 6 September Biko was taken from Walmer police station to room 619 of the Sanlam Building, an anonymous-looking office block in downtown Port Elizabeth. A suite of rooms on the sixth floor, notorious locally for the fact that its lights burnt ominously throughout the night, functioned as the local headquarters of the security police. There Biko was placed in the care, if one can use the term, of a 'day team' of security policemen led by Major Harold Snyman, and a separate 'night team', each comprising four officers. Biko was interrogated in room 619 throughout the day. He was kept overnight in the same room, manacled and chained to the wall.

At about 7 a.m. on 7 September Major Snyman and his team arrived. Biko's leg irons and handcuffs were removed. At some point before 7.30 a.m. he was beaten, sustaining a head injury that caused the brain damage that would kill him five days later. Early in the morning Snyman's superior, Colonel Goosen, was informed that there had been an 'incident'. He arrived to find Biko's speech slurred and his upper lip swollen. Two hours later, Dr Ivor Lang, a district surgeon, arrived and examined Biko in the presence of Goosen, to whom Lang gave a certificate stating that he had seen 'no evidence of any abnormality or pathology'. That evening, when police tried to continue Biko's interrogation, they found him unresponsive. He was again left chained on the office floor overnight. On the morning of 8 September Lang returned, now accompanied by the chief district surgeon, Dr Benjamin Tucker. Although Goosen told the doctors that Biko had not urinated in the previous twenty-four hours, the doctors found that his trousers and blankets were soaked in urine (after almost three weeks of complete nakedness Biko had been permitted trousers for his interrogation). Far from stubbornly refusing to go to the lavatory, as was later claimed, Biko was probably incontinent by this stage. Neither doctor questioned Biko about what had happened to him.

On the evening of 8 September a specialist physician, Dr Colin Hersch, was consulted. Hersch recommended that a lumbar puncture should be performed. Biko was transferred to a hospital within Sydenham Prison, on the edge of Port Elizabeth, where a warder apparently found Biko at 3 a.m. lying fully clothed in a bath full of water, and prostrate in the empty bath a few hours later. On 9 September the lumbar puncture was performed – the only medical intervention Biko received at Sydenham – and on 10 September its results showed that his cerebral spinal fluid was bloodstained. Another neurosurgeon, Dr Roger Keeley, was consulted by telephone. Without examining him, Keeley concluded that Biko did not have brain damage but should be kept under observation. Keeley saw no reason why Biko should not be released from the prison hospital back into the 'care' of the security police, who transferred Biko on the morning of 11 September to Walmer police station, where he was put naked under a blanket on the concrete cell floor. A few hours later a warder found Biko foaming at the mouth and glassy-eyed. Goosen was informed and sent for Tucker, who re-examined Biko at 3.20 that afternoon. Goosen then decided that rather than be returned to Sydenham Prison or placed in a civilian hospital, Biko should be driven to a prison hospital in Pretoria, 740 miles away.

Biko was to be transported not in an ambulance but lying on a felt mat on the metal floor of a Land Rover whose rear seats had been removed, with no medical personnel or equipment on board; all it carried were three of Biko's police interrogators and a container of water. Although the proposed journey would likely last over ten hours, Dr Tucker voiced no objection to Goosen's plan, and the Land Rover set off at 6.20 p.m. on 11 September. In the early hours of 12 September Biko arrived at Pretoria prison, where a warder complained that he had been brought a 'nearly dead man' to look after. Biko was examined by Dr Andries van Zyl, a newly qualified district surgeon who had no access to Biko's medical records. An orderly, Sergeant Pretorius, later said that on arrival Biko looked like he was 'seriously ill . . . I was afraid for his life'. Because Van Zyl was wrongly told that Biko had been refusing food and drink, he gave him a vitamin injection and an intravenous drip, neither of use to a patient suffering brain damage. Biko died that night.

When Donald Woods first heard of Biko's arrest, he was not unduly alarmed – after all, his friend had been arrested several times before and had never been much mishandled (at least by the standards of the security police). Although Colonel Goosen had a 'particularly savage' reputation, Woods believed that Biko was now such a well-known figure in anti-apartheid politics that the state would see to it that no serious harm befell him. But days turned into weeks, and Biko stayed in detention, out of the reach of lawyers, family or friends. His isolation from the outside world was total.

On 13 September, word got out that Biko had died the previous day. 'Within those first shocked seconds, South Africa became a different place for me,' Woods later wrote, echoing the sense of Biko's death as marking a horrific climacteric which overwhelmed so many others. Soon after, at a Nationalist Party rally, Justice Minister James Kruger explained that Biko had died as a result of having for many days refused food and water; in words that attained instant notoriety, Kruger added nonchalantly that 'the death of Biko leaves me cold' and signalled his approval when a friendly heckler shouted out that it showed what a good democracy South Africa was that Biko had been allowed to choose to starve himself to death. Kruger was already in possession of a pathologist's report which made clear that Biko had died not of malnutrition, but of a brain injury.

Seeking to forestall the growing international outcry, Kruger continued his propaganda offensive. He falsely told the media that Biko had been arrested in connection with riots in Port Elizabeth and the dissemination of 'inflammatory pamphlets which urged people to violence and arson'. The pro-government newspaper *Die Burger* duly carried the headline 'Bodies and Blood Called for in Biko Pamphlet'. Kruger insisted that far from mistreating Biko, the security police had if anything mollycoddled him, making sure not to touch him lest accusations were made, and procuring medical assistance as soon as he seemed unwell. The police were cast as victims, not murderers, and Biko as the malefactor who seemed to have committed suicide merely to smear them.

The South African legal system still accorded a deceased's next of kin certain rights. Dr Jonathan Gluckman, a liberal pathologist appointed by the Biko family, was permitted to attend his post-mortem. He discovered that the cause of death was not starvation, or anything that could be construed as suicide, but a serious contrecoup injury, causing the brain to jolt against the back of the skull, probably the result of blows to the front of the head. In the face of the sustained government disinformation campaign, Gluckman was wracked with anxiety that the truth about Biko's death might never emerge. He telephoned the editor of the *Rand Daily Mail*, Allister Sparks, and asked him to visit his house. In his garden, away from possible listening devices, he showed Sparks the death certificate jointly signed by him and the state pathologist Professor Loubser. It stated the cause of death as 'brain damage'.

'No Sign of Hunger Strike – Biko Doctors' announced the *Rand Daily Mail* front-page headline the next day, directly contradicting Kruger's account. The immediate response was a complaint by the justice minister to the South African Press Council, against the *Mail*'s editor Allister Sparks and Helen Zille, then a junior reporter who had written up the story, accusing them of publishing 'unverified' information. As we have seen, Kentridge had a long-standing professional relationship with the *Mail*, South Africa's most celebrated liberal paper. He received a call the very day of Kruger's complaint to attend an urgently convened hearing that evening before a retired Appeal Court judge, Oscar Galgut, who presided over the Press Council. Kentridge dismissed the complaint as a matter of 'syntactical trivia', but Galgut ruled that the – wholly truthful – report was 'misleading and tendentious', ordering the newspaper to print an immediate apology and retraction. It was by now one in the morning and the *Mail*'s presses had to be stopped to change the front page. Sparks later recalled: 'Kentridge was furious. I'll never forget Galgut's face as this legendary legal figure told him bluntly that his judgment was "completely unacceptable".'[11]

Nonetheless the *Mail*'s story may have forced Kruger to back away from his hunger strike story. He admitted to the *New York Times* that 'there may have been a struggle' and then conceded that Biko had indeed died of head injuries. Still he could not resist making a ghastly joke out of Biko's death: 'I can tell you that under press harassment I've often felt like banging my head against a wall too, but realising now, with the Biko autopsy, that it might be fatal, I haven't done it.'

★

The Biko family's attorney, Shun Chetty, first asked the prominent human rights lawyer and veteran of previous inquests George Bizos to be counsel at Biko's inquest. Bizos, a man of tireless dedication to the anti-apartheid cause, immediately agreed to be part of the team and recommended that Kentridge should lead it.[12] 'He was the number one choice. He was beginning to surpass even Isie Maisels' reputation,' Bizos later wrote. Kentridge was now fifty-four years old and at the peak of his career in South Africa. Still, the inquest, under the spotlight of the world's media, was a daunting prospect. The principal witnesses to the final weeks of Biko's life were security policemen and the evidently pliant physicians they picked to examine their victim, all of whom were likely to tailor their evidence to exonerate themselves from any accusation of brutality, connivance or negligence. As the inquest approached, the glare of publicity and the tensions Biko's death had kindled only increased. The funeral, on 25 September, was attended by some 10,000 people, a figure which would have been even greater had police roadblocks not turned back many more. Desmond Tutu, then bishop of Lesotho, returned to South Africa to speak, and told the mourners that, far from hating whites, Biko was in fact the least infected by racism of the many young black militant leaders that he, Tutu, had met.

Kentridge had in the autumn of 1977 been in Britain, where he had recently been called to the English Bar. After many urgent telephone calls between Johannesburg and London he hastily returned to South Africa a week before the inquest was due to begin, to devote himself to intensive study of the dozens of affidavits from the various police officers, prison warders and doctors with whom Biko had come into contact in the last few weeks of his life. Day after day, locked in the study of his house at Houghton Drive with his juniors George Bizos and Ernie Wentzel (veteran of the ffrench-Beytagh case six years earlier), Kentridge analysed the best way to approach each witness. Bizos recorded Kentridge veering between rage against the weakness of the doctors who had so willingly compromised their professional obligations and anticipation of the battle to come. 'He rubbed his hands, a sure sign of his confidence that he would smash the tissue of lies that had been put together.'[13] (Many of Kentridge's contemporaries referred to him rubbing his hands and stroking his nose as sure signs of a growing forensic excitement.)

The inquest would last for thirteen days. The venue was once again Pretoria's Old Synagogue, the familiar setting of many of Kentridge's epic legal battles over the previous two decades. Television footage shows Biko's mother and wife, 'icons of grief' as Bizos described them, accompanied by supporters in their hundreds, arriving at the courtroom. It is 14 November 1977, the first day of the hearing, at the height of the South African summer. The jacaranda trees that line the street outside are in bloom, their light purple blossom incongruous to the occasion. On the steps Winnie Kgware, president of the BPC, holds an image of Biko, framed in flowers. She keens a haunting lament:

Senzeni na?	What have we done?
Sono sethu, ubumnyama?	Our sin is that we are black?
Sono sethu yinyaniso?	Our sin is the truth
Sibulawayo	They are killing us
Mayibuye i Africa	Let Africa return

In the same footage Kentridge arrives, quick and bound up in the task awaiting him, oblivious to the cameras. He strides up the steps into the strangely exotic edifice: a venerable place of worship commandeered by the state, its exuberant polychrome brickwork effaced under coats of drab Department of Public Works cream, and now looking like a once grand early picture house fallen on hard times.

Packed into the courtroom within was a sea of people. Mourners, activists, writers and journalists occupied the pews which had accommodated the Treason Trialists almost twenty years earlier. Hilda Bernstein, one of many who left an account of the inquest, noted how what survived of the old stained-glass windows suffused the interior in green and pink light. The reverberative acoustics, better suited to the singing of psalms than to subdued exchanges between witness and advocate, were far from ideal. The tin roof would rattle loudly whenever it rained: the proceedings sometimes had to be adjourned during hailstorms.[14] To improve audibility the electric fans were switched off, turning the interior into a 'sauna bath'. 'The hall was crowded, the heat often unbearable,' recalled the solicitor David Napley, a past president of the English Law

Society, who had flown out to South Africa as an official observer to the proceedings.[15]

The inquest was presided over by the chief magistrate of Pretoria, Marthinus Prins, assisted by two medical experts, 'assessors' who had no formal say in the verdict, but could help the magistrate to weigh the medical evidence: Professor Isidor Gordon of the Natal University medical school and Professor Johannes Oliver of the University of the Orange Free State medical school. Kentridge and his team were outnumbered by lawyers who, in effect, represented various arms of the South African state. Evidence was led by Klaus von Lieres und Wilkau (the Transvaal deputy attorney general), 'a favourite of the security police', explained Bizos. The security police also had their own counsel led by Retief van Rooyen, as did the doctors who had examined Biko.

Von Lieres went straight into the police evidence. He started with the officers who had first arrested Biko, and then moved to those who had detained him over those solitary weeks at Walmer police station. Kentridge started to question a Lieutenant Gert Kuhn in English. The witness answered in Afrikaans, and formally requested that Kentridge put his questions in Afrikaans too. Prins (naturally) had no objection to this – 'Mr Kentridge, isn't it expected of counsel in our courts to be bilingual?' Kentridge was not going to fall into this trap. An inquest conducted in Afrikaans would be a parochial affair, and its vital purpose, to inform the world, would be neutered: 'I choose to ask my questions in English, one of the official languages of this country.'

As Prins dithered, Kentridge pressed home his point: 'Let me say at once that I am quite capable of cross-examining him in Afrikaans. I do not choose to do so.' An electric current seemed to course through the courtroom. Bizos recalled a 'chorus of approval in court'; a 'song of praise' followed Kentridge's words. This was no act of obtuseness. Quite apart from the ranks of international journalists present who knew no Afrikaans, for most of the black spectators English was a familiar first or second language while Afrikaans was a much-hated foreign tongue. A government policy that school teaching of black children should be conducted in Afrikaans only had been one of the sparks of the 1976 Soweto uprising.

Kuhn was followed by Sergeant Paul van Vuuren. He said he had visited Biko in his cell at the police station daily until 6 September, mostly to bring him food. Biko had not spoken to him at all; he had assumed this was out of choice. When Biko returned to Walmer on 11 September, the day before his death, Van Vuuren had found him lying on the floor, foaming at the mouth, his eyes glazed. It was Van Vuuren who had dragged the insensible Biko from his cell – 'like a lifesaver', interjected Magistrate Prins, as if Van Vuuren were deserving of a medal – and raised the alarm that led to the arrival of Dr Tucker later that day.

On the face of it, Van Vuuren's testimony was not proof of police maltreatment, only that something had happened between 6 and 11 September to cause Biko's health to suddenly deteriorate. Kentridge went to work to try to discover more about how Biko had been treated in police custody. The officer explained that he had been ordered to keep Biko naked throughout his time at Walmer, supposedly because of fears that he might use any clothing as a ligature to take his own life. Kentridge put it to Van Vuuren that the real objective had been to humiliate Biko. Van Vuuren responded blandly, complacently: 'I cannot say.' Kentridge pressed the point:

Q: How often was Mr Biko allowed out of his cell?
A: From 18 August to 6 September he was not allowed out of his cell at all.
Q: Isn't a prisoner entitled to exercise in the open air?
A: I was acting on the instructions of Colonel Goosen.

According to one observer, Van Vuuren's answers were given 'with bureaucratic smugness and with a veneer of the defensiveness of a civil servant who admits he has filched a dozen ballpoint pens from the office'.

Now came Major Harold Snyman, head of the security police daytime interrogation team. The inquest was moving towards the critical period, after Biko had been moved from the police station to room 619 in the Sanlam Building. Snyman arrived in the witness box with a briefcase, which he placed on the ledge in front of him. Kentridge's suspicion was that it contained a transmitter, which would illicitly broadcast the proceedings to his colleagues outside, who would later give evidence but were excluded from the courtroom until their turn came. This was not paranoia; it had happened before. He asked that the briefcase be removed. Snyman's face turned crimson.

Once Snyman had regained his composure he displayed even more nonchalant swagger than Van Vuuren. Prefacing every answer to the dolly questions put to him by Von Lieres with an exaggeratedly unctuous 'Your Honour', he explained that on 6 September Biko was interrogated in room 619 from 10.30 in the morning until 6 p.m. Snyman testified that although Biko had started off aggressive, he and other officers had mollified their recalcitrant detainee; removing his handcuffs, giving him a chair to sit on, offering him pies and milk; kindnesses which Biko had refused. As the day wore on, said Snyman, Biko had grown co-operative, volunteering information, even admitting responsibility for the Port Elizabeth pamphlets, which had fomented violence and fire-raising.

So apparently Biko had gone from determined non-cooperation to willing self-incrimination in the course of a few hours' gentle questioning. Kentridge rose to probe that account.

Q: What method of persuasion did you use to make an unwilling witness talk to you? That morning Biko denied all knowledge of the pamphlets, and by 6 p.m. he had admitted drawing them up?

A: Biko was confronted with certain evidence the security police had, then he admitted it.

Q: He first denied it and then admitted it? Why should he answer you at all? Why shouldn't he just whistle at you? Did you make threats?

A: No.

Q: Did you put physical pressure on him?

A: No.

Q: How did you break him down?

A: We told Biko he would remain in detention until he had answered the questions satisfactorily.

Q: Biko was in detention in 1976 for 101 days. What sort of a threat do you think it would be to him to threaten to keep him in detention unless he answered questions? What can you do to a man who insists on keeping silent?

Kentridge asked the question again – and again. There was no answer. Snyman reached for that common resort of the cornered witness: he started answering a question that had not been asked. Kentridge did not allow this distraction: 'You are evading my questions. At the beginning he gave a denial. Later on he gave proper information. How do you get him from the first stage to the second stage?'

Kentridge asked Snyman why Biko had not, at the end of his interrogation on the evening of 6 September, been returned to the Walmer police station. 'I decided not to send him back because of his importance and his aggressive attitude', came the answer; Snyman seemed not to care that five minutes earlier he had told the inquest that Biko had that day been reduced through gentle persuasion to helpful docility. A minor explosion of exasperation escaped Kentridge's lips:

> That is nonsense. He could have been taken back in the same way he was brought to the Sanlam Building – in handcuffs and in a police car – to the comparative comfort of the cell where he would not have to sleep in chains.

Instead, leg irons were placed on Biko and he was chained to a grille in room 619. Why?

A: The office was not locked.
Q: Could you not have locked it? . . . I think you will have to give a
   better answer.
A: [*No answer.*]
Q: Why did you put him in leg irons? Was it to break the man down
   or only to prevent escape?
A: It was the custom.
Q: Are these leg irons a necessary part of your equipment?
A: They are regularly kept in the office.

It was a grotesque image of entwined bureaucracy and brutality (contemporary photographs showed room 619 filled with desks, office chairs and filing cabinets). Kentridge demanded the production of those leg irons. The *Guardian*'s James MacManus reported a gasp in the courtroom as these hideous objects became visible. They were shown to Snyman. Donald Woods's wife Wendy later recalled the moment. 'They were brought in to court and we heard the chains clanking and saw the heavy rings of iron which rubbed Steve's ankles until they bled. We saw Major Snyman, in the witness stand at the time, look at them quite comfortably as if they were standard office equipment.'

Before turning to the events of the next morning, Kentridge asked Snyman how he had responded to the news of Biko's death a few days later.

A: I felt bad about it. He was worth more to us alive than dead.
Q: Is that why you were sorry?
A: I also had sympathy with the death.
Q: Were you surprised he had died?
A: I was surprised. We did not think there was so much wrong with him as . . .
Q: As what?

Snyman had returned to the Sanlam Building at 7 a.m. on 7 September, to relieve the night interrogation team which had taken charge of Biko the previous evening. In his written statement, and in answer to questions put by Von Lieres, Snyman had explained that Biko had now retreated from his confessional mode of the afternoon before: he had lashed out wildly as soon as his handcuffs and leg irons were removed ahead of a new round of questioning. Biko had 'jumped up like a man possessed, grabbed the chair and threw it at me', Snyman claimed. Then Biko had – apparently – charged at Warrant Officer Beneke and pinned him against a steel cabinet. In the melee that followed, Biko had knocked against tables in the office, and then against the wall. The force used to get him under control was, according to Snyman, 'reasonable, and only as much as was necessary to pin him down on the floor and handcuff him'. But he admitted he had not seen Biko bang his head against a wall, and had only drawn 'an inference' that he had. Snyman continued that Biko was then hand-cuffed to a radiator grille and visited at 7.30 a.m. by Colonel Goosen, who asked him questions that Biko refused to answer. Dr Lang arrived at 9.30 a.m., but again Biko refused to answer his questions.

On the inquest's second day Kentridge focused on the struggle that Snyman said had taken place in the early morning of 7 September.

> Q: In your entry [which was later made in the incident book] you said, among other things, that Mr Biko went berserk, that he threw a chair at you and that after a struggle he fell with his head against the wall. Which wall did he knock his head against?
>
> A: Against the northern wall.
>
> Q: Was it between the cabinet and the chair on which he had been sitting?
>
> A: That is correct.
>
> Q: What part of his head hit the wall?
>
> A: The back of his head, he fell several times.
>
> Q: Did you report to Colonel Goosen that he fell with his head against the wall?
>
> A: Yes, I did.
>
> Q: Were all five of you in the room when he fell with his head against the wall?
>
> A: Correct.
>
> Q: Yet Colonel Goosen did not tell the doctor that he fell with his head against the wall. He only said he feared Mr Biko might have had a stroke.
>
> A: I do not know what Colonel Goosen reported to the doctor.
>
> Q: There were 28 affidavits made in connection with the incident [on 7 September] and in none of them is mention made of Mr Biko falling with his head against a wall.

Snyman had no answer. The courtroom was heavy in its silence. Kentridge moved back to the conditions in which Biko had been kept during the weeks he had been detained at the police station. Why had he been completely naked?

> A: To prevent the detainee from committing suicide.
>
> Q: To stop them committing suicide in the police cells? For example with a pair of underpants?

Snyman misunderstood the sarcasm in Kentridge's question. 'No, the person is not wearing underpants, he is completely naked.'

Q: Do you suggest that a man could commit suicide with a pair of
   underpants?
A: It is possible.
Q: You know, we have seen a lot of statements made by the Special
   Branch in which it is said that people have committed suicide
   with their blankets. Do you know about that?
A: Yes, I know that maybe at other places, but we haven't had to deal
   with that in our section.
Q: Yes, but still you let him have blankets?
A: Yes.

In answer to questions now put to him by his counsel Van Rooyen
the major explained that Biko had 'gone beserk' that morning when
confronted with affidavits which supposedly had been made by associates of his who were also in police custody, apparently implicating
him in the bloodthirsty pamphlets. Those affidavits were produced;
copies were provided to Kentridge and his team. They soon saw that
something was very wrong with these documents. Kentridge rose
again to ask Snyman about them.

Q: Major Snyman, do I understand you right when you say that
   these *eedsverklarings* [Kentridge used the Afrikaans word for 'affidavit'] are the *eedsverklarings* which you put to Stephen Biko . . .
   what I want to know is, was it on the 6th or the morning of the
   7th?
A: It was on the morning of the 7th.

So here was an unequivocal answer. It had been extracted, without
putting the witness on his guard, by offering him a choice of two
dates (both of which Kentridge knew to be untrue). And now for the
denouement. Bizos recalled that Kentridge, normally the master of
self-control, could barely suppress his anger.

Yet the dates on these affidavits range from 14 to 30 September. All of
them, in other words, after Biko's death. They could not have been
put to him during his lifetime. What we have got here is a smear
prepared after Biko's death and I think it is a disgrace.

Snyman floundered; he tried to extract himself from the hole he had dug, mouthing that in fact it was just the substance of what the other detainees had supposedly admitted, not the documents themselves, that had been put to Biko that morning. Kentridge's anger rose to new levels: 'You are trying to convict a dead man, a man who could not be convicted when he was alive.'

'The stench of perjury was unmistakable,' noted Bizos. Van Rooyen miserably agreed that the incriminating affidavits supposedly presented to Biko, and which had set off the events leading to his fatal injury, should be withdrawn as evidence.

After Snyman came Warrant Officer Ruben Marx, who had been in the adjoining room at about 7.20 a.m. on 7 September. Marx had rushed into room 619 when he heard a commotion, and found himself having to restrain Biko, who he said – corroborating Snyman's evidence – was 'raving with fury'. Marx told the court that he had heard Biko shout out 'You are harassing me, you are intimidating me!'

Q: This morning Major Snyman used those same words. Do you know that?
A: I don't know anything about this.
Q: Eleven statements have been made about what happened in that room on the morning of the 7th. In not one of those statements is there anything about Mr Biko shouting out, and now this morning for the first time we have the exact same words from you and Major Snyman. I put it to you this is an invention.
A: It is not a fabrication.

Now came perhaps the most important witness of all: the senior officer in overall charge of Biko's detention, Colonel Pieter Goosen, chief of the security police for the Eastern Cape. He was 'a short, thick-set man, determined, unbending and resolute in his upholding of the government's wishes', observed David Napley, who sensed that Goosen had deliberately tried to degrade Biko by keeping him naked and alone until his interrogation began. Answering Von Lieres's questions, Goosen described Biko as a terrorist leader who he thought had been 'playing the fool' after the brawl in the morning of 7

September, refusing to answer questions and mumbling incoherently. Goosen said that nonetheless he had then made arrangements for Biko to be seen by Dr Hersch, who again found nothing physically wrong with him, but who still recommended a lumbar puncture. Goosen insisted that Biko had only been transferred to Pretoria 'as speedily as possible' in 'this office's comfortable Land Rover' because no military aircraft was available, and after it was ascertained that the doctors had no objection. 'Everything possible was done by me to ensure the comfort and health of Mr Biko while in detention,' simpered Goosen.

Kentridge focused first on the two days Biko had spent in room 619. The following passage has become perhaps the most infamous exchange in a South African courtroom.

Q: What right have you to keep a man in chains for 48 hours or more?

A: I have authority as divisional commander to do so to a man detained under section 6 of the Terrorism Act to prevent him committing suicide or injuring himself.

Q: Where do you get your authority from? Show me a piece of paper that gives you the right to keep a man in chains – or are you people above the law?

A: We have full authority. It is left to my sound discretion.

Q: Under what statutory authority?

A: We don't work under statutory authority.

Q: You don't work under statutory authority? Thank you very much, Colonel, that's what we have always suspected . . . I want to know what sort of a man you are. Would you keep a dog chained up in this way for 48 hours?

A: If a dog is an absolute danger I would probably do it. Here in this case this was the position.

Q: He was so dangerous he had to lie on his mat in chains for 48 hours?

A: I had to protect him.

Q: You certainly succeeded. He never got out of your hands . . . until he was let out to die.

Kentridge now moved to the preceding weeks spent in the police cell:

Q: We have been told that Mr Biko was kept naked in the police
   cell. Was this by your order?
A: That is so.
Q: Is there any reason why, for decency's sake, a man should have no
   underpants?
A: For a specific reason. It is to eliminate the risk of suicide.

Kentridge asked Goosen why Biko had not been allowed an hour's outdoor exercise each day, as prison regulations stipulated: 'What right have you to override a standing instruction?' Van Rooyen, sensitive to the eyes of the world's press looking intently at one of his clients, jumped up. Kentridge's questions had nothing to do with Biko's cause of death, he complained. They were simply part of a 'vendetta' against the police. Magistrate Prins sided with Kentridge on this point – a rare occurrence – and ruled that questions about outdoor exercise were valid. A horrifying picture of the carefully orchestrated degradation of a man over several weeks was emerging.

Kentridge moved back to the morning of 7 September. Goosen knew there had been a violent altercation with Biko. Why had he not told the doctor, who then arrived, about the possibility of a head injury?

Q: My submission will be that you knew Mr Biko might have
   suffered a head injury but wanted to draw the doctors' attention
   away from it.
A: That is not so.
. . .
Q: Do you accept that at that time he had sustained a brain injury?
A: I now know it to be possible.
Q: I will submit that a man with a brain injury was left lying in
   chains for 48 hours.
A: If I had known at the time that he had a brain injury I would not.
Q: On your own admission you did not know what was wrong with
   Mr Biko, yet he was left lying on the mat.

A: The medical doctors could find nothing wrong.

Q: That is not quite true. Dr Tucker was sufficiently worried to recommend that Mr Biko should be sent to the prison hospital to be examined by a specialist. In spite of that you left him lying on the mat.

A: I was responsible for the man's safety. I had reason to believe he was shamming. Therefore, I had to keep him like that.

Q: There is good precedent for your behaviour. I understand that in the eighteenth century this was exactly how they treated mental patients.

Van Rooyen was back on his feet again, in protest. 'This is the kind of comment which hits the headlines and should not be allowed.' One newspaper duly carried Kentridge's vivid reference, noting how the audience had responded by 'twittering in both disgust and amusement'.

On and on went Goosen's cross-examination. James MacManus noted that Goosen's 'evident dislike of Kentridge appears mutual'. Kentridge asked why Biko had not been transferred to a local hospital in Port Elizabeth, instead of being driven to Pretoria lying on a mat in the back of a Land Rover.

Q: What was wrong with Port Elizabeth? There are good hospitals in Port Elizabeth.

A: With Mr Biko's background there were good reasons why he could not be kept there.

Q: Often in hospitals, prisoners are kept under 24-hour guard? I know you made a lot of the fact that he studied yoga. Do you think he was a magician?

A: I still thought he was feigning. I thought it was possible that he could be assisted to escape and leave the country. I have often had prisoners under guard in hospitals who succeed in escaping.

Q: Wasn't the real reason that you did not want anybody to see Mr Biko in that condition? You did not think he would die and until he recovered you wanted him kept out of sight.

A: I had no reason to hide him. Neither I, nor any of my colleagues, nor the doctors saw any external injuries.

Goosen had to admit that there were 'contradictions' in Minister Kruger's widely publicised claim that Biko had been on a hunger strike. Kentridge probed how the minister could have been so misinformed. Before what James MacManus described as 'an astounded court', he continued. 'The story of a hunger strike is false, an excuse and a cover-up. Only two question arise: where did the cover-up start and how high did the cover-up go? The answers will tell us a great deal about the death of Steve Biko.' 'I have the sneaking feeling that I have been listening to a consummate piece of artistry,' interjected an angry Van Rooyen for the police. He accused Kentridge of 'speaking up on' matters that could not be introduced as evidence, and he was supported by Von Lieres, who complained that a dossier Kentridge was wielding – containing extracts from the pernicious speeches given by Kruger after Biko's death – was 'an attempt to introduce derogatory evidence which is not admissible in terms of the normal rules' and turn the inquest into a political platform in the run up to the then imminent general election. After much discussion Prins adjourned the court until the next day, 18 November, when he ruled, unsurprisingly, that Kruger's speeches were inadmissible, on the basis that they were 'irrelevant to the circumstances of Mr Biko's death' – even though the speeches had been about precisely those circumstances – and that they were also 'hearsay evidence'. It was an odd way to describe public statements by the minister of justice.

But as if to mollify Kentridge, Van Rooyen offered him a private consultation with two security police brigadiers to discuss any allegations of inaccurate statements made to, or by, Kruger ('Why not have a public consultation so that they can be asked questions in the witness box?' was Kentridge's caustic response.) Yet, although Kentridge appeared to have lost one battle, by going on the offensive he would uncover crucial evidence that would play a key role later in the inquest.

Van Rooyen's re-examination of Goosen followed. When asked how detainees held under section 6 of the Terrorism Act were interrogated, Goosen could not resist a dig at Kentridge: 'Our technique is almost that of Mr Kentridge – sometimes we talk nicely, sometimes we use sarcasm. We have no reason to assault a detainee.' Goosen then confirmed that no charges had ever been laid 'against my assaulting team'. Only after an outburst of derisive laughter in the public gallery did he correct himself: 'I mean my "interrogation team".' Goosen spoke later of the 'politeness and concern with which we treat detainees. We buy them cigarettes, cold drinks and nice things to eat.'

Then came Lieutenant Winston Wilken, part of the 'night team' on duty during Biko's period at the Sanlam Building. David Napley, sitting behind Kentridge, observed that Wilken had eyes 'of underlying anger and a degree of viciousness which I personally found to be terrifying'. But on the face of it Wilken, when initially examined by Von Lieres, was a plausible witness, showing none of Goosen's bluster and hyperbole. Only under cross-examination by Kentridge did he crumble. Was it not strange that a man chained hand and foot had to be watched overnight by a lieutenant and two warrant officers? asked Kentridge. 'Yes probably under normal circumstances. But that was the colonel's instructions.' Wilken claimed that on the evening of 6 September Biko had told him he was finally willing to give a statement, but had then fallen asleep before it could be taken. Had he not tried to wake Biko up?

A: It was . . . not my instructions to wake him up.

Q: You made a big breakthrough. You said you were pleased?

A: My instructions were to leave him and let him rest and when it seemed he was asleep, I left him.

Q: Were you not sitting there on the chair, like a night sister, to ask him a few questions?

Wilken bridled at this sarcasm:

A: I don't like the remark, Your Honour, about the night sister, but I did not ask him any questions.

Q: There were many ways of passing the time that night. I ask you to take the court into your confidence. What were you really doing?

A: [*In a hostile manner*] I don't know what you are insinuating, but nothing happened.

The court was left with the pregnant question: what had really happened that night between the shackled Biko and the three security policemen?

Wilken had accompanied Biko on the Land Rover trip to Pretoria. He had sat in the front passenger seat, a few feet away from Biko, whose condition was, he said, 'normal', except that he would start breathing more heavily when the Land Rover approached traffic lights, as if Biko was still 'shamming' and wanted to advertise his feigned malaise to any passers-by.

A: When we arrived in Pretoria Mr Biko's condition was the same, it was normal.

Q: He was 'normal' you say? We are now speaking of some twelve hours before his death?

When Wilken explained that he had told the guard at Pretoria prison that Biko could easily deceive people – again with an odd reference to his practice of yoga – Kentridge retorted with exasperation:

Why is it that you security police insist on telling people all the time that he [Biko] was shamming? . . . I suggest that it was not Biko that was shamming but members of the security police . . . This constant refrain was to draw attention away from what the security police had actually done.

Wilken's reply was inaudible. He then mumbled that Biko might have stopped 'shamming' in front of prison warders as he regarded them differently from police officers.

'Perhaps that is because prison warders did not assault him.'

Van Rooyen leapt up to complain about Kentridge's allegation of an assault on Biko, which had up to this point been implicit in Kentridge's questions, but not explicitly expressed. Kentridge told the magistrate that it would be his submission that at some point between 6 p.m. on 6 September and 7.30 a.m. on 7 September, Steve Biko had indeed suffered a head injury at the hands of the police. Van Rooyen responded that on the morning of 7 September violence had been initiated by Biko, not by the police, at which point Biko's 'head could have connected with the wall'. Kentridge retorted acidly: 'I would be vastly interested to hear from my learned colleague whether the head came to the wall or the wall came to the head.'

It was now the turn of the doctors. Dr Lang's evidence was problematic for the police. Examined by Von Lieres, he said that he had first visited Biko at 9.30 a.m. on 7 September – not midday as his original note had said – and had told Goosen that he did not think Biko had suffered a stroke. Lang testified that Biko had not complained of any symptoms other than weakness in his limbs and lack of desire to eat, and that he had duly written a report for Goosen saying that he 'could find no organic cause for Mr Biko's apparent weakness' and 'no evidence of any abnormality or pathology on the detainee'. But Dr Lang now admitted he had later prepared a report referring to a lacerated lip and 'bruising over the second vertebra'.

When pressed by Kentridge, Lang could not explain why the cursory report given to Goosen on 7 September had not mentioned any injuries. 'I can't answer, I can't. It is inexplicable,' spluttered Lang. Even Prins seemed astonished by his reply. 'You can't what?' asked the magistrate. 'It is inexplicable, I can't explain to you why,' repeated Lang, who later conceded that his medical certificate was 'highly incorrect'.

Lang now explained that when he had seen Biko's swollen lip the possibility of a head injury had come to his mind 'immediately'. Yet he could not explain why he had not asked Biko, or Goosen, whether a head injury had occurred, and if so, how. Kentridge moved to another matter: Lang had found Biko in chains, wearing urine-soaked trousers and lying under a similarly urine-soaked blanket, but he hadn't asked why, or demanded that he be given clean clothes and bedding. Lang whimpered that with hindsight he should have asked Biko to be released from his chains, and that he should have insisted that the blanket and trousers were removed. Lang said that the possibility of a brain injury was still 'at the back of his mind'; 'But it is not at the forefront of your affidavit, is it?' was Kentridge's devastating follow-up. Kentridge had remorselessly revealed Lang to be a weak doctor, unwilling to contradict or confront the security police, and apparently indifferent to Biko's welfare.

Next up was Lang's superior, Dr Tucker, who was also quickly undone by Kentridge's cross-examination. Like Lang, Tucker admitted that on 8 September Biko was still chained on the floor, with abrasions to his wrists, unable to move easily, and lying under the same urine-soaked blanket that had covered him since the morning of the day before.

Q: Were you not interested why your patient, a grown man, should have wet his bed?
A: I was.
Q: Why didn't you ask him?
A: I cannot answer.
Q: There is only one answer, you knew he couldn't answer you.
A: I'm afraid that is incorrect.
Q: Did you ask Biko how he cut his lip?
A: I did not.
Q: What sort of doctor is it who doesn't ask a patient how he got his injury?
A: Colonel Goosen told me that Biko became aggressive, had to be restrained, and I assumed that the lip injury was the result of this restraint.
. . .
Q: Why didn't you ask?
A: Because this was an assumption that I thought I was entitled to make.
Q: What right have you to make any assumption? Why didn't you ask him?
A: [Reply inaudible.]

Kentridge questioned why Tucker had reported that Biko was 'mentally alert' on 8 September. That was 'not merely misleading, [but] a plainly false statement', Kentridge suggested.

Q: Dr Tucker, if you thought the lip injury was possible evidence of a head injury, oughtn't you to have gone into it further?
. . .
A: I don't think I can reply. There was this history of restraint and the injury could have come from that period.

Q: Why did you not ask, as the obvious question, whether the man received a bump on the head?

A: I did not ask it, and that is all I can say.

Q: Was it not possible that you were reluctant to embarrass Goosen?

A: No.

Q: Either from reading about it or from your own experience, have you knowledge that the police assault people in custody?

A: I have . . . [inaudible]

Q: But on that occasion you did not ask?

A: No, I did not. Where persons are brought to me for examination, my report is completed on a special form. That is all I am required to do . . . I may put it this way, if I am called to see a patient and he has a cut to his head, then I am interested in treating him and not in how he got the cut.

MAGISTRATE PRINS: In your interests in treating the patient, is it not also essential and wise to know what caused it?

A: There was the history that Biko had become hysterical and that he had to be restrained . . .

MAGISTRATE PRINS: Why should it not have been caused by the brain injury?

A: Dr Lang said there were no signs of bruising around the head.

KENTRIDGE: Let me start again. You are a professional man and you are not doing yourself justice. Are you not aware that sometimes there are cases of people assaulted in custody? Did you not think about it?

A: No.

. . .

Q: If you see someone and you had the suspicion that he had some neurological damage and you know he was in some sort of violent incident, would you not have asked whether he had received a blow on the head?

A: [Reply inaudible.]

Q: I am suggesting to you that the reason you did not ask was because you were dealing with the security police?

A: No.

By the end of this cross-examination, punctuated by bursts of outraged laughter from the public gallery, it was clear to most people in the Old Synagogue – including even Magistrate Prins – that Tucker was either in awe of the security police, or intimidated by them.

The following day Kentridge turned to Tucker's later examination of Biko, on 11 September, the day before he died. Although Goosen had told Tucker that Biko had collapsed, frothing at the mouth and hyperventilating, Tucker spent a mere five minutes examining him. The doctor admitted he raised no objection to Biko being taken to Pretoria in the Land Rover, which he described as a 'quasi-ambulance', and added that he still thought Biko's condition was 'satisfactory'.

By raising a hypothetical example, Kentridge then revealed just how indifferent Tucker had been to Biko's plight:

Q: Let us assume that some holidaymakers from Pretoria had come to see you in Port Elizabeth about their child who had been acting in a bizarre way. The parents suspected that the child did not want to go back to school, but he was lying on the floor, had red cells in his spinal fluid, froth at the mouth, was hyperventilating and was weak in the left limbs. Would you have permitted his parents to drive 700 miles to Pretoria?

A: The circumstances were different. I would have insisted that the child should go into hospital immediately. Here there was an uncertainty.

Q: Shouldn't that have made you more careful rather than less careful? Isn't the only difference that in Biko's case Colonel Goosen insisted that he did not go into hospital?

A: I wouldn't say insisted. He was averse to the suggestion.

Q: Why didn't you stand up for the interests of your patient?

A: I didn't know that in this particular situation one could override the decisions made by a responsible police officer.

PROF. GORDON: Why didn't you say that unless Biko went to hospital you would wipe your hands of it?

A: I did not think at that stage that Mr Biko's condition would become so serious. There was still the question of possible shamming.

KENTRIDGE: Did you think that a man could feign red blood cells in his cerebral spinal fluid?

A: No.

Q: In terms of the Hippocratic oath, to which I take it you
subscribe, are not the interests of your patient paramount?

A: Yes.

Q: But in this instance they were subordinated in the interests of the
security police?

A: Yes.

It was a devastating exchange.

Kentridge reminded the court that the mark found on Biko's fore-head after his death was, according to the pathologists, between four and eight days old, and must have been visible to any doctor examining him in the last few days of his life. Tucker's pathetic response was that while the scab may have been there, it may not have been visible as it was the same colour as Biko's skin. When Kentridge put it to Dr Tucker that a report he wrote after the examination, excluding serious cerebral injury as a possibility, was a 'false statement', Tucker admitted that it 'may have been badly worded'.

The inquest was entering its final furlong. The last medical professional to see Biko before his death arrived in the witness box: Dr Andries van Zyl, who said that in the early morning of 12 September, when he arrived in Pretoria, Biko was 'medically a sick, sick man . . . he was comatose'. Kentridge then called Dr Gluckman, the pathologist appointed by the Biko family. He said that the failure of doctors to spot Biko's head injury before his death was 'beyond my comprehension'.

The inquest's penultimate day involved a surprise reappearance by Colonel Goosen. Although Kentridge had failed to get a more senior security police officer to testify about how and why Kruger came to tell the world that Biko had died of a hunger strike, he had by now obtained a copy of a telex message – presumably handed over in error – sent by Goosen to his superiors shortly after Biko's death. Although Goosen had maintained in his evidence that he had believed Biko was 'shamming', his telex made no mention of feigned illness, and stated that Biko was already in a 'semi-coma' when he was carried to the Land Rover on 11 September. Perhaps more importantly, the telex referred to an injury 'which was inflicted' (*togedien* in Afrikaans) on 7 September, suggesting that Goosen knew Biko had been deliberately assaulted, not injured accidentally while being restrained.

Here was evidence that surely destroyed Goosen's claim that Biko may have had a stroke or been shamming. It was also now apparent that Goosen had never reported to his superiors that Biko had refused food or drink. Kentridge asked the policeman once again on what basis Kruger had falsely stated that Biko had gone on hunger strike. Goosen, who had already assumed a number of contorted positions in the inquest, now sought to distance himself from the minister to whom he reported.

> Q: We are left with the situation that the Minister of Police made more than one statement in public about Mr Biko's detention which we in court have shown to be incorrect and misleading on the evidence.
> A: I have no information, only my own opinion.
> Q: We can all form our own opinions, but we can't express them in court.
> A: I reported and can't comment.

Goosen was still clinging to the proposition that, even though Biko was in a 'semi-coma' on his final journey to Pretoria, he might have been faking.

> Q: You were worried about Mr Biko, but thought he might be shamming?
> A: That is correct.
> Q: Although he was in a semi-coma?
> A: I still thought there might be some shamming.

★

On the inquest's final day, 1 December, Kentridge delivered a closing submission that has been much quoted in the years since. In advocacy devoid of bravado or showiness, he went through the mountain of evidence given at the inquest. Biko's young life been cut short not by some mysterious accident, or a stroke, or self-inflicted starvation, but because he had been violently assaulted by security policemen, woefully neglected by doctors, and then left to die alone in a cold cell.

Mr Biko was detained on the 18 August 1977, whilst in good health. He died 26 days later. What the security police themselves admit they subjected him to during this period is more than a matter for comment. The admitted assaults on his dignity under the direction of Colonel Goosen are evidence of a callous disregard for his legal and human rights and are highly relevant in assessing the evidence of those who abused him.

Goosen's statement that 'everything was done for the comfort and health of Steve Biko' was 'as cynical a statement as any heard in a court of law'. Far from being looked after, 'there is indisputable evidence', said Kentridge, that Biko 'went into the interrogation room alive and well [but] he came out a physical and mental wreck'. He had then 'died a miserable and lonely death on a mat on a stone floor in a prison cell'. Kentridge singled out the physicians who had treated – or rather mistreated – Biko for special criticism.

[As] time passed, one falsehood was compounded by another: Dr Lang's false report . . . that nothing wrong was found and Dr Tucker's claim that the dying man was in a satisfactory condition on his removal to Pretoria. The police felt confident they could rely upon the doctors to support them. And their confidence was justified. Perhaps strengthened thereby they, with gross impertinence [*what an extraordinary phrase that was*] – presented to this court a totally implausible account of Mr Biko's death – starting with a fanciful description of a struggle violent in the extreme, in which no blow was struck, a bizarre account of an alleged shamming when to any candid observer a man's progress to his death was being seen and described and all the while the refusal to acknowledge the head injury.

A court – including an inquest court – is the brake upon the abuse of power. It must be made known by this court that the penalty for falsehood contemptuously fabricated is not merely rebuke or reprimand but a firm finding adverse to the fabricators; if you create a tissue of lies it can only be that you dare not speak the truth.

Accordingly the verdict which we submit is the only one reasonably open to this court is one finding that the death of Mr Biko was due to a criminal assault upon him by one or more of the eight members of the security police in whose custody he was on the 6th or 7th September, 1977.

This inquest has exposed grave irregularity and misconduct in the treatment of a single detainee. It has, incidentally, revealed the dangers to life and liberty involved in the system of holding detainees incommunicado.

A firm and clear verdict may help to prevent further abuse of the system. In the light of further disquieting evidence before this court, any verdict which can be seen as an exoneration of the Port Elizabeth security police will unfortunately be interpreted as a licence to abuse helpless people with impunity. This court cannot allow that to happen.

As Kentridge sat down seventy people in the public gallery, including Steve Biko's family, silently left the courtroom to hold a vigil outside.

In response to the devastating directness of Kentridge's words, his opponent resorted to a common lawyerly tactic: the deployment of florid speech to mask the unattractiveness of your case. Van Rooyen proclaimed that he did not know whether to begin with the facts or with 'the irresponsible fiction that has been delivered to Your Worship this morning' by Kentridge. 'Without a pickle of evidence before Your Worship to show an unlawful assault, the way was clear to fill up the void with glorious imaginings. There is an element of fairy tale here, just like Hans Christian Andersen, or more likely the Brothers Grimm.' It is a wonder the earth did not open up to swallow the police officers' counsel.

As the hearing ended the *New York Times* recorded that 'The court's finding, scheduled to be delivered at 11 a.m. tomorrow, is widely expected to be the most important judicial ruling in South Africa's recent history.' But Magistrate Prins did not feel the heavy hand of history upon his shoulder. His verdict, delivered at the appointed time on 2 December, took some two minutes to read out.

This is my finding in terms of the Inquest Act, No. 58 of 1959:

The identity of the deceased is Stephen Bantu Biko, Black man, approximately 30 years old;

Date of death: 12 September 1977;

Cause or likely cause of death: Head injury with associated extensive brain injury, followed by contusion of the blood circulation,
disseminated intravascular coagulation as well as renal failure with
uraemia. The head injury was probably sustained during the morning
of Wednesday, the 7th of September, when the deceased was involved
in a scuffle with members of the Security Branch of the South African
Police at Port Elizabeth.

The available evidence does not prove that the death was brought
about by any act or omission involving or amounting to an offence on
the part of any person. That completes this inquest.

That was it. The public gallery seemed in shock. Biko's widow was
heard to ask, over and over, 'No one to blame?' Outside the court
protestors chanted 'They have killed Steve Biko. What have we done?
Our sin is that we are black.' Far beyond the walls of the Old Synagogue
the world recorded its astonishment at the unblushing travesty of
justice, which seemed to mock the very word 'verdict' – literally, 'the
speaking of truth'. In the face of the furore, Prins declared with sanctimonious banality: 'I have only one standard, and that's my conscience.'
It is hard to think of a more hypocritical invocation of Calvinist
doctrine.

Kentridge had half anticipated Prins's decision. 'Given the history
of previous inquests into deaths of detainees, the verdict, perverse as
it was, was by no means a surprise to us,'[16] he said decades later. Still,
the outcome put him into a state of despair. Kentridge's daughter,
Eliza, then aged fifteen, also recalls the profound effect the outcome
had on her father, as well as her pride in his work. George Bizos
wrote that his leader had been 'devastated by the magistrate's unbeliev-
ably brief and patently wrong judgment', and recalled Kentridge
asking shortly afterwards: 'Is it worthwhile continuing to practise in
the courts?'[17] That the policemen who had killed Biko had been
found guilty by the jury of international opinion was not enough:
Kentridge had by now spent almost thirty years seeking justice in the
courts of South Africa, and in one of the most important cases of his
career, justice had been outrageously denied. Undoubtedly the Biko
verdict played a part in his and his wife Felicia's decision to move to
England at the end of the 1970s, even if Kentridge only shifted his

legal practice there gradually. For the next ten years he would participate in some of the most important political cases heard in the South African courts.

The Biko inquest made Kentridge internationally famous. Laudatory profiles appeared in newspapers in the United States, Britain and beyond. The *New York Times* described a 'scholarly looking lawyer' who combined professionalism with humanity and a love of the operas of Mozart:

> Standing at the counsel's desk in the converted synagogue that serves as a courtroom, his black hair curling fashionably over his collar, he has produced a series of chilling revelations about the much-feared security police as well as damaging discrepancies in the police account of the events preceding Mr Biko's death.[18]

The *Guardian* noted Kentridge's

> cold glittering eyes, under bushy eyebrows and a forehead knitted in a permanent frown. Two unruly shocks of greying hair burst from each temple . . . His penetrating questions and forceful personality make it 'just as terrifying to be his client as it is to face him in the witness stand' said a former client . . . But as deadly as his questions are his sense of irony and sarcasm is even more dangerous. The old synagogue has echoed with laughter as Kentridge's prodding often moved the police to the point of ridicule.[19]

It is fruitless – indeed Kentridge would contend irrelevant – to ask whether the Biko inquest was the most important case of his career. It is enough to say that it was one which caught the conscience of a world whose attention had largely strayed from the evils of the apartheid regime. Perhaps its most far-reaching legacy was finally to convince the great democracies that apartheid South Africa was a rogue state that needed to be ostracised. The *New York Times* branded the verdict a 'whitewash' and said that 'the only mystery . . . is which of the security officers who interrogated Mr Biko actually administered the fatal blows'. In London, even the *Daily Telegraph*, a paper not noted for its liberalism, said that the verdict was 'very shocking'.

How had this inquest succeeded in provoking the world's collective disgust when so many other instances of deaths in custody had gone ignored? The prominence of Steve Biko was, clearly, an important factor; but the extraordinary power of effective cross-examination, described by one American jurist many years ago as 'the greatest legal engine ever invented for the discovery of the truth',[20] played a vital part in galvanising opinion. Apart from Dr Gluckman, all the witnesses who gave evidence were, in one way or another, servants of the state bent on self-exculpation and occlusion of the truth. Kentridge and his fellow counsel had almost nothing to pit against this wall of mendacity but the spoken word. Day after day he exposed the lies through questions. The fact that the inquest became instantly associated with orchestrated falsehood and state-mandated physical abuse is a function of Kentridge's advocacy. As the English barrister Lord Alexander of Weedon later said: 'Through remorseless and deadly cross-examination, sometimes with brilliant irony, Kentridge established that the founder of the Black Consciousness Movement had been killed by police brutality. The verdict of accidental death was seen as risible.'[21] Marcel Berlins, who covered the case for *The Times*, would later describe Kentridge's performance at the inquest as 'the most extraordinary feat of advocacy I have ever seen'.[22]

On 2 February 1978, founding himself on Prins's verdict, the attorney general of the Eastern Cape stated that he would not prosecute any of the security police officers who had testified at Biko's inquest. Yet this was not the end of the court proceedings that followed from his death. Kentridge and the other lawyers who had appeared in the Old Synagogue were retained again on behalf of Biko's family to sue the state for wrongful injury and medical neglect. One obstacle to the latter claim was that Professor Loubser, the state pathologist, had testified at the inquest that the injury sustained by Biko was irreversible, and that he would have died anyway even if he had received immediate medical care. A meeting took place at Kentridge's home to discuss the medical evidence. By an administrative mistake his attorney invited Loubser to join it. Kentridge was surprised to see him and engaged the professor in small talk about the motorbike

Loubser had arrived on. Once the other lawyers and medical experts had arrived, Kentridge asked ('with unaccustomed diffidence', recalled Bizos): 'Well, who would like to start?' Loubser raised his hand and said that, contrary to the evidence he had given at the inquest, he now believed that Biko might have survived if given prompt medical attention. Kentridge reacted 'as if that was what he really expected from the professor', but in reality Loubser's statement was a game-changer. As a result of it, the lawsuit never came to court: a settlement offer of 30,000 rand, later raised to 65,000 rand, was paid in July 1979. Meanwhile Tucker and Lang continued to practise as doctors. For many years legal proceedings rumbled on with a view to having them struck off for breach of the fundamental ethical rule of the profession of physician. Kentridge's fight for justice continued; he persuaded a court that the decision of the South African Medical Council not to discipline the men was irrational.[23] Eventually Tucker was found guilty of disgraceful conduct and Lang was reprimanded.

Steve Biko's memory remained a rallying cry for anti-apartheid campaigners throughout the 1980s and beyond. His life and death inspired books and songs, including Peter Gabriel's plangent anthem, simply entitled 'Biko' ('the eyes of the world are watching now'), released in 1980; needless to say, the South African government banned it. John Blair wrote a celebrated play, *The Biko Inquest*, drawn entirely from the transcripts and staged in 1984 at the Riverside Studios in London, with Albert Finney playing Kentridge. In his review for *The Times*, Bernard Levin wrote of having been over-whelmed by the experience: enraged by what the play depicted, but also inspired by a feeling of catharsis.

> Just as we do not leave *King Lear* destroyed by the horrors we have seen, we do not leave the Riverside brought low by the horrors we have heard about. Instead there is a feeling of something strangely like exal-tation, which comes – which can only come – from the realisation that, however many more Bikos have to die, in the end we shall see in South Africa one more proof that a house builded upon sand cannot stand.

As for Kentridge:

the latest in that great line of lawyers from Cicero to Clarence Darrow, who have served truth against its enemies, [he] comes to full life upon the stage, indicting wickedness in words of fire that burn the more savagely for being so carefully doused. (The hypnotic force of the 'play' is so remarkable that when, on the opening night, with the lawyer in the audience, the magistrate said 'Very well, carry on Mr Kentridge', Sydney found himself rising to his feet . . .)[24]

A year later, the play was televised, with Finney reprising his role. Reviewing the film version, the *New York Times* found itself similarly enamoured:

The hero of their piece is quite clearly Sydney Kentridge, the lawyer representing the Biko family . . . Mr Finney's Kentridge begins chipping away at the official stories until finally his questions are openly couched in sarcastic disbelief and anger. He is battling more than the familiar techniques of stonewalling. He is confronting racism, confident of its own superiority and its right to do anything where persons of a different color are concerned . . . Mr Kentridge is said to have taken the case knowing full well he wouldn't win. He did lose the case but he succeeded in his quest to win worldwide attention for the Biko story . . .[25]

In 1987 Richard Attenborough's film *Cry Freedom* – as accurate a portrayal as any of Steve Biko's life, given that Donald Woods was engaged as a consultant – was released, and was nominated for three Oscars. Starring Denzel Washington as Biko and Kevin Kline as Woods, the film had a number of leading British actors in cameo roles, including Timothy West, Ian Richardson and John Thaw as Kruger. But no actor played the part of Kentridge. Biko's inquest was reduced to one short scene in which Prins delivers his verdict to a courtroom full of startled, but unidentified, lawyers. The demands of big-budget movies meant that there was little about Black Consciousness, or how Biko came to be one of its leaders. While the last hundred pages of Donald Woods's memoir *Biko* focus on the inquest, the last hour of *Cry Freedom* is more interested in the drama of Woods's escape from South Africa on New Year's Eve 1977, disguised as a Catholic priest.

The truth of what really happened to Biko in those days in Port Elizabeth in September 1977 remained elusive. In the late 1980s George Bizos confronted Harold Snyman during another case involving the death of a detainee, and asked him about his role in Biko's death; Snyman refused to answer. It took almost twenty years to arrive at anything close to the truth. In 1996 Snyman and his interrogation team – or 'assaulting team' as he had more accurately referred to them at the inquest – sought amnesty from the Truth and Reconciliation Commission (TRC) established after the end of apartheid. The hearing before the TRC came shortly after President Mandela had unveiled a bronze stature of Biko on the twentieth anniversary of his death. The former officers now admitted that they had indeed assaulted Biko, not on the morning of 7 September 1977, but a full day earlier, almost as soon as he was put into room 619. It was revealed that Biko, brave to the end, had demanded a chair to sit on while being interrogated, and was savagely beaten for his insolence. When Biko protested at such treatment the other officers had piled in and slammed his head against the wall. On the Saturday after Biko's death all the officers involved got together with Colonel Goosen to fabricate the story they later presented to the inquest. Snyman's admission was not accompanied by much contrition. He told the TRC: 'I would agree that it was inhumane but we were acting under instructions.' One of his colleagues even had the effrontery to tell the TRC that he had felt that the killing of Biko was justified to stem the rise of Communism and ensure 'the continuation of a normal Western democracy as I know it'. Such was the indoctrination of the adherents of apartheid.

After the fall of apartheid the Sanlam Building was renamed Steve Biko House. It gradually fell into disrepair and disuse. In 2017 it was decided that it would be refurbished as a social housing project. The local council announced that 'The side handover ceremony will be preceded by the cleansing and blessing ceremony of the building to afford healing and closure to the former detainees who were tortured in the building.'

The Biko Inquest was the last significant legal proceeding to take place in the Old Synagogue. Soon after its conclusion the building was turned over to more banal government activities. It fell into disuse in 1995 and, although it was declared a national monument in 1999, the Old Synagogue has endured a long and sad decline since. Various suggestions have been made over the years to repurpose the building for cultural or educational uses; none have come to pass. Today it still stands, boarded up and crumbling, surrounded by a razor wire fence, a symbol of an era of oppression and tragedy but also of resistance and hope.

Epilogue: The London Years

IN 1976, AS he was approaching his mid fifties, Sydney Kentridge began to consider his direction. He had been practising at the Johannesburg Bar for over twenty-five years, and had been the chairman of its Bar Council in 1972/3, in which role he had been vocal in his criticism of government policy. By the early 1970s Kentridge had reached the pinnacle of his profession in South Africa. Yet there was a nagging desire to try something new – even in middle age – and the thought of practice in London took root in Kentridge's mind. His wife Felicia had always said that every twenty-five years one should reinvent oneself, and here lay an opportunity to do so.

This thirst for a new start was coupled with a growing disillusionment with legal practice in South Africa. As the 1970s wore on, opposition to the Nationalist regime seemed to wither. In the 1960s the hope that apartheid might prove a temporary aberration maintained morale and faith in the future, but the following decade it was still firmly entrenched and had acquired a sense of gloomy permanence. As we have seen, one of the characteristics of apartheid South Africa in its early period was the integrity of its judiciary and its adherence to the rule of law, even while its judges were having to apply increasingly repressive statutes. By the 1970s judicial appointments were becoming overtly political; the vacancies on the bench increasingly filled by Nationalist placemen whose primary loyalty was not to notions of justice but to the politicians who had appointed them and the pernicious creed they espoused. (Given Kentridge's status as a leading anti-apartheid advocate, it was obvious that a judicial career in South Africa was out of the question; in any event, Kentridge was not prepared to administer apartheid laws.) Any self-respecting lawyer has to believe in the quality of the justice being administered in the courts in which he or she operates; once that belief evaporates then the practice of law can become a charade. By the mid-seventies, after bitter experience of one overtly political judgment after another, Kentridge's faith in the legal system in which he practised had reached a low ebb.

At the time Kentridge knew only two English lawyers well: Michael Kerr, formerly a QC in a shipping chambers in Essex Court in the Temple, who had become a high court judge in the early 1970s (Kerr had been at Cambridge with Michael Parkington); and George Newsom QC, a chancery barrister whom Kentridge had met while on holiday in Austria. Both were benchers of Lincoln's Inn, which they encouraged Kentridge to join. Kerr was in some ways a kindred spirit of Kentridge. Born in Berlin in 1922, he and his family had fled Germany in 1933 and wound up in Britain after his father Alfred, a prominent writer and theatre critic of Jewish extraction, had managed to sell a script to the Hungarian émigré film producer Alexander Korda. The film was never made but the family settled in London in genteel penury. Kerr, whose sister Judith became a celebrated children's writer, would later claim to be the first foreign-born English judge since the thirteenth century. Kentridge consulted Kerr on how to get a foothold in a London chambers. Kerr was of the view that his former chambers were too specialist for a man of Kentridge's range. Instead he recommended that Kentridge apply to 1 Brick Court, adjacent to Essex Court, and then fast on the way to becoming the leading commercial chambers in England.[1]

An application to join a barristers' chambers in today's world invariably involves the most searching process. In the 1970s life was rather more relaxed. Kentridge recalls a meeting with the chambers' de facto head Robert (Bob) Alexander QC – then one of the most prominent barristers at the Bar – and its legendary head clerk Ronald Burley. When I asked him whether he had to present a curriculum vitae, Kentridge looked surprised. (I doubt he has ever prepared such a document in his life.) The interview clearly went well, and it ended with an offer to join 1 Brick Court as a 'door tenant' – listed with the other members of chambers on the roster traditionally painted in black lettering on a white board beside the entrance, but practising from other premises. In those days of benevolent dictatorship

Kentridge doubts whether Alexander or Burley consulted other members of chambers on the decision. As he began to spend more time in London Kentridge was given the use of the room of another member of chambers, Nicholas Lyell, who was then combining a parliamentary career with a legal practice. Kentridge's door tenancy, which formally commenced in July 1977, eventually turned into full membership, and Brick Court would remain his chambers until his retirement in 2013.

Burley, conservative both in his politics and his habits, maintained a clear divide between clerks and barristers, which he expected to be respected on both sides. He did not socialise with his 'governors' and insisted on being addressed simply as 'Burley' (whereas 'his' barristers were always Mr X or Miss Y). He would later leave clear instructions that none of his former barristers should attend his funeral (none did, though many wished to).[2] Burley would quickly mark out those barristers within his chambers who were destined for greatness, and so deserving of his support. He immediately identified Kentridge as a future star. They may not have seemed natural allies: their world views were certainly not aligned. But there was a mutual respect between them and their mutually beneficial working relationship endured until Burley retired in 1990. Kentridge tells the story that one day some members of chambers were twitting Burley about their recent South African recruit: 'But isn't Mr Kentridge very left-wing?' Burley replied approvingly that what he did know was that every time he phoned Kentridge at his home in Johannesburg the voice at the end of the line would respond that 'the Master is by the swimming pool'.

Kentridge's shift to practice in London was a gradual one. Having been called to the English Bar on 28 July 1977, he continued to practise mainly in South Africa, flying to London for a few months during the South African legal summer vacation (i.e. from the end of November to February). In 1980 he demonstrated a clear commitment to his London life by buying Bob Alexander's Georgian town house in Sandwich Street, Bloomsbury. He applied for silk in November 1982[3] but his application was refused, apparently because Lord Hailsham, the then Lord Chancellor, took the view that because of the circumstances of his birth Kentridge was ineligible to be appointed Queen's Counsel.⁴ Kentridge, who recalls that Hailsham (a staunch and prominent Conservative, once tipped for leadership of the party) seemed to harbour an animus towards him, still retains the lengthy correspondence with the Lord Chancellor's department that ensued. Kentridge persuaded the department that Hailsham's objection was baseless and took silk the next year, in 1984, apparently with the firm support of the then Attorney General Michael Havers.

The career that followed scaled the same heights that he had previously achieved in South Africa. The list of his cases is stupendous. In 1986 he acted (pro bono) in the Bar Council's challenge to the Lord Chancellor's decision to raise criminal legal aid rates (at the time set very low) by a derisory sum. Kentridge enjoyed sweet revenge against the man who had sought to thwart his English career when the Lord Chief Justice made clear during the hearing that the Bar Council's case seemed unanswerable and Hailsham capitulated.⁵ The case received much media coverage. The fact that a man who had so recently started practising in earnest in England was entrusted with this case demonstrates the status that Kentridge had achieved even by the mid-1980s.

In 1988 Kentridge was retained by P&O in the corporate manslaughter prosecution arising from the *Herald of Free Enterprise* disaster, which led to the loss of 193 lives in the Channel. His junior, Jonathan Caplan (now QC), recalls how the Old Bailey courtroom, teeming with lawyers acting for multiple parties, became like a lecture theatre as Kentridge expounded on the law. He developed his argument with such mesmeric authority that the judge, Mr Justice Turner, not a man noted for his reticence, listened spellbound. He was so in awe of Kentridge that at one point he started addressing the barrister as 'My Lord', as if he were appearing in front of Kentridge, rather than the other way round.⁶

In 1992 Kentridge appeared on behalf of Dr Nigel Cox, charged with attempted murder after having deliberately administered an overdose of potassium chloride to a terminally ill patient who had implored him to end her life. Although the doctor was found guilty, the suspended sentence reflected the fact that he had acted out of compassion. These were the only two criminal trials in which Kentridge appeared in England. However he conducted a number of criminal appeals, including acting for the Crown in responding successfully to Ernest Saunders's appeal,[7] and for the defendant in one of the longest criminal cases heard in the House of Lords in the twentieth century, *R v Preston*.[8] Kentridge also appeared pro bono in a number of appeals to the Privy Council by convicted murderers sentenced to death in various Caribbean countries. During his South African practice Kentridge had saved many lives from the gallows. Now he was continuing that task. His archive contains poignant letters from men on death row seeking his assistance.

Kentridge appeared in dozens of cases in the House of Lords, Privy Council and Supreme Court. Although these were mainly in the fields of commercial and constitutional law, he achieved the status, attained by very few advocates, of being retained in cases on appeal across the full ambit of the law. So he appeared in the leading construction case of the 1990s, *Linden Gardens v Lenesta Sludge* (the issue too recondite to merit explanation here);[9] for the *Guardian* newspaper in the Sarah Tisdall secrets case;[10] for CBS Songs in its failed attempt to sue Amstrad electronics for breach of copyright because of its sale of tape recorders to the public;[11] and for Tiny Rowland in his lengthy battle with Mohamed al-Fayed over the purchase of Harrods.[12] In the field of public law Kentridge appeared for a Zairean citizen who successfully established that the Home Secretary was in contempt of court (a legal first),[13] and shortly after he represented the Foreign Secretary in resisting William Rees-Mogg's quixotic challenge to the ratification of the Maastricht Treaty.[14] In a later lecture Kentridge deployed his characteristically sardonic humour when recalling those two cases:

> Some years ago I had the privilege of appearing in the House of Lords in a case in which my client was seeking to cite the Home Secretary for contempt of court. Sir William Wade had described that case as the most important constitutional case to come before English courts in over 200 years. Some three weeks later I appeared in a Divisional Court case on behalf of the Foreign Secretary in order to defend the constitutionality of the United Kingdom's adherence to the Maastricht Treaty. My opponent told the Court that that was the most important constitutional case for 300 years. My comment was that it was at least the most important constitutional case for three weeks.[15]

A few years later Kentridge acted on behalf of the soldiers who had been on duty during Bloody Sunday in 1972, in which twenty-six unarmed protestors in Northern Ireland were shot by British troops, fourteen of whom died. He successfully argued that their anonymity should be maintained during the Saville Inquiry into the events of that day.[16] The case involved the submission that Lord Saville, an academically brilliant member of the House of Lords, and his two colleagues, had acted irrationally in making a decision which no reasonable tribunal could have made. Given the seriousness of that submission, the legal team which acted for the soldiers had decided that a judicial review was only likely to succeed if argued by Kentridge. In the course of argument Lord Woolf, who was presiding over the Court of Appeal, asked whether there was 'any compelling justification for naming the soldiers'. It was a question which Kentridge had anticipated. In a moment of pure theatre he asked the court usher to retrieve a law report from the dusty shelves in court. He then proceeded to read a passage from a House of Lords authority in the light of which he responded to Lord Woolf's question by adding that not only was there no compelling justification for the inquiry's decision to deprive the soldiers of anonymity but that it had been 'a mistake – a vital mistake', and then added the devastating comment: 'and we all know who may have to pay the price for that mistake. And we all know who won't!'

With less success, he represented the Countryside Alliance in its attempt to overturn the anti-fox-hunting legislation enacted during the Blair government (he notes that of the fourteen judges who heard the case he did not persuade a single one of the validity of his argument).[17] Kentridge also acted over a number of years for the Chagos Islanders in their attempts to return to their homeland after their forcible eviction in the 1960s by the British government to allow the construction of the US military base on Diego Garcia.

While Kentridge became predominantly an appeal advocate, in his early years in London he appeared in numerous heavy trials. Charles Hollander (now QC), whom Kentridge led a number of times, recalls a four-week case in the Copyright Tribunal in 1991 in which they were acting for various record companies against music publishers and composers seeking an increase in their royalty rate. Hollander recalls: 'It was never clear to anyone whether Sydney's apparent complete ignorance of the pop music industry was genuine. At a conference with the two most important record company executives in the UK, he spent the entire meeting referring to the pop star "Mike" Jackson.'[18] During the trial Kentridge had to cross-examine the record producer Pete Waterman, then at the height of his fame, in preparation for which he was provided with 'the beginner's guide to Kylie Minogue', one of Waterman's star acts. Hollander records the following exchange:

Q: Mr Waterman, I understand you are in favour of an increase in
the royalty rate?
A: Yes, absolutely, I think it is incredibly important that the contri-
bution of songwriters is properly recognised.
Q: What is the current royalty rate?
A: Sorry?
Q: What do you understand to be the current royalty rate?
A: Well, I can't recall precisely what the figure is.
Q: Can you not tell us what the current figure is?
A: No.
Q: How can you be in favour of an increase if you do not know
what the current figure is?

Hollander recalls another moment in the case, when Kentridge was cross-examining a different witness, 'a slippery individual'. With great solemnity Kentridge said: 'I want you to listen to my next question very carefully and think about your answer. Because, depending on your answer I may have to put to you something I have not had to put to a single witness before this tribunal.'

'You could have heard a pin drop. The witness started backpedalling frantically and Sydney did not need to call him a liar,' Hollander continues. Kentridge won the case.[19]

Although his practice tilted towards England during the 1980s, Kentridge still appeared in numerous significant cases in South Africa (we saw in Chapter 4 that he acted for the Sharpeville Six in their much-publicised appeal) before finally giving up his South African practice at the end of the decade. In 1982 he acted for Auret van

Heerden, a student leader who had been severely tortured while in police detention. Van Heerden sued the minister of police and the case lasted several weeks. One of the defence witnesses was the notorious spy and assassin Craig Williamson. He is said to have described the experience of being cross-examined by Kentridge as one of the most terrifying of his life. Kentridge's last case in South Africa involved an application brought by the End Conscription Campaign against the minister of defence to prevent the state harassing and intimidating its employees.[20] His junior Jeremy Gauntlett (now SC and QC) recalls that the day before the hearing, counsel for the minister produced an affidavit. This sought to oust the court's jurisdiction on the basis that South Africa was under martial law (its forces were still embroiled in conflict in Namibia, with forays into Angola, Lesotho, Swaziland and Zimbabwe). Kentridge disposed of the point with the withering put-down that this would be the first time in legal history that martial law had been proclaimed by a brigadier in an affidavit.

From the 1980s Kentridge increasingly practised on a world stage. He appeared in the European Court of Human Rights and the European Court of Justice. He even submitted an amicus brief in the United States Supreme Court in the landmark Guantanamo Bay case of *Rasul v Bush*, providing a lucid analysis of the English law of habeas corpus.[21] As we saw in Chapter 1, Kentridge spent a few momentous months sitting in the South African Constitutional Court. He also sat in the Botswana, Jersey and Guernsey Courts of Appeal. Had he commenced practice in England rather earlier, many believe he would have found his way as a judge to the House of Lords.

Kentridge did not keep up with the technological revolution that radically changed the practicalities of lawyering from the 1990s onwards. The computer in his chambers was rarely put to use. Kentridge hand-wrote his skeleton arguments and opinions, or else amended in manuscript the drafts prepared by his juniors. On the occasion of Kentridge's eighty-fifth birthday Arthur Chaskalson, then the chief justice of South Africa, recalled the following story:

> Sometimes his demeanour may seem austere but that could be misleading. Ismail Mahomed told the story of his first brief with Sydney shortly after he came to the Bar. It was an appeal against a disgraceful

decision of a magistrate in a trial in the Magistrates Court. Ismail worked extremely hard on the draft, anxious to impress his renowned leader. He left it at Sydney's chambers. Later when they met, Sydney looked at him gravely and said, 'I am afraid that there is a mistake on every page.' Ismail was dismayed. Sydney then handed the draft back to him. Ismail had referred to what 'the learned magistrate' had said and done. Sydney had crossed out 'learned' wherever it appeared. That was the only change he made to the draft.

An edition of Kentridge's collected emails would not extend to many pages. He retained his distaste for self-promotion and what he would characterise as the vulgar business of marketing. He refused to entertain clients to the end. When his chambers proposed to fit an electric sign behind the reception desk he was vigorous in his objection, describing it as 'an embarrassment' and 'undignified'. He was overruled.

One of Kentridge's defining characteristics is humility. It is perhaps apt that his last case, conducted when he was ninety years old, involved representing pro bono a junior barrister who was subject to disciplinary proceedings brought by the Bar Standards Board arising from a trivial dispute with his gardener. He and his junior Gerard Rothschild prevailed.

In researching this book I have spoken to dozens of lawyers who worked with or appeared against Kentridge. If I were to quote every one of them I would have created a dull chapbook of tributes. The following testimonial from Tim Otty QC, who received a red bag (the traditional tribute from a leader to an outstanding junior, in which to keep one's wig and gown) from Kentridge for his work on the seminal Abdullah Ocalan case in the European Court of Human Rights,[22] is I think a sufficient way to end.

Sydney was the most precise, the most brilliant, the most understated and the most devastatingly effective advocate I have ever worked with or seen in action. A combination of charm, supreme intellect, simplicity of language and ruthless precision. Providing him with a draft submission you knew every proposition, every word, every comma and every semi-colon would be scrutinised with the most extreme rigour. All with the sole aim of ensuring the absolute best case could be put in the most persuasive way to every reader, sympathetic or otherwise. He is and always has been the most humane, courageous and principled of men.[23]

Acknowledgements

IN RESEARCHING AND writing this book I have received immeasur-
able assistance from many people, who have been generous with
their time, memories and insights. I am very grateful to each of
them: Gail Behrmann, Michael Beloff QC, Ian Berry, HHJ Edward
Bindloss, Geoff Budlender SC, The Honourable Edwin Cameron
SCOB, Jonathan Caplan QC, Peter Carter QC, Sir Christopher
Clarke, Professor Stephen Clingman, Professor John Dugard,
Professor Philip Frankel, Rennee Grimmbacher, Auret van Heerden,
Charles Hollander QC, Frances Jowell, Sir Jeffrey Jowell QC, Janet
Kentridge, Justice Johann Kriegler, Michael Kuper SC, Lord Leggatt,
Daniel Lightman QC, Anne McIlleron, Gilbert Marcus SC, Harry
Matovu QC, Justice Dikgang Moseneke, Ian Moyler, Colin Nicholls
QC, Tim Otty QC, Lord Pannick QC, Thomas Plewman SC QC,
Benjamin Pogrund, Sir Andrew Popplewell, Gerard Rothschild,
Justice Ivor Schwartzman SC, Pauline Schwartzman, Sir Nicholas
Stadlen, Dr Anne Stanwix, Lord Sumption, Paula Thompson,
Rhodri Thompson QC, Wim Trengove SC, Sir Alan Ward, Lwando
Xaso.

Sydney's children, Cathy, William, Eliza and Matthew, have been
incredibly helpful and supportive.

I have had a number of people walking beside me, who have
read and commented on the various chapters. Especial thanks in
this regard must go to Jeremy Gauntlett SC QC, whose profound
knowledge of South African legal history never fails to astonish
me and who has been a mentor and true friend; David Rhodes,
chief of the Kentridgians; and Peter Zombory-Moldovan, whose
historical perspective and insights have been, as ever, enormously
valuable.

The book was inspired by Edwin Glasgow QC and guided by Carolyn McCombe's endless enthusiasm.

To say that my family has been long-suffering would be trite but true. My thanks to my lovely wife for everything.

Finally, above all, thanks to my brother Alex.

Picture Credits

© Africa Media Online/Mary Evans: pages 2 above, 4 below, 6 above, centre right and below left. Alamy Stock Photo: page 7 centre left/ photo Peter Jordan. © Ian Berry/Magnum Photos: pages 3 below left, 4 above. *Encountering Darkness* by G. A. ffrench-Beytagh, Collins, 1973: page 6 below right/jacket photograph by Robert McClintock, jacket design by Ron Clark. Getty Images: page 7 above/photo Sahm Doherty. Copyright Guardian News & Media Ltd 2022: page 2 below left. Kentridge family collection: pages 1, 2 below right, 3 centre right, 8 below right. *A Life at Law: The Memoirs of I. A. Maisels, QC* by Isie Maisels (Foreword by Sydney Kentridge), ed. Keith Maisels and Benjamin Trisk, Jonathan Ball Publishers, Johannesburg, 1998: page 5 above. *Rand Daily Mail*/Gallo Images/Getty Images: page 5 below right. Shutterstock: page 8 above right. *The Sowetan*/AFP via Getty Images: page 7 below right. *Sunday Times*/Gallo Images/Getty Images: page 3 above left. *The Times*/Gallo Images/Getty Images: page 8 centre left. Times Newspapers/Shutterstock: page 4 centre left. *Die Transvaler*, 12 November 1965: page 5 centre left.

Every reasonable effort has been made to trace copyright holders, but if there are any errors or omissions, John Murray will be pleased to insert the appropriate acknowledgement in any subsequent printings or editions.

Notes

Chapter 1: Sydney Kentridge at Ninety-Nine

1. See *Prudential plc & Anor, R (on the application of) v Special Commissioner of Income Tax & Anor* [2013] UKSC 1; [2013] 2 AC 185.
2. As discussed by Kentridge in the first Ernie Wentzel Memorial lecture, 'Law and Lawyers in Changing Society', given in 1987. Printed in Kentridge, *Free Country*, p. 47.
3. Speech given to the triennial conference of the New Zealand Law Society. It was first broadcast on BBC Radio 3 on 24 November 1978 and later reproduced in *The Listener*, 30 November 1978. That radio broadcast was heard by a young Jonathan Sumption, who recalls the first time he heard 'the mesmerising quality' of Kentridge's advocacy; see *The Times*, 22 November 2012.
4. Ibid. See also Kentridge, 'The Pathology of a Legal System: Criminal Justice in South Africa', *Free Country*, p. 18.
5. Before the final abolition of the jury most black defendants would opt for trial by judge alone: juries were all-white and there was little prospect of receiving a fair hearing from such a body, especially in a multiracial case.
6. Johan Steyn, a South African barrister who later moved to England and went on to become a distinguished law lord, commented that totalitarian regimes such as that in South Africa in fact 'often achieved their oppressive aims by scrupulous observance of legality': *Democracy through Law*, p. 133.
7. Section 1 of the notorious Population Registration Act 1950 defined 'a white person [as] one who in appearance is, or who is generally accepted as, a white person, but does not include a person who, although in

appearance obviously a white person, is generally accepted as a Coloured person'; 'a native . . . [as] a person who is in fact or is generally accepted as a member of any aboriginal race or tribe of Africa'; and 'a Coloured person [as] a person who is not a white person nor a native'.

8. Kentridge, 'The South African Bar: A Moral Dilemma?', *Free Country*, p. 22.

9. Ibid., pp. 24–5. The case is reported at *Natal Law Society v S* 1985 (4) SALR 115 (N).

10. See John Dugard's recollections to the LRC Oral History Project at http://www.historicalpapers.wits.ac.za/inventories/inv_pdft/AG3298/AG3298-1-040-text.pdf Kentridge acted pro bono for Dugard, who was a friend, in mitigation. See also *Rand Daily Mail*, 17 January 1979. It is testament to Kentridge's ubiquity that in the same edition of the newspaper he is mentioned as having appeared before another judge on behalf of the *Rand Daily Mail*'s editor, who was charged with pre-empting the findings of a judicial commission.

11. See *S v Van Niekerk* 1970 (3) SA 269.

12. See *S v Van Niekerk* 1972 (3) SA 711.

13. Kentridge, 'A Barrister in the Apartheid Years', *Free Country*, pp. 177–8.

14. *2 Henry VI*, Act 4, scene 2.

15. This infamous expression is Dr Verwoerd's: see 'Hendrik Verwoerd Defines Apartheid', YouTube, 10 December 2010, https://www.youtube.com/watch?v=vPCln9czoys

16. Kentridge, 'The Ethics of Advocacy', lecture given at the Inner Temple in 1993, reprinted in *Free Country*, p. 65.

17. The Prohibition of Improper Interference Act 1968 prohibited political parties from having a multiracial membership. The Liberal Party refused to become a whites-only party and was forced to choose between disbanding or going 'underground'. It chose to disband.

18. Cyril Dunn, 'The Guilty Men of Jo'Burg', *Observer*, 13 July 1969.

19. Sampson, *Mandela*, p. 135.

20. [1969] 1 AC 645. The law report extends to 101 pages, 39 of which summarise Kentridge's oral submissions (possibly a record in the English law reports), which embraced such diverse matters as the trial of the regicides, the constitutional status of James II's deposition, the Act of Treason 1495 and the works of Grotius and Pufendorf. There can rarely have been a case which traversed so much diverse and fascinating learning. Kentridge spoke about the case, which concerned the legality of the Unilateral Declaration of Independence proclaimed by the Rhodesian

government in 1965, in his lecture 'A Judge's Duty in a Revolution', *Free Country*, chapter 7.

21. Moseneke, *My Own Liberator*, p. 78.

22. Speaking on BBC Radio 4, *Unreliable Evidence*, 29 December 2012, https://www.bbc.co.uk/programmes/b01pg54x

23. Quoted from Frances Gibb, 'Tributes at the Ritz as Sir Sydney Kentridge Turns 90', *The Times*, 22 November 2012.

24. The case went to the Appellate Division and is reported at 1979 (1) SA 14 (A). Kentridge lost (although the practical effect of the case was a relaxation of the rules). There was a powerful dissenting judgment by Corbett JA which was subsequently accepted as correct in a later decision of *Minister of Justice v Hofmeyr* 1993 (3) SA 131 (AD).

25. See generally Denis Goldberg's account of the case in his memoir *The Mission*, chapter 12.

26. Pogrund, *War of Words*, p. 222.

27. For 'The Trial of George Washington' see YouTube, 1 October 2020, https://www.youtube.com/watch?v=marOc8JpAJk Kentridge did rather better when he took part in another mock trial two years before in Middle Temple Hall, debating the question whether the author of the works commonly attributed to Shakespeare was William Shakespeare of Stratford or the Earl of Oxford. The Oxfordians' newsletter noted the event and lamented that Kentridge seemed better prepared than counsel for the Earl of Oxford. The event was even covered by the *New York Times* (29 November 1988), which quoted Kentridge as having submitted 'The Oxfordians cannot accept the fact that soaring genius can be found in the son of a glover with a good head for figures.' The judges agreed.

28. Kentridge, 'The Ethics of Advocacy', lecture given at the Inner Temple in 1993, reprinted in *Free Country*, p. 67.

29. 'The Lawyer Who Has Shattered the Police Front on Biko', *Guardian*, 25 November 1977.

30. Andrey Vyshinsky, the lead prosecutor in the Moscow show trials of the late 1930s.

31. See for instance Joffe, *The State vs Nelson Mandela*, p. xxiii.

32. See *Pogrund v Yutar* 1967 (2) SA 564.

33. There is an interesting account of Yutar's life by Emma Rathbone, 'Mandela's Prosecutor'. Johann Kriegler, who was one of the panel, ascribes the decision to allow the egregious Yutar to join the Johannesburg Bar, albeit conditionally, to 'pity'.

34. Johann Kriegler, later a judge of the Appellate Division and the Constitutional Court, was also one of the first trustees. He remembers Felicia as follows: 'I believe the kind of work a woman at the Bar could expect to be offered in those days was not what Felicia wanted from life. Her teaching at Wits and her untiring efforts in getting the LRC up and running – and continuing to run – were more her metier. Strategising, long-term planning, meeting and persuading potential funders, recruiting and inspiring supporters, above all charming while gently manipulating people, those were Felicia's talents and her calling.'

35. Felicia died in 2015. See obituary in the *Guardian*, 5 July 2015, https://www.theguardian.com/law/2015/jul/05/felicia-kentridge-obituary

36. On the Legal Resources Centre see generally Ellmann, *Arthur Chaskalson*, especially chapter 11.

37. 'The Lawyer Who Has Shattered the Police Front on Biko', *Guardian*, 25 November 1977.

38. Including as a temporary judge of the Court of Appeal of Botswana (1981–6) and, later, of Jersey and Guernsey (1988–92).

39. There have been two outstanding examples of South African lawyers reaching the highest echelons of the English judiciary: Lords Steyn and Hoffmann. Steyn was, like Kentridge, already in silk when he moved to England.

40. Chaskalson in fact asked Kentridge to agree to be a full-time judge of the court. Kentridge, then seventy-two and a full-time London resident, declined.

41. Ellman, *Chaskalson*, p. 485.

42. On the creation of the Constitutional Court see ibid., chapter 17.

43. *S v Zuma* (CCT5/94) [1995] ZACC 1.

44. *S v Makwanyane* (CCT3/94) [1995] ZACC 3.

45. At [202]–[203].

46. Arthur Chaskalson 'A Lifetime at the Bar: Kentridge at 85', *Advocate*, vol. 21, no. 1 (April 2008).

47. *Advocate*, vol. 13, no. 3 (Third Term 2000), p. 3.

48. Kentridge's choice of records was as follows: Ella Fitzgerald, 'Anything Goes'; Mozart, *The Magic Flute* ('Bei Männern, welche Liebe fühlen'); Gluck, *Orfeo and Euridice* ('Che farò senza Euridice?', sung by Kathleen Ferrier); James Johnston, 'Dark-Eyed Sailor'; Flanders and Swan, 'Ill Wind'; Schubert, Impromptu No. 3; Berlioz, *Nuits d'Été* ('Absence', sung by Janet Baker); Lord Beginner, 'Cricket Lovely Cricket'. His book was the *Jeeves Omnibus* by P. G. Wodehouse. His luxury was an endless supply of coffee and a coffee maker.

49. In this number I am including Privy Council appeals.

50. Forty years earlier Kentridge had led Mance in a commercial case. Mance then took silk and therefore technically became the senior barrister (Kentridge had not yet by this time taken silk in England). At the trial Mance introduced the parties and then sat down to let his 'junior' open the case from the second row.

Chapter 2: The Early Years

1. The first Union census of 1911 recorded a total population of 5,973,394, made up of 1,276,242 'Europeans or whites', 4,019,006 'Bantu' (i.e. blacks) and 678,146 'mixed and other coloured'. It is estimated that at that time some 52 per cent of the white population had Afrikaans (a colonial dialect of Dutch) as its first language, a proportion which was to increase gradually over the century to around 60 per cent.

2. Woolf Kentridge's personal history was a remarkable one. Lithuania was then part of the Russian Empire and Woolf became cantor of a synagogue in Utyan (Utena). He emigrated to England with his wife and children in the early 1880s to take up a similar position in Sunderland, which then had a sizeable Jewish community. In 1899 the family moved again to South Africa, where he served as cantor in the town of Vryheid, in Natal. After their arrival in South Africa the Kantrovich family changed its name to Kentridge.

3. Unless indicated otherwise, quotations from Sydney Kentridge in this chapter are taken from the transcript of interviews conducted by Paula Thompson in March–April 2008 at Brick Court Chambers in London, where Kentridge – then aged eighty-five – was still working. The interviews were conducted as part of the Legal Lives strand of National Life Stories, a British Library project, and the transcript can be read online at https://sounds.bl.uk/related-content/TRANSCRIPTS/021T-C0736X0009XX-0000A1.pdf Some of the quotes have been edited slightly for brevity and clarity.

4. Before she married Morris, May had been a waitress in a café in Johannesburg run by her mother Rose, but, like most white South African women of the time, she gave up paid work once she was married. Kentridge remembers his mother as 'an outstandingly good cook, baker, and needlewoman', and she often acted as her husband's chauffeuse. While Morris never learnt to drive a car, family folklore has it that May

had been the second woman in Johannesburg to obtain a driving licence, having passed her test in about 1918. At election time May would be a dynamic campaign organiser, marshalling canvassers and arranging transport to get voters to polling stations.

5. Arnold was born in 1927 and Leon in 1934.

6. The institutionalisation of white supremacy and racial segregation had begun with the creation of the Union, whose constitution stipulated that only whites could sit in parliament. In 1911, the Mines and Works Act gave whites a monopoly of skilled jobs; the Immigrants Restriction Act confined Indians to their province of domicile; and the Native Labour Regulation Act made strikes by black employees a criminal offence. The Native Land Act 1913 designated some 7 per cent of South African land as reserves for the rural black population.

7. Almost forty years later he would return with his wife, courtesy of a Sicilian client who was so pleased with Kentridge's handling of his claim for patent infringement that he organised a stay. Kentridge can still recall the client's words of greeting to Felicia as they arrived at Catania airport: 'Ah, Mrs Kentridge, which a great pleasure to meet you!'

8. Kentridge, 'Civil Rights in Southern Africa: The Prospect for the Future', John Foster Lecture, 4 November 1986, reprinted in *Free Country*, p. 33.

9. Paton, *Cry, the Beloved Country*, p. 137.

10. Simon Kuper later became a judge and was murdered in 1963, it is thought by a disgruntled defendant who had appeared before him.

11. This formed the basis of the later development of South Africa's defence industry, as a response to the country's international isolation and sanctions during the apartheid period, into one of the largest in the world.

12. Paton, *Cry, the Beloved Country*, p. 174.

13. See *Sachs v Donges NO* 1950 SA 265.

Chapter 3: The Treason Trial (1958–61)

1. The law firm was in Chancellor House, Fox Street. The building is now a national monument and has been recently restored. See https://www.golegal.co.za/mandela-tambo-attorneys/

2. Slovo, *Slovo*, p. 90.

3. Mandela, *Long Walk to Freedom*, p. 203.

4. Forman and Sachs, *The South African Treason Trial*, p. 11.

5. Foreword to Joseph, *If This Be Treason*, p. 7.
6. For general background to the trial see Sampson, *The Treason Cage*, and Karis, 'South African Treason Trial', p. 217.
7. See Blom-Cooper, 'South African Treason Trial: R. *v.* Adams and Others'.
8. George Bizos later recounted Kentridge telling him that 'He [the magistrate] may have been on better ground if he had held Berrangé in contempt rather than Slovo', before adding 'but as we all know it would take a particularly brave man to convict Vernon of contempt': *Odyssey to Freedom*, p. 180.
9. Born in 1908, Maisels was not primarily a human rights specialist: it is said that by the late 1950s he was the highest-earning QC at the South African commercial Bar. He accepted an appointment to the High Court of Southern Rhodesia in Salisbury but returned to practise at the Johannesburg Bar in aversion to the drift towards racialism in Salisbury.
10. About Fischer see generally Chapter 5.
11. Maisels's memoirs *A Life at Law* devotes a substantial amount of space to the Treason Trial. Kentridge wrote an appreciation of Maisels when he retired from the Bar in *Consultus*, vol. 6, no. 1 (April 1993), https://www.gcbsa.co.za/law-journals/1993/april/1993-april-vol006-no1-pp71-72.pdf
12. Maisels, *Life at Law*, p. 141.
13. He had won the coveted Whewell scholarship in international law at Cambridge.
14. Kentridge had acted for the Congress Alliance that had organised the boycott and against which the Rembrandt Group sought an injunction.
15. Joseph, *If This Be Treason*, p. 24.
16. See the interesting account of the synagogue's history: Fran Buntman and Barbara Buntman '"Old Synagogue" and Apartheid Court: Constructing a South African Heritage Site', *South African Historical Journal*, vol. 62 (2010), pp. 183–201.
17. Though not for much longer: South Africa became a republic in 1961. A referendum on 5 October 1960 on whether South Africa should leave the Commonwealth and become a republic was narrowly won by the republicans.
18. Pritt recounts his conversation with Pirow in the third volume of his autobiography, *The Defence Accuses*, p. 160. On Pirow see F. A. Mouton, *The Opportunist*.

19. Mandela, *Long Walk to Freedom*, p. 274.

20. Joseph, *If This Be Treason*, p. 29.

21. See the decision in *R v Adams* 1959 (1) SA 646 (T).

22. See Slovo's account of the party, *Slovo*, pp. 102–3.

23. In fact they were quashed in April 1959.

24. De Vos was a former fascist sympathiser who had been a *kommandant* in the Ossewabrandwag, a pro-German Afrikaner organisation. He had been interned during the war by the South African government.

25. See Luthuli's account in his autobiography, *Let My People Go*, p. 224.

26. Clingman, *Bram Fischer*, p. 253.

27. In September 1966 Verwoerd suffered a second assassination attempt, a stabbing by a parliamentary messenger named Dimitri Tsafendas, which proved fatal.

28. Clingman, *Bram Fischer*, p. 102.

29. Ibid., p. 104.

30. Sophiatown was a vibrant black suburb of Johannesburg which was the subject of a forced clearance and then demolition between 1955 and 1959, carried out under the Natives Resettlement Act 1954.

31. Clingman, *Bram Fischer*, p. 258.

32. Mandela, *Long Walk to Freedom*, p. 308.

33. Kentridge discusses this in his lecture 'The Pathology of a Legal System', in *Free Country*.

34. In her introduction she specifically thanks Kentridge, who had (along with Diana Athill) read the manuscript.

35. Maisels, *A Life at Law*, p. 212.

36. Most of the transcript is available from the University of Witwatersrand's Historical Papers Research Archive, http://www.historicalpapers.wits. ac.za/?inventory/U/collections&c=AD1812/R/

37. Mandela, *Long Walk to Freedom*, p. 300.

38. Trengove's son, Wim, who would himself go on to become one of South Africa's leading advocates, confirms that during his evidence Mandela 'impressed even the prosecution by his open and forthright manner': 'Rivonia Days', *London Review of Books*, vol. 29, no. 18 (20 September 2007).

39. Serote, *To Every Birth*, p. 188.

40. Griswold discusses the trial and his meeting with Kentridge in *Ould Fields, New Corne*, pp. 203–5.

41. When Kentridge and Felicia later came to London they had lunch with West and her notoriously lecherous husband, Henry Maxwell Andrews.

Kentridge recalls with amusement Andrews's futile attempts to flirt with Felicia.

42. See Haus der Kunst, 'In Conversation: William Kentridge and Sir Sydney Kentridge', YouTube, 24 April 2013, https://www.youtube.com/watch?v=fsLXipKe7n8

43. The Sydney and Felicia Kentridge Award is awarded annually by the General Counsel of the Bar of South Africa for outstanding achievements in public interest law.

44. *Advocate*, vol. 13, no. 3 (Third Term 2000), p. 3.

Chapter 4: The Sharpeville Inquiry (1960)

1. Jones attended on behalf of the International Commission of Jurists. See his memoirs, *In My Time*, pp. 170–1.

2. Lodge, *Sharpeville*, p. 82. Lodge's book and an earlier book by Philip Frankel, *An Ordinary Atrocity*, provide a detailed account of the massacre, its background and its place in South African history.

3. Coincidentally, on 3 February 1960 the British prime minister Harold Macmillan addressed the South African parliament in Cape Town, declaring: 'The wind of change is blowing through this continent, and, whether we like it or not, this growth of national consciousness is a political fact . . . and our national policies must take account of it . . . [It] is our earnest desire to give South Africa our support and encouragement, but I hope you won't mind my saying frankly that there are some aspects of your policies which make it impossible for us to do this without being false to our own deep convictions about the political destinies of free men.' Despite the gentlemanly tone, this clear condemnation of apartheid signalled a major shift in British policy towards South Africa. Widely reported and discussed, the 'Wind of Change' speech gave heart to the resistance movement while hardening the determination of an increasingly isolated Nationalist government to use all the means at its disposal to crush it.

4. In fact the number was significantly larger: see Frankel, *Ordinary Atrocity*, p. 108.

5. Conversation with the author, July 2021.

6. Frankel, *Ordinary Atrocity*, p. 124.

7. Tyler, *Life in the Time of Sharpeville*, p. 18.

8. Quoted in 'Appeal to Whites by Dr Verwoerd', *The Times*, 28 March 1960.

9. Frankel, *Ordinary Atrocity*, p. 187.

10. To this day, the inquiry transcript exists only as a photocopy of a typewritten original – Michael Parkington's own copy, and carrying his handwritten notes – which is incomplete and in places barely legible. Many volumes (though not all) can be read online at the University of California, Los Angeles's International Digital Ephemera Project, idep.library.ucla.edu/search#!/q=sharpeville&collection=Sharpeville+Massacre; another incomplete set is held in Britain at the University of York's Borthwick Institute for Archives, www.york.ac.uk/borthwick.

11. Frankel, *Ordinary Atrocity*, p. 194.

12. Gordimer, *Burger's Daughter*, p. 152.

13. Churchill had said these words in the parliamentary debates on 8 July 1920 after the Amritsar massacre in 1919. The quote originated with Macaulay: '*the* most *frightful of all spectacles* [is] *the* strength of *civilisation without its mercy*' (*Memoirs of the Life of Hastings*, 1841).

14. Haus der Kunst, 'In Conversation: William Kentridge and Sir Sydney Kentridge', YouTube, 24 April 2013, https://www.youtube.com/watch?v=fsLXipKe7n8

15. Canetti, *Crowds and Power*, pp. 60–1.

16. See e.g. Frankel, *Ordinary Atrocity*, p. 192.

17. With no apparent sense of irony, most of *Zulu* was shot on location in South Africa in 1963 – something of a public relations coup for the government in the aftermath of Sharpeville. Cast and crew were required to observe apartheid laws on social mixing throughout production.

18. Frankel, *Ordinary Atrocity*, p. 192.

19. A few years earlier the government had instituted a new form of black-led local authority structure to try to legitimise what Edwin Cameron describes as 'its increasingly precarious rule over the black urban population': see Mr Justice Edwin Cameron, 'When Judges Fail', *Current Legal Problems*, vol. 58 (2005), p. 83.

20. S v Safatsa and Others 1988 (1) SA 868 (A).

21. There is a substantial literature concerning the Sharpeville Six. See the excellent Parker and Mokhesi-Parker, *In the Shadow of Sharpeville*. The attorney for the Six, Prakash Diar, produced his own memoir, *The Sharpeville Six*.

22. David Beresford, 'Top Legal Talent for Sharpeville', *Guardian*, 7 September 1988.

23. Parker and Mokhesi-Parker, *In the Shadow of Sharpeville*, p. 287.

24. Ibid., p. 239.
25. David Beresford, 'Barrister Appeals to "Heart of Court"', *Guardian*, 8 September 1988.
26. Quoted in Snyckers (ed.), *Group 621 Centenary*, a book celebrating the centenary of Kentridge's Johannesburg chambers, p. 42.
27. *Safatsa and Others v Attorney General, Transvaal* 1989 (1) SA 815 (A).

Chapter 5: Defending Bram Fischer (1965)

1. For a full account of the events described in this chapter see the superb Clingman, *Bram Fischer*.
2. Technically the General Law Amendment Act No. 76 of 1962.
3. The trial was recorded and has recently been digitised. One can hear Fischer making submissions at the trial in the BBC World Service documentary, *Remembering Rivonia*, 14 July 2018, available on YouTube at https://www.youtube.com/watch?v=y68on3fZoA4
4. Only Lionel 'Rusty' Bernstein was acquitted. The case against another accused, James Kantor, an attorney, had been dismissed at the end of the prosecution case.
5. The definitive account of the trial is contained in Joffe, *State vs Nelson Mandela*. Joffe had been the attorney for the accused. A documentary film by Nick Stadlen titled *Life is Wonderful* (2018) provides a compelling and moving account of the trial.
6. See for instance 'Queen's Counsel on Bail', *The Times*, 16 October 1964.
7. President Mandela gave the first Bram Fischer Memorial Lecture on 9 June 1995. In it he said: 'Bram was a courageous man who followed the most difficult course any person could choose to follow. He challenged his own people because he felt that what they were doing was morally wrong. As an Afrikaner whose conscience forced him to reject his own heritage and be ostracised by his own people, he showed a level of courage and sacrifice that was in a class by itself. I fought only against injustice not against my own people.'
8. G. J. Marcus SC and J. Kentridge, 'The Striking Off of Abram Fischer QC', in Eiselen (ed.), *Johannesburg Bar*. Janet Kentridge is Sydney's daughter-in-law.
9. 'Word from Missing QC', *Observer*, 7 February 1965.
10. Clingman, *Bram Fischer*, p. 368.
11. *Incorporated Law Society, Transvaal v Mandela* 1954 (3) SA 102 (T).

12. *Ex p Krause* 1905 TS 221. Krause lived to a great age. For an obituary see A. A. Roberts 'The Late F. E. T. Krause', *South African Law Journal*, vol. 364 (1959).

13. 'Fischer Disbarment Hearing', *Rand Daily Mail*, 29 October 1965.

14. *Society of Advocates of S.A. v Fischer* 1966 (1) SA 133 (T).

15. Bizos, *Odyssey to Freedom*, p. 301.

16. As remembered by Benson in her memoir *A Far Cry*, p. 176.

17. Clingman, *Bram Fischer*, p. 401.

18. Until South Africa became a republic the concept of King/Queen's Counsel prevailed. From 1961 the title changed, for future appointments, to Senior Counsel. Existing South African QCs retained that title.

19. Clingman, *Bram Fischer*, pp. 406–7.

20. In truth, there were close and vital links between the ANC and the SACP throughout the apartheid period. Nelson Mandela, who remained coy about his clandestine SACP membership, was revealed after his death to have served on its Central Committee. As he teasingly put it in his autobiography, 'The cynical have always suggested that the Communists were using us. But who is to say that we were not using them?'

21. Hlapane and his wife were assassinated by an ANC gunman in their Soweto home on 16 December 1982, nine months after Hlapane claimed in testimony to a United States Senate committee that the SACP still controlled the ANC.

22. 'Fischer Defends Belief in Communism', *The Times*, 29 March 1966.

23. See for instance Edwin Cameron's Bram Fischer Lecture, 16 June 2015, available on YouTube, https://www.youtube.com/watch?v=aK3aI N9N4Io

24. Ellman, 'To Live Outside the Law'.

25. Mandela, *Long Walk to Freedom*, p. 104.

26. Budlender, 'Bram Fischer: The Man and The Lawyer', *Consultus*, vol. 8, no. 2 (November 1995).

Chapter 6: The Trials of Winnie Mandela (1970–86)

1. Winnie Mandela, *Part of My Soul*, p. 57.

2. The house is now a museum.

3. In English 'Spear of the Nation' (generally abbreviated to MK), founded in the wake of the Sharpeville massacre.

4. See Hepple, *Young Man with a Red Tie*, p. 139. Hepple became a distinguished lawyer in England and was later knighted.

5. Herbstein, *White Lies*, p. 161.

6. Hepple, *Young Man with a Red Tie*, p. 123.

7. Madikizela-Mandela, *491 Days*, p. 9.

8. Carlson was already well known from his role in the first trial under the Terrorism Act, *The State v Tuhadeleni and 36 Others*, in 1967. He defended thirty-seven Namibians who had been beaten and tortured during months of secret, solitary confinement and faced the death penalty on conviction. Carlson took advantage of a recess in the trial to fly to the United States, where he secured the help of Senators Edward and Robert Kennedy, State Department officials and Arthur J. Goldberg, the American representative at the United Nations. 'Nobody wanted to defend us, but Mr Carlson took up our case and he saved us from the gallows,' said the lead defendant in the case, Andimba Toivo Ya Toivo, later secretary general of the South West Africa People's Organization (SWAPO) and a minister in Namibia's first democratic government. 'His actions embarrassed the authorities. That's why they had to sentence us to prison, not death.'

9. Carlson, *No Neutral Ground*, pp. 154–5.

10. Accused Number One was a trade unionist called Samson Ndou.

11. Bekker died aged only sixty-one in 1974. For tributes paid to him by his fellow judges see *South African Law Journal*, vol. 92 (1975), p. 207.

12. Bizos, *Odyssey to Freedom*, p. 359.

13. Carlson, *No Neutral Ground*, p. 202.

14. Ibid., p. 203.

15. When the daughter of a Cape judge, P. W. B. Baker, was murdered in a botched break-in in the late 1970s, the judge flown in to hear the case was Theron. The killer was sentenced to death.

16. See e.g. Dugard, 'Courts and Section 6 of the Terrorism Act', p. 289.

17. Carlson, *No Neutral Ground*, p. 212.

18. Now Michael Kuper SC and a former chairman of the Johannesburg Bar.

19. Conversation with the author, 2021.

20. Bizos, *Odyssey to Freedom*, p. 360.

21. He was subsequently promoted to the Appellate Division (South Africa's appeal court), and was an invariable member of the panel hearing appeals in security cases in the court headed by Chief Justice Pierre Rabie.

22. *A-G of Israel v Eichmann* [1961] 36 ILR 5.

23. The essence of Kentridge's argument was later vindicated in *S v Ebrahim* 1991 (2) SA 553 (A), where South African security policemen had snatched the accused from Swaziland.
24. Carlson, *No Neutral Ground*, p. 217.
25. Extracted from Snyckers (ed.), *Group 621*, p. 132.
26. Madikizela-Mandela, *491 Days*, p. 195.
27. Carlson, *No Neutral Ground*, p. 219.
28. 'Amandla! Ngawethu!' ('Power! It is ours!') was an ANC cry. Ramotse would go on to be sentenced to fifteen years in prison.
29. 'The Acquittals in Pretoria', *The Times*, 15 September 1970.
30. 'Justice in South Africa', *New York Times*, 16 September 1970.
31. The state appealed but the Court of Appeal rejected it in December 1970: see 1971 (1) SA 668 (A).
32. Quoted in Sampson, *Mandela*, p. 248.
33. Winnie Mandela, *Part of My Soul*, p. 26.
34. See *S v Waite* 1978 (3) SA 896 (O).
35. See Gilbey, *The Lady*, p. 128.
36. J. M. Coetzee, 'Waiting for Mandela', *New York Review of Books*, 8 May 1986.
37. Conversations with the author, 2021.
38. *Kadalie v Hemsworth NO* 1928 TPD 495 at 506, per Feetham J.
39. *Nkondo v Minister of Law and Order* 1986 (2) SA 756 (A).

Chapter 7: 'The Dean': Gonville ffrench-Beytagh (1971–2)

1. Sparks, *Mind of South Africa*, p. 28.
2. Walshe, *Church Versus State*, p. 63.
3. Kentridge, *Free Country*, p. 173.
4. Herbstein, *White Lies*, p. 161.
5. 'Good and Fearless Shepherd', *Guardian*, 14 May 1991.
6. All quotations ascribed to ffrench-Beytagh are from his memoir, *Encountering Darkness*.
7. Herbstein, *White Lies*, p. 160.
8. Although Joseph had been acquitted along with all the others at the end of the Treason Trial in 1961, she was later banned after the publication of her account of the trial, *If This Be Treason*, which Kentridge had read in draft.
9. Herbstein, *White Lies*, p. 160.

10. Pogrund, *War of Words*, p. 222. All subsequent quotations are from this volume.

11. Cyril Dunn, 'The Guilty Men of Jo'Burg', *Observer*, 13 July 1969.

12. When the much more liberal Mr Justice Simon Bekker (see Chapters 3 and 6) learnt of Cillié's elevation he telephoned the justice minister in a fury telling him: 'if you wanted to appoint any damn fool to be Judge President you could have chosen me'.

13. Further, the Terrorism Act itself required trial by judge alone: section 5(a).

14. Cameron, *Justice*, pp. 15–16.

15. Ibid., pp. 17–18.

16. Ibid., p. 28.

17. For extracts from ffrench-Beytagh's interview with the BBC, 15 April 1972, see YouTube, https://www.youtube.com/watch?v=mMsyYZ_d5Rk

Chapter 8: The Biko Inquest (1977)

1. See Introduction to Biko, *I Write What I Like*, p. 1.

2. Zille, *Not Without a Fight*, p. 46.

3. See generally Kentridge's Steve Biko Memorial Lecture, 'Evil Under the Sun: The Death of Steve Biko', University of Cape Town, 11 September 2011, reprinted in *Free Country*, p. 159.

4. A selection of Biko's writings was gathered after his death in the book *I Write What I Like* (1988).

5. Steve Biko, 'White Racism and Black Consciousness'.

6. See Bizos's account of the trial in *Odyssey to Freedom*, pp. 426ff.

7. Biko, *I Write What I Like*, p. 172.

8. Sydney Kentridge, *South Africa*, lecture, BBC Radio 3, 24 November 1978.

9. See generally Bizos, *No One to Blame?*, a harrowing account of various deaths in custody and the inquests that followed.

10. Kentridge, *South Africa*.

11. Sparks, *Sword and Pen*, p. 352.

12. After his death in 2020 Bizos was given a state funeral.

13. Bizos, *No One to Blame?*, p. 52.

14. Bernstein's account, published by International Defence and Aid Fund in London in April 1978, was entitled *No. 46 – Steve Biko*. Biko was the

forty-sixth person to die in security police detention in South Africa since 1963.

15. Napley, *Not Without Prejudice*, p. 378.
16. Kentridge, *Free Country*, p. 164.
17. Bizos, *No One to Blame*, p. 72.
18. 'The Man Who Speaks for Biko', *New York Times*, 17 November 1977.
19. 'The Lawyer Who Has Shattered the Police Front on Biko', *Guardian*, 25 November 1977.
20. 3 Wigmore, Evidence §1367, p. 27 (2d ed. 1923).
21. Quoted in Robert Verkaik, 'The Barrister's Barrister', *Independent*, 3 July 2001.
22. Quoted in Duncan Campbell, 'Mandela's QC Goes into Battle for the Hunters', *Guardian*, 4 October 2004.
23. *Veriava v President, SA Medical And Dental Council* 1985 (2) SA 293.
24. Bernard Levin, 'Verdict: Death that Others Might Be Free', *The Times*, 11 February 1984.
25. John J. O'Connor, 'TV Review: *The Biko Inquest* on *Showtime*', *New York Times*, 12 September 1985.

Epilogue: The London Years

1. Brick Court Chambers, as it now is, celebrated in 2021 its hundredth anniversary. See Hollander, *Hundred Years of Brick Court*.
2. Burley has the distinction of being the only barristers' clerk ever to be the subject of a *Times* obituary (8 April 2010).
3. Lawyers reading this will be interested to learn that in those days the application form to become a Queen's Counsel was one-page long, had a specific section about 'Service with H.M. Forces', and required only two referees.
4. This was based on a perverse reading of section 3 of the Act of Settlement 1701. It also ignored the fact that Johan Steyn, also South African-born, had been granted silk just two years before.
5. See the account in Hollander, *Hundred Years of Brick Court*, pp. 59–60.
6. *R v P&O European Ferries (Dover) Ltd* (1991) 93 Cr. App.R. 72. For Kentridge's court presence, as remembered by prosecuting counsel David Jeffreys QC, see 'Lives Remembered', *The Times*, 1 December 2018.
7. *R v Saunders* [1996] 1 Cr App R 463. Saunders was one of the so-called Guinness Four, who attempted dishonestly to manipulate the company's share price in one of the great business scandals of the 1980s.

8. [1994] 2 AC 130. The issue in the appeal was whether the Crown was obliged to disclose evidence helpful to the accused which had been obtained by authorised phone tapping. Their Lordships held that it was not.

9. [1994] 1 AC 85.

10. *Secretary of State for Defence v Guardian Newspapers Ltd* [1985] AC 339.

11. *CBS Songs Ltd v Amstrad Consumer Electronics* [1988] AC 1013.

12. *Lonrho v Fayed* [1992] 1 AC 448.

13. *M v Home Office* [1994] 1 AC 377.

14. *Regina v Secretary of State for Foreign and Commonwealth Affairs, Ex parte Rees-Mogg* [1994] QB 552.

15. The Tanner Lectures on Human Values, 'Human Rights: A Sense of Proportion', Brasenose College, Oxford, 26–27 February 2001, https://tannerlectures.utah.edu/_resources/documents/a-to-z/k/Kentridge_02.pdf

16. *R v Lord Saville of Newdigate* [2000] 1 WLR 1855.

17. *R (Jackson) v Attorney General* [2006] 1 AC 262.

18. Hollander, *Hundred Years of Brick Court*, pp. 7–8.

19. *British Phonographic Industry Ltd v Mechanical-Copyright Protection Society Ltd (No. 2)* [1993] EMLR 86.

20. *End Conscription Campaign v Minister of Defence* 1989 (2) SA 180 (C).

21. *Rasul v Bush*, 542 U.S. 466 (2004). The judgment of the majority drew heavily on Kentridge's submission. In 1962 Kentridge had written a note on *Habeas Corpus Procedure in South Africa* which in successive states of emergency in the 1980s was regularly drawn on ((79) 1962 SALJ 283).

22. Abdullah Ocalan was the founder of the Kurdistan Workers Party (PKK), who had been captured in Kenya by operatives of the Turkish state and rendered back to Turkey.

23. Correspondence with the author, 2021.

Select Bibliography

Much of the source material for this book derives from Sydney Kentridge's personal archive and press cuttings. Transcripts of many of the trials discussed are available on the internet. Other invaluable sources have been the *Rand Daily Mail*, *New York Times*, *Washington Post*, *Sunday Times*, *Guardian*, *Observer* and *The Times*. The lengthy series of interviews which Paula Thompson conducted with Kentridge for the British Library's National Life Stories project in 2008 (see https://sounds.bl.uk /related-content/TRANSCRIPTS/021T-C0736X0009XX-0000A1. pdf) has been invaluable, as has Kentridge's collected speeches and lectures, *Free Country* (Oxford: Hart, 2012), edited by Sir David Lloyd Jones and Sir George Leggatt (as they then were).

I have divided the bibliography by chapter. A number of books are significant for more than one chapter. I have identified them only in the first chapter to which they are relevant.

Chapter 1: Sydney Kentridge at Ninety-Nine

Ellmann, Stephen, *Arthur Chaskalson: A Life Dedicated to Justice for All* (Johannesburg: Picador Africa, 2019)

Goldberg, Denis, *The Mission: A Life for Freedom in South Africa* (Johannesburg: Real African Publishers, 2010)

Gordimer, Nadine, *The Late Bourgeois World* (London: Gollancz, 1966)

Kentridge, Catherine, *The Book of Cathy: A South African Childhood* (Newmarket, Ontario: Davies Slate, 2013)

Kentridge, Eliza, *Signs for an Exhibition* (Cape Town: Modjaji Books, 2015)

Kentridge, Sydney, *Free Country: Selected Lectures and Talks* (ed. David Lloyd Jones and George Leggatt) (Oxford: Hart, 2012)

Joffe, Joel, *The State vs Nelson Mandela: The Trial that Changed South Africa* (London: Oneworld, 2007)

Moseneke, Dikgang, *My Own Liberator: A Memoir* (Johannesburg: Picador Africa, 2016)

Pogrund, Benjamin, *War of Words: Memoir of a South African Journalist* (New York: Seven Stories Press, 2010)

Rathbone, Emma, 'Mandela's Prosecutor', *Virginia Quarterly Review*, vol. 89, no. 4 (Fall 2013), pp. 158–68

Sampson, Anthony, *Mandela: The Authorised Biography* (Johannesburg: Jonathan Ball, 1999)

Steyn, Johan, *Democracy through Law: Selected Speeches and Judgments* (Abingdon and Burlington, VT: Ashgate, 2004)

Chapter 2: The Early Years

Kentridge, Morris, *I Recall: Memoirs of Morris Kentridge* (New York: Free Press, 1959)

Paton, Alan, *Cry, the Beloved Country* (1948; Harmondsworth: Penguin Modern Classics, 1973)

Chapter 3: The Treason Trial (1958–61)

Bizos, George, *Odyssey to Freedom* (Cape Town: Random House, 2009)

Blom-Cooper, Louis, 'The South African Treason Trial: R. *v.* Adams and Others', *International & Comparative Law Quarterly*, vol. 8, no. 1 (January 1959), pp. 59–72

Forman, Lionel, and Solly Sachs, *The South African Treason Trial* (London: John Calder, 1957)

Griswold, Erwin, *Ould Fields, New Corne* (Saint Paul, MN: West Academic Publishing, 1992)

Joseph, Helen, *If This Be Treason* (London: Andre Deutsch, 1963)

Karis, Thomas, 'The South African Treason Trial', *Political Science Quarterly*, vol. 76, no. 2 (June 1961), p. 217

Luthuli, Chief Albert, *Let My People Go: An Autobiography* (Johannesburg and London: Collins, 1962)

Maisels, Isie, *A Life at Law: The Memoirs of I. A. Maisels, QC* (Johannesburg: Jonathan Ball, 1995)

Mandela, Nelson, *Long Walk to Freedom: The Autobiography of Nelson Mandela* (London: Little, Brown, 1994)

Mouton, F. A., *The Opportunist: The Political Life of Oswald Pirow 1915–1959* (Pretoria: Protea, 2020)

Parker, Peter, and Joyce Mokhesi-Parker, *In the Shadow of Sharpeville: Apartheid and Criminal Justice* (Basingstoke: Macmillan, 1998)

Pritt, D. N., *The Defence Accuses* (London: Lawrence & Wishart, 1966)

Sampson, Anthony, *The Treason Cage: The Opposition on Trial in South Africa* (London: Heinemann, 1958)

Serote, Mongane, *To Every Birth Its Blood* (Johannesburg: Raven Press, 1981)

Slovo, Joe, *Slovo: The Unfinished Autobiography* (Johannesburg: Ravan Press, 1995)

Chapter 4: The Sharpeville Inquiry (1960)

Cameron, Edwin, 'When Judges Fail', *Current Legal Problems*, vol. 58 (2005), p. 83

Canetti, Elias, *Crowds and Power* (London: Gollancz, 1961)

Diar, Prakash, *The Sharpeville Six: The South African Trial that Shocked the World* (Toronto, ON: McLelland & Stewart, 1990)

Frankel, Philip, *An Ordinary Atrocity: Sharpeville and Its Massacre* (New Haven and London: Yale University Press, 2001)

Gordimer, Nadine, *Burger's Daughter* (London: Jonathan Cape, 1979)

Jones, Elwyn, *In My Time: An Autobiography* (London: Weidenfeld & Nicolson, 1983)

Lodge, Tom, *Sharpeville: An Apartheid Massacre and Its Consequences* (Oxford: Oxford University Press, 2011)

Reeves, Ambrose, *Shooting at Sharpeville: The Agony of South Africa* (London: Gollancz, 1960)

Snyckers QC, F. (ed.), *Group 621 Centenary: 1913–2013* (Durban: LexisNexis Butterworths, 2013)

Tyler, Humphrey, *Life in the Time of Sharpeville: And Wayward Seeds of a New South Africa* (Cape Town: Kwela Books, 1995)

Chapter 5: Defending Bram Fischer (1965)

Benson, Mary, *A Far Cry: The Making of a South African* (London: Penguin, 1990)

Clingman, Stephen, *Bram Fischer: Afrikaner Revolutionary* (Cape Town: David Philip, 1998)

Eiselen, G. T. S. (ed.), *The Johannesburg Bar: 100 Years in Pursuit of Excellence* (Durban: LexisNexis Butterworths, 2002)

Ellmann, Stephen, 'To Live Outside the Law You Must be Honest: Bram Fischer and the Meaning of Integrity' *North Carolina Journal of International Law & Commercial Regulation*, vol. 26 (2000), p. 767

Gordimer, Nadine, *The Essential Gesture: Writing, Politics and Places* (London: Jonathan Cape, 1988)

Chapter 6: The Trials of Winnie Mandela (1970–86)

Carlson, Joel, *No Neutral Ground* (London: Quartet, 1977)

Dugard, John, 'The Courts and Section 6 of the Terrorism Act', *South African Law Journal*, vol. 87 (1970), p. 289

Gilbey, Emma, *The Lady: The Life and Times of Winnie Mandela* (London: Jonathan Cape, 1993)

Herbstein, Denis, *White Lies: Canon Collins and the Secret War Against Apartheid* (London: James Currey, 2004)

Hepple, Bob, *Young Man with a Red Tie: A Memoir of Mandela and the Failed Revolution, 1960–1963* (Johannesburg: Jacana, 2013)

Madikizela-Mandela, Winnie, *491 Days: Prisoner Number 1323/69* (Athens, OH: Ohio University Press, 2013)

Mandela, Winnie, *Part of My Soul* (London: Penguin, 1985)

Chapter 7: 'The Dean': Gonville ffrench-Beytagh (1971–2)

Cameron, Edwin, *Justice: A Personal Account* (Cape Town: Tafelberg, 2014)

ffrench-Beytagh, Gonville, *Encountering Darkness* (London: Collins, 1973)

Sparks, Allister, *The Mind of South Africa* (London: William Heinemann, 1990)

The State v The Dean of Johannesburg (Johannesburg: South African Institute of Race Relations, 1972)

Walshe, Peter, *Church Versus State in South Africa: The Case of the Christian Institute* (London: C. Hurst, 1983)

Chapter 8: The Biko Inquest (1977)

Bernstein, Hilda, *No. 46 – Steve Biko* (London: International Defence & Aid Fund, 1978)

Biko, Steve, 'White Racism and Black Consciousness', in Hendrik van der Merwe and David Welsh (eds), *Student Perspectives on South Africa* (Cape Town: David Philip, 1972)

———, *I Write What I Like: A Selection of Writings* (London: Penguin, 1988)

Bizos, George, *No One to Blame? In Pursuit of Justice in South Africa* (Cape Town: David Philip, 1998)

Fanon, Fritz, *The Wretched of the Earth* (London: Penguin Modern Classics, 2001)

Napley, David, *Not Without Prejudice* (London: Harrap, 1982)

Sparks, Allister, *The Sword and the Pen: Six Decades on the Political Frontier* (Johannesburg: Jonathan Ball, 2016)

Woods, Donald, *Biko* (London: Penguin, 1979)

Zille, Helen, *Not Without a Fight: The Autobiography* (London: Penguin, 2016)

Epilogue: The London Years

Hollander QC, Charles, *A Hundred Years of Brick Court* (London: Wilton 65, 2021)

Kentridge QC, Sydney, 'Habeas Corpus Procedure in South Africa', *South African Law Journal*, vol. 79 (1962), p. 283

———, 'Human Rights: A Sense of Proportion', The Tanner Lectures, Brasenose College, Oxford, 26–27 February 2021

Index

Index

Page references to notes are indicated by n.

West, Rebecca 90
white opposition 41
white supremacy 76, 300n6
Wilde, Oscar 161
Wilken, Lieutenant Winston 263–4
Williams, Cecil 27
Williamson, Craig 286
Witwatersrand, University of the
  27, 29–30, 34
women 94; *see also* Black Sash

Woods, Donald 242, 246–7, 277
Woods, Wendy 255
Woolf, Harry (Baron Woolf) 285

Yutar, Dr Percy 15–17, 297n33

Zille, Helen 239, 248
Zimbabwe *see* Rhodesia
Zulu (film) 125, 304n17
Zwart, Nicholaas 220–4, 225, 234